RENÉ DESCARTES was born in 1596 at La Haye (now called Descartes) near Tours, and educated at the Jesuit College at La Flèche. Like many of his contemporaries he contested the value of an education based on Aristotelianism and, after leaving college, attempted to resolve the sceptical crisis of his age by devising a method of reasoning modelled on the rigour and certainty of mathematics. Despite claiming to avoid theological questions and stay within the scope of human reason, his writings involved him in numerous disputes with theologians of both the Catholic and (especially) the Reformed persuasion. In 1621, after a period spent in the Netherlands, Bohemia and Hungary as a soldier, he left the army and devoted himself to the study of science and philosophy. He retired to the Netherlands in 1628 and spent the next twenty-one years there, living and working in seclusion. Then in late 1649, after an invitation the previous year, he went to Sweden to take up a post instructing Queen Christina in philosophy. Descartes' habit for many years was to rise not much before midmorning but the Queen wished to be tutored at five o'clock in the morning, three days a week. This and the cold weather placed a severe strain on Descartes' health and he contracted pneumonia, dying in Stockholm in early 1650, having only just begun to teach the Queen. His last words were reportedly *a mon âme, il faut partir* ('my soul, it is time to depart').

DESMOND CLARKE was educated in Ireland, France and the United States. He is Professor of Philosophy at the National University of Ireland, Cork, and a member of the Royal Irish Academy. His publications include *Descartes' Philosophy of Science* (1982), *Church & State* (1984), *Descartes' Theory of Mind* (Oxford, 2003), and two translations of early Cartesian authors: Poulain de la Barre's *The Equality of Sexes* (1990), and Louis de la Forge's *Treatise on the Human Mind* (1997). He is co-editor with Karl Ameriks of the series Cambridge Texts in the History of Philosophy. He is married, with two daughters, Nora and Ann.

This new Penguin Classics edition of Descartes includes this volume of metaphysical writings and a companion volume, *Discourse on Method and Related Writings*.

RENÉ DESCARTES

Meditations

and Other Metaphysical Writings

Translated with an Introduction by

DESMOND M. CLARKE

PENGUIN BOOKS

For Nora

PENGUIN BOOKS

Published by the Penguin Group
Penguin Books Ltd, 80 Strand, London WC2R 0RL, England
Penguin Putnam Inc., 375 Hudson Street, New York, New York 10014, USA
Penguin Books Australia Ltd, 250 Camberwell Road, Camberwell, Victoria 3124, Australia
Penguin Books Canada Ltd, 10 Alcorn Avenue, Toronto, Ontario, Canada M4V 3B2
Penguin Books India (P) Ltd, 11, Community Centre, Panchsheel Park, New Delhi – 110 017, India
Penguin Books (NZ) Ltd, Cnr Rosedale and Airborne Roads, Albany, Auckland, New Zealand
Penguin Books (South Africa) (Pty) Ltd, 24 Sturdee Avenue, Rosebank 2196, South Africa

Penguin Books Ltd, Registered Offices: 80 Strand, London WC2R 0RL, England

This translation first published 1998
Reprinted with corrections 2000
Reprinted with a new Chronology and updated Further Reading 2003
10

Set in 10.25/12.5 pt Monotype Van Dijck
Typeset by Rowland Phototypesetting Ltd, Bury St Edmunds, Suffolk
Printed in England by Clays Ltd, St Ives plc

Contents

The Penguin Descartes

Descartes' publications extend over a very wide range. They include new developments in mathematics, scientific explanations of natural phenomena, and essays on what is usually classified today as philosophy. They were written in Latin when the issues discussed were philosophical in a technical sense and where the intended readership was limited to those who knew some philosophy. In other cases, they were written in French for a wider, non-academic audience. Besides the range and diversity of subject matter, Descartes produced a large volume of writings which extends to twelve large tomes in the standard edition by Adam and Tannery.

In selecting texts for the new Penguin edition, it was decided to focus on the two most famous Cartesian texts, the *Meditations* and the *Discourse*, and on the issues raised by them. The *Meditations* (1641) was written in Latin and, together with the Objections and Replies, represented a major contribution to seventeeth-century metaphysics. Descartes subsequently rewrote his metaphysics in a different style as Part I of the *Principles* (1644). He also began to take seriously objections to mind–body dualism and some of these were discussed in correspondence, especially with Princess Elizabeth. This volume includes selections from the metaphysical texts, and Descartes' replies to another critic, the *Comments on a Certain Manifesto* (1648). Together they provide a representative sample of Descartes' work on metaphysics, from 1641 to 1649.

Before writing extensively on basic issues in philosophy, Descartes had published his first book in 1637: three scientific essays on geometry, dioptrics and meteorology. He wrote a special preface for that publication, the *Discourse on Method*, which was intended as a summary statement of Cartesian scientific method. The *Discourse* provides the focus for a companion volume of texts, which includes the *Rules* and selected writings from correspondence and other publications in which Descartes clarified his theory of scientific method.

Acknowledgements

In preparing this translation, I had the benefit of consulting the work of others who have embarked on the same project in the recent past. In particular, I learned much from the French translation of the *Meditations* by Michelle Beyssade (*Méditations métaphysiques*, Paris: Le Livre de Poche, 1990), the English translation by John Cottingham (*The Philosophical Writings of Descartes*, vol. 2, Cambridge University Press, 1984) and the recent translation of the works of Descartes into Italian (*Opere Filosofiche di René Descartes*, ed. E. Lojacono, Turin: 1994). I also gratefully acknowledge a grant from the Arts Faculty Research Fund, University College, Cork, which made it possible to consult the first editions of the texts at the Bibliothèque Nationale, Paris. Finally, Stephen Gaukroger was kind enough to read an earlier draft of my translation of the *Meditations* and made many helpful suggestions.

Desmond M. Clarke
Cork, 10 March 1997

NOTE TO CORRECTED EDITION

In this reprint, I have included a short paragraph which had been omitted on page 59. I am grateful to Meindert Kok for bringing it to my attention. I have also taken advantage of the reprint to make a number of other corrections and stylistic improvements.

July, 2000

Note on References to Descartes

The standard edition of Descartes' works was prepared by Charles Adam and Paul Tannery at the beginning of the twentieth century and was published in twelve volumes (Paris: L. Cerf, 1897–1913). These have been revised under the general direction of the Centre National de la Recherche Scientifique, France and have been reissued as *Oeuvres de Descartes*, ed. C. Adam and P. Tannery (Paris: Vrin, 1964–74). All references in notes to Descartes' works are to this latter edition, and are identified as AT, followed by the volume and page number.

Chronology

31 March 1596 Born at La Haye (since renamed Descartes), France
16 May 1597 Descartes' mother died
1607–1615 Attended Jesuit College of La Flèche
14 May 1610 Henry IV assassinated
9/10 November 1616 Graduated in Law, University of Poitiers
1618–19 At Breda, in the United Provinces
1618–48 Thirty Years War
1619–21 Travels to Poland and Germany
10 November 1619 Dreams of a 'great discovery' at Neuberg (Bavaria)
1620 Bacon publishes the *New Organon*
March 1621 Hugo Grotius escapes from prison and goes into exile in Paris
1623–28 Travels to Italy, and resides in Paris and Brittany
1627–8 Siege of La Rochelle
1628 Abandons writing the *Rules for Guiding One's Intelligence in Searching for the Truth*
1628–49 Lives at various places in the United Provinces
1633 Galileo's *Dialogue* condemned by the Roman Inquisition
1633 Decides not to publish *The World*
1637 Publishes *Discourse on the Method for Guiding One's Reason*, *the Dioptrics*, *the Meteors*, *and the Geometry*
1639 Campanella dies in exile in Paris, having been imprisoned in Italy for thirty years
1641 Publishes *Meditations on First Philosophy*
1642 Second edition, expanded and corrected, of the *Meditations*
1644 Published *The Principles of Philosophy*
1647 Published the French edition of *The Principles of Philosophy*
1648 Published response to Regius: *Comments on a Certain Manifesto*

1649 Published *The Passions of the Soul*
October 1649 Arrives in Sweden, at the Court of Queen Christina
11 February 1650 Dies at Stockholm
1662 *Treatise on Man* published in Latin
1664 *Treatise on Man* and *The World* published in French
1657, 1659, 1667 Three volumes of Descartes' letters edited by Clerselier
1701 *Rules for Guiding One's Intelligence* published

Introduction

When Descartes was grappling with the questions raised in these texts, in the early decades of the seventeenth century, the intellectual context in which he was writing was dominated by a number of major cultural, political and philosophical movements. One was the Protestant challenge to the traditional authority of the Catholic Church, expressed in the writings of Luther and Calvin among others, and the doctrinal and ecclesiastical counter-reformation which that provoked in predominantly Catholic countries such as France. Another significant development was what we describe in retrospect as the beginning of the scientific revolution. This included contributions by some of Descartes' famous scientific contemporaries, such as Kepler and Galileo in astronomy, William Harvey in physiology and, slightly later, Robert Boyle in chemistry. Third, every intellectual initiative of the period was challenged by the prevalence of various forms of scepticism, so that it was a commonplace for any theologian or philosopher to address the implications, for their own work, of this pervasive spirit of doubt. In a period of intellectual flux such as this, there might have been some refuge for innovative thinkers had the disciplines in which they worked been clearly demarcated, as they have become to a great extent since then. But those involved in the intellectual life of the early seventeenth century did not enjoy the protective benefits of clear disciplinary divisions; they had to cope with queries and objections from many different sources, ranging from astrology and magic to biblical studies and the new sciences. Thus the originality of the theories that emerged in this period was matched by the complexity and fluidity of the intellectual environment in which they had to compete.

Novel ideas in science, medicine, philosophy or law faced another challenge, which was not purely academic or intellectual. To the extent that those expressing new theories publicly were at odds with relevant authorities, they risked censure, dismissal from office, imprisonment or worse. The relevant authorities may have been one's colleagues in the same faculty or university, any church that objected to what it classified as unorthodox or, evidently, the political authorities, which showed remarkable zeal and an exaggerated competence in supporting churches or suppressing theories when it seemed politically opportune to do so. Giordano Bruno was put to death, by order of the Inquisition, in 1600 for reasons that are confused enough, even still, to include dabbling in magic, confounding the faith of the simple or an unwelcome involvement in international diplomacy. Galileo found to his cost, during the 1620s and 1630s, that the discussion of biblical interpretation was best left to others. Campanella spent more than a quarter of a century in jail but, despite that, was still publishing in the 1630s; and in the Netherlands, Hugo Grotius was sentenced to life imprisonment in the aftermath of the Synod of Dort, in which Calvinists and Arminians disputed the theology of predestination. Fortunately for the history of jurisprudence, he managed to escape from prison in a book chest in 1621 and went into exile in France.

Descartes was active during this momentous, revolutionary period in the history of ideas. Born on 31 March 1596 in La Haye, near Tours, in central France, he was educated initially at home and then followed his older brother to one of the recently founded Jesuit colleges at La Flèche. Descartes studied there for over eight years. The curriculum was the standard course of studies for Jesuit schools, which included Latin and Greek, mathematics and scholastic philosophy. It also included recent developments in the sciences that were relevant to the education of a young Catholic gentleman. When he left La Flèche in 1615, at the age of nineteen, Descartes enrolled at the University of Poitiers, from which he graduated in law in 1616. It might have seemed natural for him, at that stage, to follow in his father's footsteps and pursue a career in law. Instead he went to Breda, in the Netherlands, where he joined the army of the Prince of Orange, Maurice of Nassau. Given the indifferent health Descartes had experienced since his childhood, it is surprising that he even considered a military career; however, his sojourn at Breda was more like an induction into the applied mathematics of military science than the life of an ordinary soldier. It raised his awareness of recent developments in mathematics and, more generally, in the sciences.

It was during this period, in 1619, that Descartes had his famous dream in which he conceived the project of a fundamental renewal and unification of the sciences. Following some travel abroad to Germany and Denmark, he returned to the Netherlands where, for most of his adult life, he enjoyed the seclusion he claimed was necessary to pursue his intellectual project. He changed residence frequently, protecting his privacy and opportunities for study, travelling, corresponding with others who were involved in similar research programmes and, above all, doing experiments and writing. His objective was not a modest one: it was nothing less than constructing a new system of philosophy that would replace the scholastic style of philosophy almost universally taught at colleges and universities in Europe.

Apart from intermittent brief travel abroad, Descartes spent almost all the rest of his life in the Netherlands until he agreed, in 1649, to accept a post as philosopher in residence to Queen Christina of Sweden. The cold weather and early-morning philosophy lessons proved too much for his frail health and he died in Stockholm on 11 February 1650. Descartes never held a teaching post at a university or college; in fact, he supported himself from private resources during his whole adult life and devoted his time exclusively to thinking, doing experiments and writing. In doing so he addressed many of the issues uppermost in the minds of his contemporaries; in particular, he explicitly confronted the challenges raised by a form of scepticism that had become endemic in European intellectual circles.

SCEPTICISM

Scepticism, either as a thesis to the effect that it is impossible to know anything or, as a less dogmatic claim, that all our beliefs are more or less doubtful, was widely discussed for at least a hundred years before Descartes published the *Meditations*.[1] The question of how we can know anything with certainty, especially religious or philosophical beliefs, became a focus of theological discussions when Luther first challenged the Church's authority in the early sixteenth century. Church reformers cast doubt on the authenticity of texts that had been traditionally accepted as having been, in some sense, revealed or inspired by God. Even if there was agreement on this issue, there was a further question about how texts that had been written in Hebrew or Aramaic in a much earlier historical context should be interpreted. This suggested a fundamental problem for any church about the use of sacred texts, such as the Bible, to establish a church's authenticity. If one relies on a church to identify authentic sacred scriptures and to interpret them correctly, is it not arguing in a circle to appeal to the same scriptures to establish the authority of that church?

Besides these theologically motivated doubts, a philosophical strain of scepticism was cultivated by the reintroduction into Europe of sceptical writings from Greek philosophy. Pyrrhonism was a form of scepticism, named after the Greek philosopher Pyrrho of Elis (*c.* 365–275 BC). It avoided dogmatic claims about anything and argued, instead, that all our beliefs are subject to doubt. The Pyrrhonist writings of Sextus Empiricus were translated into Latin and published in Paris in 1562.[2] The writings of Cicero, especially the *Academics* and *Tusculan Disputations*, were also read widely during the sixteenth century and were integrated into a general negative assessment of the limits of human understanding. The general uncertainty created by theological division and the popular discussion of sceptical arguments is reflected in writings such as Erasmus' *The Praise of Folly* (Paris, 1511), where he says: 'human affairs are so manifold and obscure that nothing can be clearly known, as is rightly taught by my friends the Academics, the least arrogant of the philosophers'.[3] However, the writings of Michel de Montaigne were by far the most influential sceptical essays in the period immediately preceding Descartes.

Montaigne, in his famous *Apology for Raymond Sebond*, which is found in Book II of his *Essays* (1580–88), rehearses many familiar arguments for the Pyrrhonist thesis that none of our beliefs is beyond doubt. He introduces his discussion of human weakness with a lengthy comparison of human and animal achievements, which often reflects unfavourably on the former. 'Does anyone doubt that a child . . . would know how to go in search of food? . . . Animals do many actions which surpass our understanding.'[4] Montaigne thinks that the relative poverty of humans, both in skills and virtues, is best expressed by Pyrrhonism: 'No system discovered by man has greater usefulness nor a greater appearance of truth [than Pyrrhonism] which shows us Man naked, empty, aware of his natural weakness, fit to accept outside help from on high.'[5] The feebleness of human understanding and the arrogance that masks it is most apparent when we try to reduce the transcendent reality of God to the limits of human concepts. Thus, among all the areas in which we err, our talk of the divine is most wide of the mark.[6] But the uncertainty of human knowledge is not limited to speculation about God. Our senses frequently deceive us: 'Anybody can provide as many examples as he pleases of the ways our senses deceive or cheat us, since so many of their faults or deceptions are quite banal';[7] and 'since all knowledge comes to us through them and by them, we have nothing left to hold on to if they fail in their reports to us'.[8] We cannot even be certain that we are not dreaming when we seem to be clearly aware of our own present experiences and, if we are only dreaming, then whatever we are thinking may be a mere figment of our imagination. 'Why should we therefore not doubt whether our thinking and acting are but another dream; our waking, some other species of sleep?'[9] These doubts about sensory knowledge, and about the veridical character of what we are currently aware of, may be generalized by using an argument later exploited by Descartes: if we are deceived by someone even once, how do we know subsequently when to trust them? When applied to our cognitive faculties, the objection is: if the faculties by which we gain knowledge are sometimes mistaken, how can we know when, if ever, to trust them? 'If this appearance has once deceived me, if my touchstone regularly proves unreliable and my scales wrong and out of true, why should I trust them this time, rather than all the others?'[10] The depth and range of doubts surveyed by Montaigne seem to undermine our confidence that we know anything with certainty. In the simple formula with which Montaigne summarized his conclusion, the question is: what do we know (*Que sais-je?*)? The implied answer is: very little.

The wide scope of Montaigne's scepticism, extending from religious belief to human affairs and from politics to medical knowledge, is presented in a positive light as an antidote to irrational dogmatism. It gives rise to a form of fideism or uncritical belief; in other words, once we acknowledge the limits of what we can know by using our native intelligence, we can do no better than put our trust in what is generally believed. Thus Montaigne consistently favours conservatism both in religious belief and politics – not because we have indubitable reasons for our beliefs, but because it is not possible to have anything better than belief in tradition. When applied to religious belief this gave rise to a negative theology, of faith in a *hidden* God, which was subsequently favoured by some of Descartes' contemporaries such as St Francis de Sales and Blaise Pascal. Montaigne's version of scepticism was extremely influential during the early decades of the seventeenth century, and found supporters at the highest political levels in Mazarin and Richelieu. It was also adopted, paradoxically, as a weapon against Calvinism, which was described by some critics as granting a privileged place to unaided human understanding in deciding between competing religious beliefs. Such critics argued that human reason is so unreliable that we cannot even be sure of the rules of logic; therefore, when there is a question about the existence of God or the salvation of our souls, it is preferable to trust the authority of the Church rather than the apparent certainties of reason.

While this version of scepticism was favoured by many prominent Catholic writers in support of the counter-reformation, there were others whose sceptical motivation was more philosophical, such as Descartes' contemporary Pierre Gassendi, or more literary or fashionable, such as another of Descartes' contemporaries La Mothe le Vayer. Even Marin Mersenne, Descartes' most frequent correspondent and a sympathetic supporter of the new sciences, was persuaded by sceptical objections that we cannot hope to acquire anything more than probable knowledge of the world around us. The prevalence of sceptical arguments, and the frequency with which similar questions were raised by different authors, is very obvious from two books published by Jean de Silhon in 1626 and 1634. They identified the two questions that Silhon thought were crucial for sceptical debates: the existence of God and the immortality of the soul, the same issues Descartes addressed in the *Meditations*.[11]

Descartes could not possibly have been unaware of the almost constant public discussion of various forms of scepticism in the early seventeenth century and of its implications for science, religious belief and philosophy. There are frequent references in his correspondence to the writings of many of the sceptics mentioned above. He also adverts to the continuing popularity of Pyrrhonism in his replies to Pierre Bourdin's objections to the *Meditations*, where he rejects the suggestion that the influence of scepticism had waned. 'We should not believe that the sect of sceptics has been extinct for a long time. It is very much alive today, and almost everyone who regards themselves as more intelligent than others takes refuge in scepticism, when they find nothing in the commonly accepted philosophy to satisfy them and cannot see any alternative which is more true.'[12] However, it was unfortunately one of the risks associated with discussing scepticism that one might appear to readers as a supporter rather than a critic. Descartes' presentation of some standard sceptical doubts in the First Meditation gave many readers the impression, both during his lifetime and subsequently, that he was endorsing the very opinions he claimed to reject. In defence of his strategy, he draws the analogy with Galen's discussion of the causes of disease. Surely it would be unfair to describe Galen's work as a scientific method for getting sick; likewise, he claims, 'I did not propose any reasons for doubt with the intention of teaching them but, on the contrary, in order to refute them.'[13] In reading Descartes' analysis of sceptical objections in the first two meditations, we should take him at his word. He was rehearsing some of the most familiar Pyrrhonist objections of the period, and his objective was to answer them as best he could.

THE REFORMATION AND COUNTER-REFORMATION

Descartes associates his project in the *Meditations* with the Catholic counter-reformation by his reference, in the Letter of Dedication, to the Fifth Lateran Council (1512–17). This was a general council of bishops, meeting during the papacy of Leo X, at which Luther's teachings were condemned and the Catholic Church formally agreed on the doctrinal defences it planned to develop against the reformers.

One of the central issues that divided the churches was the capacity of human understanding to establish truths that are certain, independently of divine revelation or religious faith, and to specify the role of the senses in providing reliable information on the basis of which reason could reach reliable conclusions. Reformers were no more unanimous in their approaches to these issues than were their Catholic counterparts. In particular, the predominantly French form of Protestantism during the seventeenth century was based on the writings of Jean Calvin, whose supporters put much more trust in what our senses seem to teach and what our reason seems to conclude from empirical evidence, than in the authority of tradition or any other source of belief apart from the Bible.[14]

Descartes addressed questions about the scope of human knowledge and the competence of our cognitive faculties by asking whether our minds, independently of what may be taught by the Bible, can provide convincing arguments in favour of the existence of God and the immortality of the soul. His answer was unambiguously in the affirmative, and he was directly in line with the teaching of the counter-reformation Councils of the Catholic Church, both at Lateran and Trent, in adopting this position. Hence his annoyance at the suggestions, in the *Manifesto* published by Regius, that these truths could be known with certainty only from the Scriptures.

However, his unequivocal orthodoxy on this issue was not enough to prevent Descartes from becoming embroiled in other theological controversies. During the early 1630s, he showed remarkable caution when he was preparing for publication one of his most revolutionary works, *The World*, in which heliocentric astronomy was defended. When he heard about the fate of Galileo in Italy, he withheld the manuscript from publication and it remained unpublished during his lifetime. This unwillingness to challenge Church teaching in public is consistent with his often repeated claim that he did not wish to discuss theological questions and, as he conceded at the conclusion of the *Principles of Philosophy* (Part IV, art. 207), that anything he had written should be subject to correction by learned theologians and the Roman Catholic Church.

Despite all this caution and his apparently deferential attitude towards the Sorbonne theologians, Descartes was unwise enough to offer an opinion about one of the most contested theological issues of the seventeenth century, namely transubstantiation. The Council of Trent had considered this doctrine at length and eventually proposed, as Catholic doctrine, that the substance of bread and wine is changed during the Eucharist while the appearances of bread and wine (what the Council described in Latin as *species*) remain unchanged. Thus Catholics were invited to believe that, after the consecration of the Mass, they were presented with the substance of Christ and the appearances normally associated with bread and wine. This teaching of the Council of Trent was understood by many scholastic theologians as indirectly endorsing their philosophical account of a distinction between substances and accidents; in their view, the colour, taste, etc., of bread remained as accidents (or as nonsubstantial qualities) even though the underlying substance had been changed. Descartes thought that it was possible to provide a better theology of the Eucharist (consistent with the teaching of Trent), by using his own philosophical account of substance and qualities. According to the Cartesian theory, it is impossible for qualities to survive without the substances of which they are manifestations. Thus, in the Eucharist, the substance of bread or wine and their qualities are changed completely into the substance of Christ, and nothing remains of the original bread and wine. However, the new substance is able (by divine intervention) to cause us to have mental perceptions usually associated with the presence of genuine bread and wine. On this account, there are no qualities that are separated from their usual host substance. Instead, what is present is exclusively the substance of Christ; but by divine arrangement it succeeds in deluding us into apparently perceiving the presence of bread and wine.

Descartes' temerity in even discussing this question was compounded by the apparent implication, in his theory of animal machines, that many features of animal activity, such as moving, hearing, etc., could be explained without the hypothesis of an animal soul. Scholastic critics of Cartesianism had a well-founded intimation of the likely development of that theory. It was a short step from explaining all animal functions and actions in a purely mechanical way to attempting to explain human thought likewise without relying on the hypothesis of a human soul. La Mettrie's publication of *Machine Man* (1747) later confirmed the worst fears of Descartes' scholastic critics.

However, the fundamental issue that made Descartes suspect in the estimation of his theological contemporaries was the role he attributed to the human mind, unaided by divine revelation, in discovering the truth. There is a clear indication of this in his *Comments on a Certain Manifesto*, where he discusses the compatibility of faith and reason and the relative priority of reason in deciding which beliefs we should accept from among those offered to our faith. 'Since we were born human before we were made Christian, it is not credible that, in order to cling to the faith which makes someone a Christian, they would seriously adopt views that they believe are inconsistent with the right reason which makes them human.'[15] This confidence in the powers of the human mind, even if its limitations were acknowledged when confronted with mysteries such as the Incarnation or the Trinity, and his opposition to the kind of fideism associated with Pyrrhonism, left Descartes open to the charge that he had more in common with Calvinism than with the type of Catholicism officially in favour in his own day.

Any involvement in theological disputes in the seventeenth century was bound to lead to problems with ecclesiastical authorities. But, for reasons already mentioned, it was probably impossible to present any novel ideas in philosophy that were not perceived as unorthodox by some church or religious sect. In this respect, Descartes was typical of other innovators of the period. He spent considerable time and energy in answering objections from the reformed churches in the Netherlands.

One might anticipate that the opposition of reformed churches would be complemented by support from Catholicism. However, Descartes' reception in Rome was equally unfavourable. The Index of Forbidden Books, in 1663, prohibited printing, reading or even possessing copies of his works until such time as they were corrected.

THE SCIENTIFIC REVOLUTION

The texts included in this volume were all written from about 1640 onwards, that is, during the last ten years of Descartes' life. For the previous twenty years, Descartes had dedicated most of his time and energy to natural philosophy and mathematics or to what is today classified as science rather than philosophy. For example, he had contributed significantly to mathematics in his *Geometry* (1637), and had done novel work on optics and the explanation of the rainbow. But most fundamentally he had suggested that all natural phenomena could be explained mechanically, and that there are basic laws of nature that describe the patterns according to which all natural phenomena occur.

The hypothesis in favour of a general mechanization of nature was not exclusive to Descartes. This was a theme endorsed, to a greater or less extent, by many contributors to the scientific revolution. For example, Robert Boyle argued famously against thinking of 'nature' as some kind of universal agent independent of God, which could explain why natural phenomena occur as they do.[16] He also argued, just as vigorously, against any appeal to what scholastic philosophers called faculties and forms because the multiplication of such occult powers did nothing to explain the natural phenomena that required an explanation. Thus Boyle argued that, if a key opens a lock, it does so in virtue of its shape, size and rigidity, and it adds nothing to our understanding to say that the key has a 'lock-opening' faculty or form. Descartes' project in *The World* was similar to Boyle's. During the 1630s and 1640s, he focused on the question: what would it mean to *explain* a particular natural phenomenon, such as the attraction of iron filings by a magnet or the characteristic shape and colours of the rainbow? He argued that it is not an explanation to say that iron has an attractive power, or that rain and sunlight have a rainbow-making faculty or, in the example borrowed from Cartesianism and made famous by Molière, that a sleeping powder puts us to sleep because it has a dormitive or sleep-inducing power. A genuine explanation of any of these natural phenomena requires a description of the small parts of matter of which they are formed, the shapes and motions of those particles, and the ways in which the interaction of particles causes the phenomenon in question.

After 1630 this mechanistic agenda, of substituting explanations of natural phenomena in terms of parts of matter and their motions for traditional philosophical explanations in terms of forms and faculties, was central to Descartes' concerns. This project also required him to identify the basic laws according to which pieces of matter move and interact as they apparently do. These were provided by the three laws of nature, which were first introduced in *The World* and subsequently amended and published in the *Principles of Philosophy* (1644). The laws of nature were the ultimate theoretical elements on which the mechanical explanation of all natural phenomena relied. If this picture is correct – of Descartes as a dedicated proponent of a mechanical natural philosophy – then it raises a question about why he became involved with metaphysics and why he devoted so much of his time after 1640 to correspondence about metaphysical questions.

The answer to this question depends on how Descartes might have hoped to introduce the new natural philosophy to his readers, especially those who taught in colleges like La Flèche and universities such as Utrecht or the Sorbonne. In order to succeed he had to respond to the widespread scepticism which, if adopted, would undermine any pretensions he might have had to acquiring scientific knowledge. Descartes' metaphysics was a pre-emptive response to sceptical objections against the viability of the new science, an effort to establish foundations on which the mechanization of the physical world could proceed securely. He also needed to address the apparent implications of such a project for traditional philosophy as taught in the schools, and to explain the extent to which it was possible to retain scholastic philosophy while grafting on to it a revolutionary scientific world view. Even more seriously, Descartes had to consider the possible impact of his novel theories on the theological beliefs of the various churches with which he hoped to cultivate peaceful relations. Thus the *Meditations* and related philosophical writings were Descartes' attempt to come to terms with scepticism, with the entrenched philosophy of the schools, and with the theological sensitivities of the churches. He was confronting the political and intellectual influence of these competing forces, and attempting to carve out a space in the intellectual landscape in which the new natural philosophy could flourish.

The foundational role of metaphysics is explained in the tree metaphor, which was used, in the preface to the French edition of the *Principles* (1647), to describe how the various sciences depend on each other.[17] The root of the tree of knowledge is metaphysics, the trunk is physics, and the branches are all the applied sciences. Whether the roots are metaphysical or otherwise, it does not follow that one should continually replant the tree or, once planted, that one should obsessively dig up the roots to check that all is in order. An experienced gardener plants a tree carefully in well-prepared soil; any subsequent interference with the roots is likely to damage the tree rather than strengthen or secure its growth. Descartes seems to have accepted this implication of the tree metaphor in relation to metaphysics. In a letter to Princess Elizabeth in 1643, he explains the need to address radical metaphysical questions only once in a lifetime. In this context he also explains the need to use all our intellectual faculties, including the senses and the imagination, to make progress in understanding and not to focus exclusively on metaphysical insights, which depend on understanding alone:

> I can also say truthfully that the main rule that I followed in my study – and the rule that I believe has helped me most to acquire some knowledge – is that I never gave more than very few hours a day to thoughts which occupy the imagination, and very few hours a year to thoughts that occupy the understanding on its own; . . . although I think that it is very necessary to have understood well, once in a lifetime, the principles of metaphysics, because they provide us with knowledge of God and our soul, I also think that it would be very harmful to occupy one's understanding frequently in thinking about them because the understanding would find it difficult to leave itself free for using the imagination and the senses.[18]

The proposed division of time between natural philosophy (the study of which requires us to use our imagination and senses), and metaphysics (which is studied by using the understanding alone, without any other cognitive faculties), reflects Descartes' account of the role of metaphysics as the roots of the tree of knowledge: the roots should be established carefully, once only, before cultivating all the other branches of knowledge.

It has often been suggested that Descartes claimed to have found a single, indubitable truth in the certainty of 'I think, therefore I am', and that he logically deduced all other knowledge from this unshakeable foundation. This is evidently impossible and was never thought to be otherwise, even by the author of the *Meditations*. However, Descartes was certainly involved in a foundationalist enterprise: he was inquiring into the reliability of our cognitive faculties and the plausibility of scepticism, the apparent independence and superiority of faith and its theological interpretation, and the capacity of the human mind to establish some basic truths as a benchmark against which the kind of certainty possible in different areas of knowledge could be tested. In that sense, he was establishing the foundations of his whole project; he was removing sceptical objections to the reconstruction of natural philosophy and, at the same time, trying to make peace with the established schools of philosophy and theology.

This is the reason why Descartes wrote most of these texts in Latin. He had broken with tradition four years earlier by deciding to publish his first book in French: the *Discourse on Method* and scientific essays of 1637. The intention on that occasion was to make it accessible to a wider public, including women readers who had not followed the standard school curriculum. But the objective of the metaphysics was different. Descartes hoped to influence academic readers in many different European countries. He was especially interested in the possibility that religious orders which had established networks of colleges, such as the Oratorians or Jesuits, might consider integrating his new philosophy into their standard curriculum. Besides, his own travels, an extensive correspondence over many years with authors in England, Italy, France and the Netherlands, and his reading of the most recent publications on scientific and philosophical topics showed how difficult it was to reach international readers by writing in one's vernacular. It was not a casual decision, then, to choose the academic language in which metaphysics was usually written and to return to Latin as the medium for expressing his philosophical insights in the *Meditations*, *The Principles of Philosophy* and his *Comments on a Certain Manifesto*.

THE MEDITATIONS AND THE PRINCIPLES

Here Descartes pushed the challenge of scepticism to its limits by raising the possibility that our cognitive faculties may be constitutionally unreliable because God or Nature designed them defectively or because, despite a satisfactory design, they are subject to the distorting influence of powerful external factors. If this were true, then it would seem to be impossible to use the very same faculties, the reliability of which is in doubt, to provide a ladder by which to escape from scepticism. Undaunted by the magnitude of this challenge and rejecting the charge that he was arguing in a circle, Descartes tried to establish some very basic truths, the certainty of which was beyond the reach of even the most fundamental sceptical objections.

In the course of arguing against scepticism in the *Meditations*, Descartes defends a theory of human nature for which he has since become famous. According to this theory, human beings are composed of two completely distinct kinds of substance, matter and mind, each of which is defined in terms of a different basic property. Mind is defined by the ability to think, and matter is defined in terms of extension in three dimensions. This distinction provided Descartes with as neat a division as one could hope for between the domain of the sciences, that is, natural phenomena, which are material, and the domain of the mind, which is non-material, and it facilitated the construction of a purely mechanistic natural philosophy.

In making the mind–body distinction as he does, Descartes adapts the language and conceptual resources of scholastic philosophy to his own purposes.[19] The Cartesian distinction relies on the concept of a substance and its modes, which is not significantly different from the conceptual framework of scholastic metaphysics. Thus Descartes defines the mind as a faculty for thinking and the will as a faculty for willing. Since both are mere faculties, that is, capacities for performing distinctive actions, they cannot exist on their own as free-standing realities but must be predicated of something else that can enjoy an independent existence. This latter type of reality was traditionally called a substance. Descartes' use of faculty language prompted Hobbes to object that he seemed to be going back to the scholastic way of talking, as if the understanding understands, sight sees, the will wills and, at a stretch, walking walks.[20] Hobbes might seem to be quibbling over words here, but the issue was important. Descartes himself had mocked the explanatory uselessness of scholastic faculties in natural philosophy. However, if we cannot explain magnetic phenomena by attributing a 'magnetic power' to magnets, in what sense do we explain how human beings manage to think by attributing a 'thinking faculty' to them? Is explanation in metaphysics not subject to the same strict standards as explanation in physics?

This question is a special case of a more general problem with which Descartes struggled during the years following publication of the *Meditations*. He was proposing a quasi-scholastic foundation for a revolutionary new natural philosophy which seemed to be conceptually incompatible with it. He was trying to pour the new wine of modern science into the old wine-bottles of scholastic categories. For modern readers, then, the *Meditations* and the first book of *The Principles of Philosophy* may be read either as a bungled adaptation of scholastic philosophy – which provoked objections from its traditional proponents that their familiar theories did not need improvement – or as a radically new philosophy that was attempting to build bridges to the tradition it was discarding. The same ambivalence is apparent in Descartes' followers after his death in 1650. Some argued that scholastic philosophy should be abandoned because it had long outlived its usefulness; others argued that Descartes' principles were unobjectionable because they were hardly different from those of Aristotle!

Once embarked on this project, Descartes presents a traditional picture of the soul as a spiritual or non-physical substance which is united, inexplicably, with a body that functions like a biological machine. The machine of the body works by analogy with a hydraulic automaton. There are very narrow tubes through which an extremely subtle matter flows. The subtle matter is called animal spirits but, despite apparent connotations of the word 'spirits', it is just as material as any matter observable to the unaided eye. The tubes carry messages to and from the brain, in both directions. There are outgoing signals when the brain stimulates our limbs to move, and there are incoming signals from our sensory organs to the brain when we observe something. Observation is initiated by the physical action of external objects on the surface of our sensory organs. When appropriately stimulated, they transmit patterned impressions to the brain and to the central processing centre of the brain which, following scholastic terminology, is called 'common sense'.

The patterns of brain activity are sometimes called 'ideas' but Descartes was anxious not to confuse ideas in this sense – which are evidently physical events or dispositions in the brain – with their mental counterparts in the mind. Memory is a function, initially, of the brain. When sensory impressions reach the brain, they open up pathways in the narrow tubes through which they move and, by stretching the internal dimensions of the tubes, they make it easier for later flows of animal spirits to travel the same path. In this way, sense impressions leave behind in the brain dispositions that facilitate the subsequent occurrence of similar brain events. Thus there is a whole set of patterned events and after-effects in the brain, which are parallel to the mental activities of having thoughts and remembering previous ideas.

The interaction of mind and body was something his correspondent Princess Elizabeth found extremely difficult to understand. Descartes was often dismissive of people who raised good objections to his theories, accusing their authors of stupidity or bad faith. But he seems to have made a genuine effort for this correspondent to answer the objections raised; perhaps he was more open than usual to being questioned or more patient in his answers because she was a princess. Or perhaps he recognized the obvious validity of the questions she sent him. After repeated attempts to answer the question, how is it possible for something which is physical to interact with something else which, by definition, is not physical?, Descartes concedes that he cannot explain how it is possible. The reason, he says, is that to explain the union of mind and body is to think of them as a single entity, whereas to think of them as distinct substances is to think of them as not a single entity, and it is impossible to think of them in both ways at the same time. However, the fact that mind and body interact is something that each of us knows from experience, from our feelings and the experience of the passions.[21] For this reason Descartes talks about the substantial unity of human beings even though each person may be analysed into two distinct substances.

The unity of disparate substances in human nature is only one of the philosophical problems that emerge from these texts. Descartes also exploited the scholastic theory of the intentionality of ideas to construct a novel proof of God's existence. He argued that ideas are realities in their own right; they are events that take place in the mind of the individual thinker. But they are distinctive, not simply because of what they are as mental events occurring in a particular spiritual substance, but also because of their capacity to point to realities outside themselves. This particular feature, representing or pointing to realities other than themselves, is what makes one idea an idea of God while another idea, in the same human mind, is merely the idea of a horse or a heap of mud. Understandably, many readers questioned whether the intentional or representative character of ideas could support a proof of God's existence and Descartes' efforts to defend his analysis provided many opportunities for explaining his theory of ideas.

Apart from supporting proofs of God's existence, the theory of ideas outlined in the *Meditations* also addresses one of the themes that was to remain a central question in the theory of knowledge for centuries. Galileo had argued in *The Assayer* (1623) that, in many cases, our sensations of objects do not resemble the objects or events that cause them. For example, if the soles of someone's feet are lightly touched with a feather, they have a sensation of tickling. But it would make no sense to conclude from our sensation that there is an external reality – some kind of objective tickling – which resembles the sensation; the only realities that are relevant to explain our characteristic feeling, apart from our sensory organs and our consciousness, is the physical movement of the feather and its contact with our skin. Descartes uses this same example as Galileo to support a similar conclusion in the opening chapter of *The World*. He also adds another argument along the following lines. It is widely accepted that when we hear words, we consistently think of the appropriate object and that this happens even though the words do not resemble the objects in question. The word 'dog', for example, does not look like a dog nor, when pronounced, does it usually sound like a dog. Yet despite the lack of similarity, the word 'dog' in English makes us think about a dog. Now if words can get us to think about specific things without resembling them, purely as a result of a convention, why could it not happen naturally (that is, by divine prearrangement) that external objects would trigger appropriate ideas or sensations in our minds without resembling them either?

By generalizing this argument, one arrives at the insight that underpinned the distinction between what are often called primary and secondary qualities.[22] The name 'primary quality' was used to refer to certain fundamental or primitive qualities that substances have independently of our thinking about them. The size or shape of a piece of matter would be an example. In contrast, the term 'secondary quality' was used to denote either objective qualities, which could be explained in terms of primary qualities (for example, the magnetic properties of certain pieces of iron), or in some cases our perceptions or ideas of such secondary qualities. This implies a distinction between qualities that really exist in the way in which we think of them and may not be analysed into other more basic qualities, and qualities that, despite appearances, are reducible to primary qualities. For example, our perception of a particular natural phenomenon may be consistently what we call 'blue', but the external reality that causes us to have this sensation may not have the same qualities as our perception. If this is so, how can we make inferences from the qualitative character of our sensations to claims about the objective features of the external world? Evidently we cannot. Therefore our theorizing about the world outside our minds, about the kinds of realities it includes and the ways in which they interact, must ultimately be hypothetical. Our knowledge of the external world is a hypothesis about the kinds of external realities that are most likely to cause our perceptions. The logic of this strategy is exactly similar to that of a code-breaker.[23] If we think of a translation that makes sense of a string of coded symbols, we cannot be certain that this translation is unique or that we have the correct translation. On the other hand, we cannot do any better than construct translations that make sense of all the strings of symbols with which we are confronted. Likewise, the human mind has no direct access to the external world or its intrinsic properties. We have only the ideas we gain from experience. Our knowledge of the external world, then, is a hypothetical construction, a plausible theory about the kind of external objects that could cause us to have the perceptions we experience.

The anti-sceptical conclusion of the *Meditations* is that the most potent arguments of the sceptics fail, and that human beings are capable of knowing some truths with such clarity and distinctness that they are indubitable. At the same time, Descartes is clear that he should not prove too much – for example, that we are infallible or that our cognitive capacities are so well designed that they rarely mislead us. Having secured the foundations of human knowledge against Pyrrhonism, his task was to specify ways in which we could reasonably claim to have knowledge in all the areas that human understanding, without the assistance of divine revelation, is competent to explore.

Once the *Meditations* was published in 1641, Descartes continued to work on the original project of mechanizing nature that had been outlined in *The World*. The success of his metaphysical encounter with scepticism, and the range of objections and replies it provoked, encouraged Descartes to try to integrate first philosophy and natural philosophy into a new synthesis in the *Principles*. On this occasion, he changed the presentation of his theories from what he called an 'analytic' to a 'synthetic' style. That suggested a systematic exposition of his whole system, beginning from first principles, and an ordered presentation, such that if anything is required for the knowledge or explanation of a given phenomenon it has to have been explained or proved, as appropriate, prior to its use. This was the pattern followed by textbooks at the time, and Descartes hoped that the *Principles* might be adopted as a college text. Part I presents a revised version of the *Meditations*, Part II a general theory of matter and the laws of nature, and the remaining Parts III and IV a mechanical explanation of astronomical phenomena, of light, magnetism and other similar physical realities. This was also the occasion on which Descartes explicitly spelt out his account of substance and modes, of the concept of space and time, and the definition and explanation of motion on which he was to rely in his physics.

The publication of Descartes' metaphysics continued to provoke discussion from both supporters and opponents during the 1640s. Among the most sympathetic of critics was Princess Elizabeth, who carried on a philosophical correspondence with Descartes from 1643 to 1649. Elizabeth's letters often reported the busy distractions of life at the royal court. She also wrote about her own poor health and asked Descartes to suggest remedies for what seemed, to both of them, conditions caused by psychological factors. This correspondence encouraged Descartes to think more systematically about mind–body interaction, and particularly about the way in which the passions arise from the intimate relation between body and mind. Evidently if mind and body interacted, as his theory suggested, then any mental aberration could trigger a corresponding bodily illness and, in turn, a bodily illness could induce psychological sicknesses such as depression. The questions raised in these letters and the preliminary draft replies were eventually synthesized in the last work published during Descartes' life, *The Passions of the Soul* (1649).

For many years prior to his departure for Stockholm in 1649, Descartes lived in the Netherlands and won for his philosophy some of its earliest academic supporters. One of the first among the Dutch Cartesians was Henricus Regius, or Henri De Roy, a professor of theoretical medicine and botany at the University of Utrecht. Regius was more enthusiastic than discerning in his public teaching and defence of the new philosophy. This resulted in a series of theological and philosophical disputes that Descartes seems genuinely to have wished to avoid. On some occasions he advised his local supporter not to be so explicit or categorical in rejecting the philosophy of the schools. He even suggested introducing Cartesian ideas into his teaching as alternatives that left intact and unchallenged the traditional theories of the theology faculty at Utrecht.

However, Regius overtaxed Descartes' patience when he published an anonymous tract or manifesto which purported to explain the main principles of Cartesian philosophy in a series of very synoptic propositions. Some of these claims were obviously very different from what Descartes had published in the *Meditations* and the *Principles*, or were at least a significant misrepresentation of his views. More seriously, they erred in the direction of attributing to Descartes philosophical positions that attracted unwarranted theological censures. It was necessary, then, for Descartes to clarify his own position on the questions introduced by Regius and other Dutch critics, and this resulted in his *Comments on a Certain Manifesto*. In contrast with the correspondence with Elizabeth, we get a taste here of the more usual style of Descartes' replies: he sharply corrects misinterpretations and clarifies what he suggests is the obvious meaning of his various metaphysical doctrines.

THE LEGACY OF DESCARTES

During the period following Descartes' death in 1650, the impact of his theories on the intellectual life of Europe, especially in France and the Netherlands, was immense. Many professors of philosophy adapted his ideas to the prevailing programme of studies in colleges and universities, so that natural philosophy and even metaphysics were gradually Cartesianized much more than might have been expected from the initial reception of his publications. However, as already mentioned, Descartes' works were banned by Rome; consequently those who persisted in teaching such an unorthodox philosophy were often dismissed or censured for their views. The fate of Cartesianism also became entangled with new theological disputes in the French Church, especially those associated with Jansenism. When Jansenism was condemned by Rome, the court of Louis XIV provided civil support for the implementation of Church censures. In the years leading up to the revocation of the Edict of Nantes, in 1685, when the limited measures for religious toleration in France were officially cancelled, it was almost impossible for philosophers to avoid censure, by the state or the Church, except by repeating the well-known formulae of the scholastic tradition. Yet despite the extensive censorship of the times and the unavoidable conflicts with theologians of different religious traditions, Cartesianism prospered both as a method for philosophizing and as a widely accepted research programme in natural philosophy.

One of the central features of the Cartesian enterprise was confidence in the powers of human understanding when applied to objects of knowledge within the scope of its limited powers. This was expressed clearly by Nicolas Malebranche, the most famous of Descartes' followers, in 1675: 'Be advised, then, once and for all, that reason alone should stand in judgement on all human opinions not related to faith.'[24] If Descartes was right, there are many things that we can know, although the degree of certainty that we can achieve depends on what kind of belief is involved. Even the certainty of religious faith depends, ultimately, on our ability to prove God's existence because, if we cannot prove that a non-deceptive God exists, we have no reason to believe that he has revealed any credible mysteries to us.[25]

This extensive competence of human understanding was innate; it certainly was not something acquired by years of study in scholastic philosophy. In fact, the artificial training of scholastic philosophy was more of an impediment than a help in preparing the human mind for knowledge. Not surprisingly, Cartesians argued that those who did not have the benefits of a traditional schooling were in a better position to acquire knowledge than those whose minds were clouded by the obscurities of school philosophy. That implied that women, who usually missed the dubious benefits of a formal education, were better placed than most to use their native intelligence in the pursuit of the truth. This was a position argued at length by another Cartesian, Poulain de la Barre.[26]

The subsequent history of Cartesianism is a history of confronting the methodological and conceptual choices made by Descartes in order to facilitate the emergence of a new science of nature. Even those who famously disagreed with his philosophy – such as Newton in physics, Leibniz or Locke in philosophy, and Pascal or Samuel Clarke in their understanding of God's relation to nature – were forced to express the novelty of their own theories by situating themselves in relation to the world described by Descartes. In that sense, Descartes quickly acquired the status of one of the canonical philosophical writers of the early modern period. He joined the ranks of Aristotle and Aquinas and, subsequently, of Locke, Hume, Kant and Hegel as foremost among Western philosophers who have helped shape the way in which we currently think about the nature and limits of human understanding. Likewise, the scientific revolution that began in the seventeenth century relied on the work of a large number of experimental scientists, from lens grinders and alchemists to astronomers and mathematicians. But it was also indebted to philosophers, such as Descartes, who defended the competence of human understanding to explain the natural world and who provided the methodological and metaphysical foundations that underpinned what we now call scientific knowledge.

TEXTS SELECTED FOR THIS EDITION

Any abridgement of historical texts risks imposing on them the values or interests of readers from a later period. Ideally, they should be reproduced in their entirety. However, this is often impossible for practical reasons, usually because they are too long, and one is obliged to compromise between the integrity of the original text and its availability to modern readers. In preparing this new edition for Penguin Books, it was decided to focus on the two most famous texts by Descartes, the *Discourse on Method* (1637) and the *Meditations on First Philosophy* (1641), and to translate them without abridgement from French and Latin respectively. The former is the most accessible version of Descartes' theory of scientific method, and the latter is his most well-known contribution to metaphysical questions. Since both texts raise a cluster of related issues, it was thought best to publish them in separate editions and to supplement the core texts with selected writings by Descartes that clarify or develop the questions raised in the two principal texts.

The *Meditations* was Descartes' principal contribution to seventeenth-century metaphysics. He subsequently rewrote its central theses in a different style as Part I of *The Principles of Philosophy* (1644). As already indicated, he also began during the early 1640s to take seriously objections to mind–body dualism and some of these were discussed in correspondence, especially with Princess Elizabeth and Henry More.

This volume focuses on Descartes' metaphysical writings. It includes the *Meditations*, together with selections from the Objections and Replies, which were published in the first editions of the *Meditations*; Part I of *The Principles of Philosophy*; a selection from Descartes' correspondence in which he discussed some of the metaphysical issues raised in the *Meditations*; and finally Descartes' replies to a sympathetic critic of his metaphysics, the *Comments on a Certain Manifesto* (1648). Together they provide a representative sample of Descartes' work on metaphysics from 1641 to 1649.

Before writing extensively on metaphysical issues, Descartes had published his first book in 1637: it included three scientific essays on geometry, dioptrics and meteorology and a specially written Preface, the *Discourse on Method*, which was intended as a summary statement of Cartesian scientific method. The *Discourse* provides the focus for a companion volume of texts, which also include the *Rules* and other writings in which Descartes clarified his theory of scientific method.

NOTES

1. See Richard H. Popkin, *The History of Scepticism from Erasmus to Descartes*, rev. ed. (Assen: Van Gorcum, 1964).
2. Sextus Empiricus, *Pyrrhonian Hypotyposes* (Paris: 1562). The Greek text was subsequently published in France (and elsewhere) in 1621.
3. Erasmus, *The Praise of Folly*, trans. C. H. Miller (New Haven: Yale University Press, 1979), p. 71.
4. Michel de Montaigne, *The Complete Essays*, trans. M. A. Screech (Harmondsworth: Penguin Classics, 1993), pp. 511, 523.
5. Ibid., p. 564.
6. Ibid., pp. 572, 581.
7. Ibid., p. 669.
8. Ibid., p. 667.
9. Ibid., p. 674.
10. Ibid., pp. 634–4.
11. Jean de Silhon, *Les deux véritez de Silhon* (*The Two Truths of Silhon*) (Paris, 1626), and *De l'immortalité de l'âme* (*The Immortality of the Soul*) (Paris, 1634).
12. Descartes' reply to the Seventh Objections, AT VIII, 548–9.

13. Ibid., 573–4.

14. See, for example, a book published in the same year as Descartes' *Meditations* by a French Calvinist professor of theology at Saumur, Moise Amyraut: *De l'elévation de la foy et de l'abaissement de la raison en la créance des mystères de la religion (The Elevation of Faith and the Depression of Reason when Believing in the Mysteries of Religion)* (Saumur: Jean Lesnier, 1641).

15. *Comments on a Certain Manifesto*, p. 192. Compare this with the opposite view expressed by one of Descartes' later critics, Louis de la Ville: 'Since we know that our reason is liable to deceive us and frequently to represent what is false with the same appearance of truth as the truth itself; and since we are assured, on the other hand, that the faith is infallible and that what it teaches cannot be false; what should the Christian philosopher do when reason seems to contradict the faith? . . . Should he not cling more to his faith and assume that his reason has only a false appearance of truth?' *Sentimens de M. Des Cartes* (1672), pp. 12–13.

16. Robert Boyle, *A Free Enquiry into the Vulgarly Received Notion of Nature*, ed. E. Davis and M. Hunter (Cambridge: Cambridge University Press, 1996).

17. *Principles*, AT IX, Part 2, 14. 'Thus the whole of philosophy is like a tree, the roots of which are metaphysics, the trunk is physics, and the branches which emerge from the trunk are all the other sciences, which are reducible to three principal sciences, viz. medicine, mechanics and morals.'

18. Descartes to Elizabeth, 28 June 1643.

19. In Rule III of *Rules for Guiding One's Intelligence*, Descartes adverts to the need to use traditional Latin terms with a new meaning. 'I hereby advise them, as a general point, that I am not thinking at all about the way in which these terms have been used in recent times in the schools . . .' AT X, 369.

20. Hobbes, Third Objections against the Meditations, AT VII, 177.

21. See Descartes' *Conversation with Burman*, AT V, 163.

22. Some version of this distinction became almost a commonplace in seventeenth-century philosophy. It was adopted by Galileo, Boyle and, most famously, by John Locke and George Berkeley. It was also endorsed by Descartes' followers in France, for example by Jacques Rohault and Nicolas Malebranche.

23. *Principles*, Part IV, art. 205 (AT VIII, 1, 327–8).

24. *Search after Truth*, trans. by T. Lennon and Olscamp (Cambridge: Cambridge University Press, 1997), p. xxviii.

25. Ibid., pp. 291, 482.

26. See François Poulain de la Barre, *The Equality of the Sexes*, trans. by D. M. Clarke (Manchester: Manchester University Press, 1990).

Further Reading

Ariew, Roger, John Cottingham and Tom Sorrell, eds. *Descartes' Meditations: Background Source Materials* (Cambridge: Cambridge University Press, 1998).

Ariew, R., and M. Grene, eds. *Descartes and his Contemporaries: Meditations, Objections, and Replies* (Chicago and London: University of Chicago Press, 1995).

Armogathe, Jean-Robert. *Theologia cartesiana: l'explication physique de l'eucharistie chez Descartes et Dom Desgabets* (The Hague: Nijhoff, 1977).

Beyssade, Jean-Marie. *La Philosophie première de Descartes* (Paris: Flammarion, 1979).

Blackwell, Richard J. *Galileo, Bellarmine, and the Bible* (Notre Dame and London: University of Notre Dame Press, 1991).

Broughton, Janet. *Descartes's Method of Doubt* (Princeton and Oxford: Princeton University Press, 2002).

Clarke, Desmond M. *Descartes's Theory of Mind* (Oxford: Clarendon Press, 2003)

Clarke, Desmond M. *Occult Powers and Hypotheses: Cartesian Natural Philosophy under Louis XIV* (Oxford: Clarendon Press, 1989).

Cottingham, John. *Descartes* (Oxford: Blackwell, 1986).

Cottingham, John. *A Descartes Dictionary* (Oxford: Blackwell, 1993).

Cottingham, John, ed. *The Cambridge Companion to Descartes* (Cambridge and New York: Cambridge University Press, 1992).

Curley, Edwin. *Descartes against the Sceptics* (Oxford: Blackwell, 1978).

Doney, Willis, ed. *Descartes: A Collection of Critical Essays* (New York: Doubleday, 1967).

Frankfurt, Harry G. *Demons, Dreamers, and Madmen* (Indianapolis: Bobbs-Merrill, 1970).

Garber, Daniel. *Descartes Embodied* (Cambridge: Cambridge University Press, 2001).

Garber, Daniel. *Descartes' Metaphysical Physics* (Chicago and London: University of Chicago Press, 1992).

Gaukroger, Stephen. *Descartes: An Intellectual Biography* (Oxford: Clarendon Press, 1995).

Gaukroger, Stephen, et al. eds. *Descartes' Natural Philosophy* (London and New York: Routledge, 2000).

Gaukroger, Stephen, *Descartes' System of Natural Philosophy* (Cambridge: Cambridge University Press, 2002).

Jolley, Nicholas. *The Light of the Soul: Theories of Ideas in Leibniz, Malebranche and Descartes* (Oxford: Oxford University Press, 1990).

Marion, Jean-Luc. *Sur la théologie blanche de Descartes* (Paris: Presses Universitaires de France, 1981; 2nd ed. 1991).

Montaigne, Michel de. *The Complete Essays*, trans. and ed. M. A. Screech (Harmondsworth: Penguin Books, 1993).

Nadler, Steven M. *Arnauld and the Cartesian Philosophy of Ideas* (Manchester: Manchester University Press, 1989).

Popkin, Richard H. *The History of Scepticism from Erasmus to Descartes*, rev. ed. (Assen: Van Gorcum, 1964).

Rodis-Lewis, Geneviève. *Descartes: biographie* (Paris: Calmann-Lévy, 1995).

Rozemond, Marleen. *Descartes's Dualism* (Cambridge, Mass., and London: Harvard University Press, 1998).

Verbeek, Theo. *Descartes and the Dutch: Early Reactions to Cartesian Philosophy, 1637–1650* (Carbondale, Ill.: Southern Illinois University Press, 1992).

Williams, Bernard. *Descartes: The Project of Pure Inquiry* (Harmondsworth: Penguin Books, 1978).

Wilson, Margaret D. *Descartes* (London: Routledge, 1978).

RENATI

DES-CARTES,

MEDITATIONES

De Prima

PHILOSOPHIA,

In quibus Dei existentia, & animæ humanæ à corpore distinctio, demonstrantur.

His adjunctæ sunt variæ objectiones doctorum virorum in istas de Deo & anima demonstrationes;

Cum Responsionibus Authoris.

Secunda editio septimis objectionibus antehac non visis aucta.

Amstelodami,

Apud Ludovicum Elzevirium. 1642.

Meditations on First Philosophy,
in which God's Existence
and the Distinction between the Human Soul and the Body
are Demonstrated

1641

NOTE ON THE TEXT AND TRANSLATION

The first edition of the *Meditations* was written in Latin, and was published by Michael Soly, Paris, in 1641 under the title: *Meditationes de prima philosophia, in qua Dei existentia & animae immortalitas demonstratur* (*Meditations on First Philosophy, in which God's Existence and the Immortality of the Soul are Demonstrated*). This edition included the first six sets of objections and Descartes' replies to them. In the royal permission to publish, which was printed at the end of the book, the title was given as *Meditationes Metaphysicae* (*Metaphysical Meditations*); this was also the title used by Descartes in transferring the copyright to Soly, and it was often used by correspondents in referring to the book subsequently. The second edition was published by Elzevier, Amsterdam, in 1642, under a slightly different title: *Meditationes de prima philosophia, in quibus Dei existentia, & animae humanae a corpore distinctio, demonstrantur* (*Meditations on First Philosophy, in which God's Existence and the Distinction between the Human Soul and the Body are Demonstrated*). This edition also included, for the first time, the seventh set of objections and replies.

The first French edition was published in 1647 as *Les Méditations Métaphysiques de René Descartes touchant la première philosophie* (*The Metaphysical Meditations of René Descartes concerning First Philosophy*). Apart from being a relatively loose translation, this text also included frequent minor additions to the original text in which the translator, presumably with Descartes' agreement, elaborated on the meaning of the Latin text.

In preparing this translation I have followed the Latin text of the second edition. There were no paragraph indentions in the first three meditations of this edition, and the following three meditations included only a relatively small number of new paragraphs. The first French translation initiated what later became standard practice by inserting new paragraphs whenever they seemed appropriate for the structure of the argument or the meaning of the text. I have adopted the same practice, although I have not followed the Adam and Tannery text in every instance.

It might seem from the structure of the text that Descartes published the *Meditations* initially as a separate book, and that he invited readers to send in objections or comments on the text. If that had happened, the *Meditations* could stand alone and the subsequent material might be considered secondary. However, there is good reason to believe that Descartes planned the *Metaphysical Meditations* so as to include, as an integral part, the Objections and Replies. The Objections provided an opportunity to clarify ideas that appeared in outline in the initial *Meditations* and to engage in print both with sympathetic critics and with those, such as Hobbes, who obviously disagreed with his central theses. Thus the very first edition of the text included the six sets of Objections and Replies; the six Meditations occupied 116 pages, and the Objections and Replies appeared on pages 117–602. Descartes asked readers, in the Preface, not 'to pass judgement on the *Meditations* until they have taken the trouble to read through these objections and my replies'. However, despite the integrity Descartes claimed for the full published text, it is now common to read the *Meditations* independently of the rest of the book. This edition represents a compromise between Descartes' published text and the usual practice of twentieth-century readers. It includes translations of selected parts of the Objections, together with Descartes' Replies. In making a selection, I have been guided by the extent to which the Replies throw genuine new light on what Descartes wrote in the Meditations and, in each case, I have included the text of the Objection that provoked the clarification.

Descartes' Latin is remarkably compact. He also used rather long sentences. Since any English translation is likely to be longer, sentence by sentence, than the original, it is tempting to subdivide the original sentences into more manageable phrases. However, I have tried to reflect the style of the original by keeping Descartes' own sentences as much as possible.

Finally, there is one phrase in Latin that causes special problems for the translator. Descartes writes about a feature of ideas which he calls, in Latin, their '*realitas objectiva*'. This is usually translated as the 'objective reality' of ideas. However, the phrase 'objective reality' in modern English means almost the exact opposite to what Descartes meant. Given his debt to late scholastic philosophers (especially to Suarez) and their discussion of the so-called intentional reality of ideas, I thought it best to use the phrase 'intentional reality' to translate Descartes' '*realitas objectiva*'.

LETTER OF DEDICATION TO THE SORBONNE

To the very wise and renowned Dean and Professors of the Faculty of Sacred Theology of Paris, from René Descartes.

My reason for offering you this book is very persuasive, and I am confident that you will have an equally strong reason for defending it once you understand why I wrote it; thus the best way of commending it to you is to say a few words about my objectives in writing it.

I have always thought that two questions, about God and the soul, are foremost among those which should be demonstrated philosophically rather than theologically. Although, for those of us who are believers, it is enough to accept on faith that the human soul does not die with the body and that God exists, it certainly seems impossible in the case of non-believers to convince them of any religion or of almost any moral virtue unless they are first convinced by natural reason[1] of these two truths. Besides, since there are often greater rewards for vice than for virtue in this life, few will prefer what is right to what is profitable if they neither fear God nor expect an afterlife. It is perfectly true that we should believe in God's existence because it is taught by Sacred Scripture and, conversely, that we should believe in Sacred Scripture because it comes from God, for faith is a gift of God and the same person who gives us grace to believe other things can also provide the grace to believe that he exists. However, that is not something that can be proposed to non-believers, because they would think it is circular. I have also noticed that, like other theologians, you all claim not only that God's existence can be proved by natural reason, but that Sacred Scripture implies that knowledge of God is easier than the knowledge available about many created things, and that it is so easy to know God that those who lack this knowledge are at fault. This is clear from these words of the Book of Wisdom, chapter 13: 'Nor should they be ignorant of these. For if they were able to know so much as to make a judgement of the world; how did they not more easily find out the Lord thereof?'[2] And in chapter 1 of the Epistle to the Romans, the same people are said to be 'inexcusable'. We seem to be reminded in the same text by the words 'what is known about God is manifest to them'[3] that everything that can be known about God can be shown from reasons that derive from no other source but our own mind. Therefore I thought it was appropriate to inquire how that is possible, and how God may be known more easily and more certainly than worldly things. As regards the soul, many people thought that its nature cannot easily be investigated, and some have even dared say that human reason shows us that the soul dies with the body and that the contrary view is held by faith alone; however, the Lateran Council, held under Leo X (Session 8), condemns them and explicitly commands Christian philosophers to defeat their arguments and prove the truth to the best of their abilities, and therefore I too have not hesitated to take on this challenge.

Besides, I know that many impious people refuse to believe that God exists and that the human soul is distinguishable from the body for no other reason, they claim, except that no one has so far been able to prove these two truths. Although I do not agree with them at all and believe, on the contrary, that almost all the reasons which have been adduced by eminent men in support of these truths, when they are adequately understood, have the force of demonstrations, and although I am convinced that hardly any other reasons could be given which were not found previously by others, still I think that there can be nothing more useful to philosophy than if, once and for all, the best of all those reasons are carefully sought and expounded accurately and clearly, so that it is established for everyone for the future that they are demonstrations.

Finally, I have been strongly encouraged to do this by some people who knew that I had once developed a method for resolving certain difficulties in the sciences[4] – not, however, a new method because nothing is older than the truth, but one that they had seen me use often with success in other areas. For that reason, I thought it was my duty to attempt something in this area.

Everything I have been able to accomplish is contained in this treatise. I have not tried to include every argument that could be used to prove the same conclusion, nor would that seem worthwhile unless none is considered satisfactory. Instead I have chosen only the most basic and most important arguments, so that I now dare to propose them as the most certain and evident demonstrations. I would even add that these arguments are such that I do not think there is any way in which human intelligence could ever discover better ones. Both the importance of the issues and the glory of God, which is the purpose of the whole discussion, make me speak a little more freely about my arguments than I usually do. Even though I think they are certain and evident, I am not convinced as a result that everyone has the ability to grasp them. There are many writings in geometry from Archimedes, Apollonius, Pappus and others which, although accepted by all as most certain and evident – because they clearly include nothing which is not very easy to understand when considered on its own, and there is nothing in the consequences which does not fit exactly with the antecedents – are, nonetheless, understood by very few people, because they are rather long and require a very careful reader. In a similar way, although the arguments I use here compare with or surpass in certainty and evidence the proofs of geometry, I fear that they may not be understood adequately by many readers, both because they are rather long, some depend on others, and especially because they require a mind that is completely free from prejudices and can easily withdraw itself from dependence on the senses. Moreover, it is certainly the case that the number of people in the world who are adept at metaphysics is not greater than those who are adept at geometry. There is also this difference, that everyone is convinced that nothing should be written in geometry which is not demonstrated with certainty, and beginners are more mistaken by accepting what is false rather than by rejecting what is true, because they wish to appear as if they understand; in philosophy, by contrast, since it is believed that there is no thesis which cannot be argued either way, few pursue the truth while many others seek a reputation for intelligence by daring to challenge what is most solidly established.

Thus whatever the merits of my arguments, since they are concerned with philosophy I do not expect them to succeed in achieving anything worthwhile unless you assist me with your patronage. The reputation of your Faculty is so high in everyone's estimation and the name of the Sorbonne has such great authority, that not only has no institution apart from the Church Councils as much credibility as yours in matters of faith but, even in secular philosophy, no one is thought to have a greater insight and reliability, and a greater integrity and wisdom in making judgements.[5] I am mindful not only of my humanity but especially of my ignorance, and hence I do not claim that this book contains no mistakes. Thus if you deigned merely to pay enough attention to it so that, in the first place, it may be corrected; secondly, so that arguments which are defective, incomplete, or require more explanation can be completed, perfected or clarified, either by you or at least by me after being advised by you; and finally, so that the arguments included here, which prove that God exists or that the soul is distinct from the body, may be made as clear as I think they can be and, as a result, these arguments may be considered very rigorous demonstrations and you may be willing to say this and to testify to it publicly; if this were to happen, I have no doubt that all the errors which have ever been made about these issues would be erased quickly from human minds. The truth itself would easily cause other intelligent and wise people to agree with your judgement, and your authority would cause atheists (who are usually classified as learners, rather than as intelligent and learned) to give up the spirit of contradiction and even, lest they appear not to understand, to defend those arguments that they would recognize are accepted as demonstrations by everyone who is intellectually gifted. Finally, everyone else would so easily accept so many testimonies that there would be no one in the world who dares doubt that God exists or that the human soul is really distinct from the body. You yourselves, because of your exceptional wisdom, can estimate better than anyone else the great benefits of this, and it would not be appropriate for me here to commend any further the cause of God and of religion to you, who have always been the sturdiest pillar of the Catholic Church.

PREFACE TO THE READER

I have already briefly discussed questions about God and the human mind in the *Discourse on the Method for Guiding One's Reason and Searching for Truth in the Sciences*, published in French in 1637. I did not intend to discuss them in detail in that book, but simply to provide an introduction and to learn from readers' reactions how they should be presented subsequently. I thought that these questions were so important that they should be discussed more than once, and that the way in which I explain them is so novel and so different from what is usually done that it was unhelpful to teach it in greater detail in a book written in French and available to be read by everyone, lest minds even less gifted than mine might believe that they should follow the same path.

Although I asked in the *Discourse* that anyone who found anything objectionable in my writings should kindly bring it to my notice,[6] only two objections worth mentioning were raised concerning these questions, to which I will now reply briefly before undertaking a more detailed explanation.

The first objection is: from the fact that the human mind reflecting on itself does not perceive itself as anything other than a thinking thing, it does not follow that its nature or essence consists merely in the fact that it is a thinking thing, where the word 'merely' excludes everything else that might also be said to belong to the nature of the soul. I reply to this objection that, in that context, I did not wish to exclude other things with respect to the truth of the question (which I was not discussing at that stage) but merely with respect to my own perception. Thus what I meant was: I did not discover anything clearly that I knew belonged to my essence except that I was a thinking thing or a thing that possesses in itself a thinking faculty. I will show below how, from the fact that I do not know anything else that belongs to my essence, it follows that nothing else does in fact belong to it.

The other objection is: from the fact that I have within me an idea of something which is more perfect than me, it does not follow that the idea itself is more perfect than me and, much less, that the reality which the idea represents exists. I reply that the word 'idea' is equivocal here. It can be understood either materially, as an operation of the intellect and, in this sense, it cannot be said to be more perfect than me. Or it can be understood intentionally,[7] as the thing represented by the idea and, even if this thing is not assumed to exist outside the mind, it may be more perfect than me with respect to its essence. But how, from the fact that I have an idea of something which is more perfect than me, it follows that this thing really exists, will be explained in detail below.

Apart from those two objections, I also saw two fairly long pieces that challenged my conclusions rather than my reasoning on these questions, by means of arguments borrowed from standard atheists' sources. Since such arguments cannot have any influence on those who understand my reasons, and since many people's judgements are so perverse and foolish that they are more convinced by the first views they hear, no matter how false and unreasonable they are, than by a true and sound refutation which they hear later, I do not wish to reply to these objections here lest I be the first to report them. I will say simply, in general terms, that all the things commonly invoked by atheists to challenge the existence of God always depend either on falsely attributing human affections to God, or on arrogating so much power and wisdom to our minds that we try to determine and comprehend what God can and should do. Therefore, as long as we remember that our minds should be considered finite but that God is infinite and incomprehensible, they will not pose any difficulty for us.

Now that I have finished examining the judgements of others, I return to the same questions of God and the human mind and to the beginnings of the whole of First Philosophy,[8] but without waiting for popular approval or a wide readership. Indeed, I would not encourage anyone to read these pages unless they are willing and able to meditate with me seriously and to detach their minds from the senses and simultaneously from all prejudices, and I know that there are few such readers. As for those who do not bother to understand the order and interconnection of my arguments but try to snipe at individual sentences, as they usually do, they will derive little benefit from reading this book. They may find an opportunity to cavil in many places, but they will not easily raise any objection that is significant or deserves a response.

However, I do not even promise to satisfy the remaining readers on all questions on their first reading, and I am not so arrogant as to believe that I can anticipate everything with which readers may find some difficulty. For that reason I initially expound, in the *Meditations*, precisely those thoughts by which I think I have reached a certain and evident knowledge of the truth in order to test if I might be able to convince others by the very same reasons that convinced me. After that, I will reply to the objections of some eminently intelligent and learned people to whom these *Meditations* were sent for comments before they were printed. Their objections were so numerous and varied that I dare hope that no objection – at least no significant objection – will easily occur to anyone else which they have not already raised. Therefore I repeat that readers should not pass judgement on the *Meditations* until they have taken the trouble to read through these objections and my replies.

SUMMARY OF THE FOLLOWING SIX MEDITATIONS

The First Meditation introduces reasons why we can have doubts about everything, especially about material things, as long as we have no other foundations for the sciences apart from those that we have had to date. Although the usefulness of such an extensive doubt may not be apparent initially, it is extremely useful because it frees us from all prejudices, provides the easiest way to detach the mind from the senses and eventually makes us such that we cannot subject to further doubt the things that we later discover to be true.

In the Second Meditation the mind, by exercising its own freedom, assumes that nothing exists if its existence can be even slightly doubted, and realizes that it is impossible that it does not exist itself during that time. This is extremely beneficial because it thereby distinguishes what belongs only to itself, that is to an intellectual nature, and what belongs to the body.

But since some readers may expect to find arguments about the immortality of the soul in this section, I should warn them immediately that I tried to write nothing that I was unable to demonstrate rigorously. Therefore I could not follow any method apart from that used by geometers, which is to write down first everything on which some proposition that is sought depends before deriving any conclusion from it. Now, the first and principal prerequisite for knowing the soul's immortality is that we form as clear a concept of the soul as possible, and one which is clearly distinct from every concept of body. That is what has been done in this Meditation. Furthermore, we also need to know that all those things which we clearly and distinctly understand are true in the way in which we have understood them. It was impossible to prove this before the Fourth Meditation. One also needs a clear concept of bodily nature, which is partly in the Second Meditation itself and partly in the Fifth and Sixth Meditations. From these one ought to conclude that all those things which are conceived clearly and distinctly as distinct substances – and mind and body are so conceived – are truly substances that are really distinct from each other, and I came to that conclusion in the Sixth Meditation. That is also confirmed in the same place by the fact that we can understand body only as divisible whereas, in contrast, we can understand the mind only as indivisible. Nor can we conceive of half a mind, as we can of even the smallest body. Thus their natures are recognized as being not only distinct but even in some sense opposites.

However, I have not discussed this question any further in this book, both because these considerations are enough to show that the annihilation of the mind does not follow from the corruption of the body and thus to provide mortals with hope for an afterlife, and because the premises from which one can conclude that the mind really is immortal presuppose an explanation of the whole of physics. First one needs to know that all substances – that is, things which, in order to exist, have to be created by God – are without exception incorruptible by their nature, and they can never cease to exist unless they are reduced to nothingness by the same God if he stops maintaining their existence. Then we need to acknowledge that even body, considered in general, is a substance and therefore can never perish either. But the human body, insofar as it is distinct from other bodies, is constituted merely by a certain combination of parts and other variable features of the same sort; the human mind, however, is not composed of variable features in this way, but is a pure substance and even if all its variable features change so that it understands different things, wills different things, senses different things, and so on, the mind itself does not thereby become a different mind. The human body, however, does become a different body by the mere fact that the shape of some of its parts is changed. It follows that the body may indeed perish very easily but that the mind is by its own nature immortal.

In the Third Meditation I think I have explained in sufficient detail my principal argument for proving the existence of God. However, since, in order to detach my readers' minds as much as possible from the senses, I did not wish to use any comparisons drawn from bodily things, many obscurities may have remained but I hope they will later be resolved completely in the Replies to Objections. One example, among others, is this: how does the idea of a supremely perfect being which is found in us contain so much intentional reality that it is impossible for it not to result from a supremely perfect cause? This is illustrated, in the Replies, by analogy with a very perfect machine, the idea of which is in the mind of some designer. Just as the intentional artifice of this idea must have some cause, namely the knowledge of the designer or of someone else from whom they got it, so likewise the idea of God that we have must have God himself as its cause.

In the Fourth Meditation, everything that we clearly and distinctly perceive is proved to be true, and I also explain at the same time what is the essence of falsehood. These must be known both in order to confirm earlier arguments and to understand what comes later. (Meantime one should note that there is no discussion there about sin, that is, a mistake made in pursuing good and evil, but merely of mistakes that occur in deciding truth and falsehood. Nor does it apply to anything related to religious belief or to human conduct, but only to theoretical truths, which are known by means of the natural light of reason.)[9]

In the Fifth Meditation, apart from what is explained about bodily nature in general, there is a new argument to demonstrate God's existence. Here, too, there may be some difficulties, which are resolved later in the Replies to Objections. Finally, it is shown in what sense it is true that even the certainty of geometrical demonstrations depends on knowledge of God.

Lastly, in the Sixth Meditation, the intellect is distinguished from the imagination; the criteria for this distinction are explained; the mind is proved to be really distinct from the body, but it is shown to be so closely joined with it that together they form a single entity; all the errors that usually arise from the senses are reviewed; ways by which errors may be avoided are presented; and finally, all the reasons from which the existence of material things may be deduced are introduced. I do not think that these arguments are very useful on account of the fact that they prove what they establish – namely, that there really is a world, that human beings have bodies, and similar things – for no one of sound mind has ever seriously doubted these things. Rather, by considering these arguments, they are recognized as being less sound and clear than those by which we acquire knowledge of our own mind and of God. Thus the latter are the most certain and evident of all the arguments that can be known by human intelligence. My only objective in these Meditations was to prove that one thing. Therefore I will not review here the various other questions which also happen to be discussed as they arise in the Meditations.

MEDITATIONS ON FIRST PHILOSOPHY

in which God's existence
and the distinction between the human soul and the body
are demonstrated

FIRST MEDITATION

Things which can be called into Doubt

Some years ago I noticed how many false things I had accepted as true in my childhood, and how doubtful were the things that I subsequently built on them and therefore that, once in a lifetime, everything should be completely overturned and I should begin again from the most basic foundations if I ever wished to establish anything firm and durable in the sciences. But that task seemed enormous, and I waited to reach such a mature age that no more appropriate age for learning would follow. Thus I waited so long that, from now on, I could be blamed if I wasted in further deliberation whatever time remains for me to begin the project. Therefore today I appropriately cleared my mind of all cares and arranged for myself some time free from interruption. I am alone and, at long last, I will devote myself seriously and freely to this general overturning of my beliefs.

To do this it is not necessary to show that they are all false – something I might never be able to accomplish! But since reason already convinces us that we should withhold assent just as carefully from whatever is not completely certain and indubitable as from what is clearly false, if I find some reason for doubt in each of my beliefs, that will be enough to reject all of them. However, they need not all be reviewed individually, for that would be an infinite task; as soon as foundations are undermined everything built on them collapses of its own accord, and therefore I will challenge directly all the first principles on which everything I formerly believed rests.

Everything that I accepted as being most true up to now I acquired from the senses or through the senses. However, I have occasionally found that they deceive me, and it is prudent never to trust those who have deceived us, even if only once.

But despite the fact that the senses occasionally deceive us about things that are very small or very far away, perhaps there are many other things about which one surely cannot have doubts, even if they are derived from the senses; for example, the fact that I am here, sitting by the fire, wearing a dressing gown, holding this page in my hand and other things like that. Indeed, how could I deny that these hands or that this body is mine, unless perhaps I think that I am like some of those mad people whose brains are so impaired by the strong vapour of black bile that they confidently claim to be kings when they are paupers, that they are dressed up in purple when they are naked, that they have an earthenware head, or that they are a totally hollowed-out shell or are made of glass. But those people are insane, and I would seem to be equally insane if I followed their example in any way.

Very well. But am I not a man who is used to sleeping at night and having all the same experiences while asleep or, sometimes, even more improbable experiences than insane people have while awake? How often does the nocturnal quietness convince me of familiar things, for example, that I am here, dressed in my gown, sitting by the fire, when I am really undressed and asleep in my bed? But at the moment I certainly see this sheet of paper with my eyes wide open, the head I shake is not asleep, I extend and feel this hand, carefully and knowingly; things which are as clear as this would not occur to someone who is asleep. As if I do not remember having been deluded by similar thoughts while asleep on other occasions! When I think about this more carefully, I see so clearly that I can never distinguish, by reliable signs, being awake from being asleep, that I am confused and this feeling of confusion almost confirms me in believing that I am asleep.

Let us assume therefore that we are asleep and that those things are not true – that I open my eyes, move my head, extend my hand – and that we do not even have such hands nor this whole body. But it must be admitted that the things we see while asleep are like certain familiar images, which can be painted only as copies of things which are real. Therefore at least these general things – eyes, head, hands, the whole body – exist as real things rather than as some kind of imaginary things. For clearly even painters, when they try to imagine the most unusual sirens or satyrs, cannot assign natures to them which are completely new; rather, they simply mix up the parts of different animals. Even if they happen to think up something so novel that nothing like it was ever seen before – so that it is therefore very clearly fictitious and false – nonetheless, at least the colours from which they paint it must surely be real. In a similar way even if these general things – the eyes, the head, the hands and so on – were imaginary, it must still be admitted that at least some other things are real, that they are even more simple and general and that it is from them, as if from true colours, that all those images of things in our thought, both true and false, are constructed. Physical nature in general and its extension seem to be of this kind; likewise, the shape of extended things; also quantity, or their size and number; similarly the place in which they exist, the time through which they last, and similar things.

Thus we might conclude reasonably from these considerations that physics, astronomy, medicine, and all other disciplines that involve an examination of composite things are indeed doubtful; but that arithmetic, geometry, and other such disciplines that discuss only very simple and general things, and are not concerned with whether or not they exist in nature, contain something that is certain and beyond doubt. For whether I am awake or asleep, two and three added together make five and a quadrilateral figure has no more than four sides. It seems impossible that one could ever suspect that such clear truths are false.

However, there is an ancient belief somehow fixed in my mind that God can do everything and that I was created by him with the kind of existence I enjoy. But how do I know that, although he created absolutely no earth, no sky, no extended things, no shape, no magnitude, no place, he still arranged that all these things would appear to exist, as they currently do? Besides, just as other people are sometimes mistaken about things that they think they know perfectly, is it not possible that God may have caused me to be mistaken in a similar way when I add two and three together, or think about the number of sides in a quadrilateral figure, or something even simpler if that can be imagined? But perhaps God did not allow me to be deceived like that, for he is said to be good in the highest degree; however, if it is inconsistent with God's goodness for him to create me in such a way that I am always mistaken, it would seem to be equally foreign to his goodness to allow me to be occasionally mistaken. But this last claim cannot be made.

There may be some people who would prefer to deny the existence of such a powerful God rather than believe that everything else is uncertain. But let us not contradict them and let us assume that everything said about God above is fictitious. Assume that I have arrived at my present condition by fate, by chance, by some uninterrupted series of events, or by any other means one wishes. Since to be deceived and mistaken seems to be some kind of imperfection, the less powerful the author they assign to my origin, the more likely it is that I was made in such a way that I am always mistaken. I have no reply to such arguments, but I am forced to concede eventually that there is nothing among my former beliefs that cannot be doubted and that this is so not as a result of levity or lack of reflection but for sound and considered reasons. Therefore, I should carefully withhold assent in future from those beliefs just as much as from others that are clearly false, if I wish to discover anything that is certain.

But it is not enough simply to know this; I must try to keep it in mind. For familiar beliefs return constantly and, almost in spite of me, they seize hold of my judgement as if it were bound to them by established custom and the law of familiarity. And I shall never overcome the habit of relaxing in them and believing them as long as I think they are as they are in fact, namely, in some way doubtful (as has been shown) and yet, despite that, very probable and such that it would be much more reasonable to believe them than to deny them. Therefore, I think I shall not act badly if, having turned my will around in exactly the opposite direction, I deceive myself and pretend for a while that these beliefs are completely false and imaginary until at length, as if I were balanced by an equal weight of prejudices on both sides, no bad habit would any longer turn my judgement from the correct perception of things. For I know that no danger or error will result from this in the mean time, and that I cannot exaggerate my cautiousness since I am concerned here not with doing things but merely with knowing them.

Therefore, I will suppose that, not God who is the source of truth but some evil mind, who is all powerful and cunning, has devoted all their energies to deceiving me. I will imagine that the sky, air, earth, colours, shapes, sounds and everything external to me are nothing more than the creatures of dreams by means of which an evil spirit entraps my credulity. I shall imagine myself as if I had no hands, no eyes, no flesh, no blood, no senses at all, but as if my beliefs in all these things were false. I will remain resolutely steady in this meditation and, in that way, if I cannot discover anything true, I will certainly do what is possible for me, namely, I will take great care not to assent to what is false, nor can that deceiver – no matter how powerful or cunning they may be – impose anything on me. But this is a tiring project and a kind of laziness brings me back to what is more habitual in my life. I am like a prisoner who happens to enjoy an imaginary freedom in his dreams and who subsequently begins to suspect that he is asleep and, afraid of being awakened, conspires silently with his agreeable illusions. Likewise, I spontaneously lapse into my earlier beliefs and am afraid of being awakened from them, in case my peaceful sleep is followed by a laborious awakening and I live in future, not in the light, but amid the inextricable darkness of the problems just discussed.

SECOND MEDITATION

The Nature of the Human Mind, and that it is better known than the Body

I was thrown into such serious difficulties in yesterday's Meditation that I can no longer forget them; however, I cannot see how they can be resolved either. In fact, I am so tossed about, as if I had fallen suddenly into a deep whirlpool, that I can neither put my foot on the bottom nor swim to the surface. However, I will work my way up and test once more the same strategy on which I embarked yesterday, that is, setting aside everything which is subject to the least doubt as if I had found that it was completely false. I will follow this strategy until I discover something that is certain or, at least, until I discover that it is certain only that nothing is certain. Archimedes looked for only one firm and immovable point in order to move the whole earth; likewise, I could hope for great things if I found even the smallest thing that is certain and unmoved.

Thus I will assume that everything I see is false. I believe that, among the things that a deceptive memory represents, nothing ever existed; I have no senses at all; body, shape, extension, motion, and place are unreal. Perhaps that is all there is, that there is nothing certain.

How do I know that, apart from all the things I have just listed, there is not something else about which there is not even the least opportunity for doubting? Is there not some God, or whatever I might call him, who puts these very thoughts into me? Why should I think that, when I myself may perhaps be the author of those thoughts? Is it not true then, at the very least, that I myself am something? However, I have already denied that I have any senses or any body. I still cannot make any progress, for what follows from that? Am I so tied to a body and senses that I am incapable of existing without them? Nonetheless I convinced myself that there is nothing at all in the world, no sky, no earth, no minds, no bodies; is it not therefore also true that I do not exist? However, I certainly did exist, if I convinced myself of something. There is some unidentified deceiver, however, all powerful and cunning, who is dedicated to deceiving me constantly. Therefore, it is indubitable that I also exist, if he deceives me. And let him deceive me as much as he wishes, he will still never bring it about that I am nothing as long as I think I am something. Thus, having weighed up everything adequately, it must finally be stated that this proposition 'I am, I exist' is necessarily true whenever it is stated by me or conceived in my mind.

However, I do not yet understand sufficiently who this 'I' is who now necessarily exists. I must be careful in future that I do not perhaps carelessly substitute something else in place of me, thereby being mistaken in the very knowledge that I claim is the most certain and evident of all. I shall therefore meditate once again about what I formerly believed I was before I began to think along these lines, and from that concept I will subtract anything that can be weakened, however slightly, by these arguments, and thus eventually there will remain precisely only that which is certain and unshakeable.

Up to the present, then, what did I think I was? A human being, surely. But what is a human being? Will I not say: a rational animal? No, because then the following questions would arise: what is an animal? and what is rational? Thus I would lapse from one question into two more difficult questions, and I do not have so much free time that I wish to spend it on such subtleties. But I will look instead at what used to come into my mind spontaneously and naturally whenever, formerly, I wondered about what I was. What used to occur to me first was that I had a face, hands, arms and this whole machine of limbs, which is also observed in a corpse and which I used to call a body. It also occurred to me that I was nourished, that I walked, sensed and thought; I referred these actions to the soul. Now, what this soul was, either I did not consider or else I imagined it was some unknown thing, which was subtle, like wind, fire or ether, and which was infused into the more observable parts of me. As regards the body, however, I had no doubts. I thought I knew its nature clearly and, if I ever tried to describe how I conceived it in my mind, I would have explained it as follows: by a body I understand anything that can be limited by some shape, can be circumscribed in a place, and can so fill a space that every other body is excluded from it. It can be perceived by touch, sight, hearing, taste or smell and can be moved in various ways – however, not by itself but by whatever else touches it. For I thought that it did not belong in any way to the nature of body to have a power to move itself, any more than it has the power of sensing or thinking. In fact, I was surprised to find such powers in certain bodies.

But what will I say now about myself, when I suppose there is some very powerful and, if I may say so, evil deceiver who is committed to deceiving me in everything possible? May I claim to have even the least of all those things I just said belonged to the nature of the body? I consider them, think about them, reflect on them, but nothing occurs to me; it is tiring to repeat the process with the same lack of success as before. What about the things, then, that I attributed to the soul? To be nourished or to walk? Since I no longer have a body, these are only fictions. To sense? But even this cannot be done without a body and I seemed to sense many things while dreaming that I later realized I had not sensed. To think? That's it. It is thought. This alone cannot be detached from me. I am, I exist; that is certain. But for how long? As long as I think, for it might possibly happen if I ceased completely to think that I would thereby cease to exist at all. I do not accept anything at present that is not necessarily true. I am, therefore, precisely only a thinking thing, that is, a mind, soul, intellect or reason – words the meaning of which was formerly unknown to me. But I am a genuine thing and I truly exist. But what kind of thing? I just said: a thinking thing.

What else? I shall imagine that I am not the collection of limbs that is called a human body, nor some subtle air that is infused into those limbs; I am not a wind, fire, vapour or breath, nor anything that I imagine, for I have supposed that those things do not exist. That supposition stands but, nonetheless, I am still something. Is it possible that these very things, which, I am supposing, do not exist because I have no knowledge of them, are not in fact distinct from the me that I knew? I do not know, and I am not discussing that issue for the moment. I can make a judgement only about those things that I do know. I know that I exist, and I am asking who is this 'I' whom I know. I can be quite sure that knowledge of this 'I', in that precise sense, does not depend on things that I did not know existed, nor therefore on any of those things that I construct in my imagination. This verb 'to construct' warns me about my mistake. For I would really be constructing if I imagined myself to be something, because imagining is only the contemplation of the shape or image of a physical thing. However, I already know that I exist and, at the same time, that it is possible that all those images and, in general, whatever pertains to the nature of bodies may be merely dreams. Having recognized that, it seems to be just as foolish to say, 'I imagine, in order to understand more clearly what I am,' as to say, 'I am now clearly awake and I see something true, but because I do not yet see it clearly enough I shall fall asleep so that my dreams will represent it to me more truly and clearly.' Thus I know that none of those things that I can understand with the help of my imagination is relevant to what I know of myself, and that the mind must be turned away carefully from those things so that it can perceive its own nature as distinctly as possible.

But what, then, am I? A thinking thing. And what is that? A thing which doubts, understands, affirms, denies, wills, does not will, and which also imagines and senses. That is obviously a fair number of things, if they all apply to me. Am I not the very one who was just doubting almost everything, who still, however, understands something, who affirms that this one thing is true, who denies the rest, who wishes to know more, who does not wish to be deceived, who imagines many things even despite myself and who notices many things as if they came from the senses? Which of these is not as true as the fact that I exist, even if I am constantly asleep and even if whoever created me deludes me as much as they can? Which of these is distinct from my thought? Which of them can be said to be distinct from myself? For the fact that it is I who doubt, who understand, who will, is so obvious that there is nothing which could make it more evident. In fact, I am also identical with the 'I' who imagines because even if it happened, as I supposed, that none of the things I imagined were any longer true, the power of imagining itself truly exists and is part of my thought. Thus I am the same subject who senses, or who notices physical things as if through the senses; for example, I already see light, hear sound and feel heat. Those are false, because I am asleep. But I certainly seem to see, to hear and to get warm. This cannot be false. This is what is meant, strictly speaking, by me having a sensation and, understood precisely in this way, it is nothing other than thinking.

From these considerations I begin to know somewhat better what I am. However, it still seems to me – and I cannot prevent myself from thinking – that physical things, the images of which are formed in my thought and which the senses themselves explore, are much more distinctly known than the unknown me who is outside the scope of the imagination, although it really is surprising that I understand more distinctly things which I realize are doubtful, unknown and foreign to me than what is true, what is known and, ultimately, what is myself. But I see what the problem is. My mind likes to wander and is not yet willing to stay within the boundaries of the truth. Let it be and allow it once again to be completely unconstrained so that soon afterwards, when the constraints are reimposed, it will find it easier to be directed.

Consider those things that are commonly thought to be understood most distinctly, namely bodies which we touch and see – not bodies in general, because such general perceptions are usually inclined to be more confused – but a single body in particular. For example, let us take this wax. It has just been extracted from the honeycomb. It has not yet completely lost the taste of honey and it still retains some of the scent of the flowers from which it was collected. Its colour, shape and size are obvious. It is hard, cold, easy to touch and, if tapped with a finger, it emits a sound. Thus it has everything that seems to be required for a body to be known as distinctly as possible. But notice that, as I speak, it is moved close to the fire. It loses what remains of its taste, its smell is lost, the colour changes, it loses its shape, increases in size, becomes a liquid, becomes hot and can barely be touched. Nor does it still emit a sound if tapped. But does the same wax not remain? It must be agreed that it does; no one denies that, no one thinks otherwise.

What was it about it, then, which was understood so distinctly? Certainly none of those things that I reached through the senses, for whatever fell within the scope of taste, smell, sight, touch or hearing has already changed. The wax remains. Was it perhaps what I now think, namely, that the wax itself was not really that sweetness of honey, nor the fragrance of flowers, nor that whiteness, shape or sound, but the body, which a short time ago presented itself to me with those modes and which now appears with different modes? But what exactly is this thing that I imagine? Let us pay attention and, having removed whatever does not belong to the wax, let us see what remains. It is nothing but something that is extended, flexible and changeable. But what do the words 'flexible' and 'changeable' mean? Is it what I imagine, namely, that this wax can change shape from being round to square or from square to triangular? Not at all. For I understand that it is capable of innumerable similar changes, even though I cannot review whatever is innumerable in my imagination and therefore this understanding does not result from the faculty of imagining. What is meant by 'extended'? Is it not the case that even its very extension is unknown? For melting wax increases in volume, increases further when it boils and increases further again if the temperature rises further. Nor could I correctly judge what this wax is unless I thought it could assume many more variations in extension than I have ever grasped in my imagination. I have to concede, then, that I cannot in any way imagine what this wax is, but that I can perceive it only with my mind. I say this about a particular piece of wax; it is even clearer about wax in general. What, then, is this wax that can be perceived only by the mind? It is the same wax that I see, touch, imagine, and finally the same wax that I thought was there from the beginning. But what should be noticed is that perceiving it is not a case of seeing, touching or imagining, nor was it ever such although it seemed that way earlier, but it is an inspection of the mind alone, which may be either imperfect and confused as it was earlier, or clear and distinct as it is now, depending on whether I pay more or less attention to what it is composed of.

Meanwhile, I am surprised at how much my mind is inclined to errors. For although I think about these things to myself, silently and without speaking, I am still restricted to these words and am almost deceived by ordinary language. For we say that we see the wax itself if it is present, not that we judge that it is there from its colour and shape. From this way of talking I might conclude immediately that the wax is therefore known by how the eye sees and not by an inspection of the mind alone, had I not looked out of the window at people passing on the street below and said, in the same customary way as in the case of the wax, that I saw the people themselves. But what do I see apart from hats and coats, under which it may be the case that there are automata hidden? Nonetheless, I judge that they are people. In this case, however, what I thought I saw with my eyes I understand only by the faculty of judging, which is in my mind.

But whoever wishes to know things better than they are commonly known should be ashamed to find reasons for doubt in commonly used ways of talking. Let us continue, then, by considering whether I perceived what wax is more perfectly and clearly when I first looked at it and thought I knew it by means of the external senses or, at least, by the so-called common sense, that is, the faculty of imagining; or do I know it better now, having carefully investigated both what it is and how it is known? It would surely be foolish to doubt this, for what was distinct in the first perception? What did it include that was not apparently available to any animal whatsoever? However, when I distinguish the wax from its external forms and consider it as if it were bare and without its clothes on, then, although there may still be a mistake in my judgement, I cannot perceive the wax correctly without a human mind.

What shall I say, however, about this mind itself, or about myself, for I do not yet admit that there is anything in me apart from a mind? What, I ask, am I, who seem to perceive this wax so distinctly? Do I not know myself much more truly and certainly and also more clearly and distinctly? For if I judge that the wax exists from the fact that I see it, it would certainly follow much more clearly, from the fact that I see it, that I myself exist. For it may be the case that what I see is not really wax; it might even be true that I have no eyes, by which to see anything; but obviously it cannot be the case, while I see or while I seem to see (something that, so far, I have not distinguished from seeing), that I myself am nothing as long as I am thinking. Likewise, if, from the fact that I touch it, I judge that the wax exists, it follows again that I exist. If I judge the same from the fact that I imagine it or for any other reason, clearly the same conclusion follows. Now what I notice about the wax may be applied to everything else that exists outside me. Besides, if the perception of the wax was more distinctly seen after it became known to me not only by sight and touch but from many other causes, must I not grant that I now know myself much more distinctly, because all the reasons that could assist in perceiving the wax or any other body establish the nature of my mind better. But there are also so many other things in the mind itself, by which knowledge of the mind can be made more distinct, that it hardly seems worth considering those that emanate from the body to the mind.

Here at last I have returned unaided to where I wished to be. I know now that even bodies are not perceived by the senses or the faculty of imagining, but are perceived only by the mind, and that they are not perceived by being touched or seen but only by being understood, and therefore I know clearly that there is nothing that can be perceived by me more easily or more clearly than my own mind. However, since the habit of old views cannot be changed so quickly, it is appropriate that I rest here so that this new knowledge may be lodged more deeply in my memory by the length of my meditation.

THIRD MEDITATION

The Existence of God

I will now close my eyes, block my ears and shut down all my senses. I will erase from my thought all images of physical things or, since this is almost impossible, I will regard them as nothing, as false and empty, addressing only myself and looking more deeply into myself. I will try to make myself gradually better known and more familiar to myself. I am a thinking thing, that is, something which is doubting, affirming, denying, understanding a few things, not knowing many, willing, not willing, even imagining and sensing. As I already mentioned, even if the things that I sense or imagine happened not to exist, I am still certain that the modes of thinking that I call sensations and imaginings, insofar as they are simply certain modes of thinking, are in me. And in these few things I have listed everything that I know or, at least, what I have so far noticed that I know.

I will now look about more carefully to see if there happen to be other things in me which I have not yet examined. I am certain that I am a thinking thing. Do I not therefore also know what is required in order for me to be certain of anything, namely, that there is nothing in this first thought other than a certain clear and distinct perception of what I claim? Evidently that would not be enough to make me certain about something if it could ever happen that what I perceived clearly and distinctly in this way could be false. It seems, therefore, that I could establish as a general rule that everything that I perceive very clearly and distinctly is true.

However, I have in the past accepted as completely clear and distinct many things that I later discovered were doubtful. What kinds of things were they? The earth, sky, stars and all the other things that I used to perceive by means of the senses. But what was it that I used to perceive clearly about them? It was that the very ideas or thoughts of those things were presented to my mind. Even now I still have no doubt that these ideas are in me. But there was something else that I used to claim, and I even thought that I perceived it clearly as a result of believing it whereas, in fact, I did not perceive it clearly: that was, that some things existed outside me from which those ideas originated and which they resembled in every way. But I was either mistaken in that or, at least, if I judged correctly, it did not result from my faculty of perceiving.

However, when I used to think of something very simple and easy in arithmetic or geometry – for example, that two and three together make five, or other things like that – did I not see at least those things sufficiently clearly to claim that they are true? Indeed, I subsequently decided that I should doubt them simply because it occurred to me that some God may have endowed me with such a nature that I could be deceived even about things that seemed most evident. For whenever this preconceived belief about the supreme power of God occurs to me, I cannot avoid conceding that, at least if he wishes, it is easy for him to make me err even about things that I think I see most clearly with my mind's eye. On the other hand, whenever I turn to those things that I think I perceive very clearly, I am so completely convinced by them that I spontaneously say: let me be deceived by whoever can deceive me, but it will never happen that I am nothing as long as I think I am something, that it could ever be true that I never existed when it is already true that I am, or even perhaps that two and three added together are more or less than five, and similar things in which I recognize a manifest contradiction. Certainly, since I have no reason to think there is such a deceptive God and, in fact, I do not even know yet if any God exists, any reason for doubting which depends exclusively on that belief is a very flimsy and, I would say, a metaphysical reason for doubting. In order to remove even this reason as soon as possible, I should examine whether God exists and, if he exists, whether it is possible that he is a deceiver. As long as this is unknown, I cannot see how I can ever be certain of anything else.

Now, order seems to require that I classify all my thoughts into certain kinds and that I find out in which kinds truth or falsehood are properly found. Some thoughts are like the images of things, and the term 'idea' applies in a strict sense to them alone: for example, when I think of a person, a chimera, the sky, an angel or God. Other thoughts, however, also have additional forms; for example, when I will, fear, affirm, or deny, I always grasp something as the subject of my thoughts but I include in my thought something more than a resemblance of the thing in question. Some of these thoughts are called volitions or emotions, and others are called judgements.

When ideas are considered only in themselves, since I do not refer them to anything else they cannot, strictly speaking, be false; for whether I imagine a goat or a chimera, it is no less true that I imagine one thing rather than the other. Likewise, there is no danger of falsehood in volitions as such, or in emotions; for although I can choose what is evil or even what does not exist, it does not follow that it is not true that I choose them. That leaves only judgements and this is where I have to be careful not to be mistaken. The principal error, however, and the one most likely to occur here consists in the fact that I judge that the ideas, which are in me, resemble or correspond to things which are outside me. For if I consider the ideas merely as certain modes of my thought, and if I do not refer them to anything else, they can hardly provide me with any material for error.

Among these ideas, some seem to be innate, some acquired and some seem to have been fabricated by me. The fact that I understand what a thing is, what truth is and what thought is, seems to result from my own nature alone. However, up to now I have thought that, when I hear a noise, see the sun, or feel the fire, these result from certain things which are external to me. Finally, sirens, hippogriffs and the like are fabricated by me. Perhaps, however, I can think that they are all adventitious, or all innate, or all fabricated, for I have not yet seen clearly what is their true origin.

But the main question I wish to ask here is about ideas that I think originate from things which are external to me, namely: what reason would persuade me to believe that those ideas are similar to the things in question? I do indeed seem to be taught this by nature; and I also experience the fact that these ideas do not depend on my will nor, therefore, on me, because they are often present against my will. For example, I now feel heat whether I want to or not, and therefore I think that the sensation or idea of heat comes to me from something that is distinct from me, namely, from the heat of the fire beside which I am sitting. The most natural thing for me to judge is that the external thing sends me its own likeness rather than something else.

I will now see whether these reasons are convincing enough. When I say here that I was taught this by nature I only mean that I am led to believe it by some spontaneous impulse and not that I have been shown that it is true by some natural light. There is a big difference between the two. For whatever is shown to me by the natural light of reason – for example, that from the fact that I doubt it follows that I exist, and similar things – cannot in any way be doubtful, because there cannot be another faculty which I trust as much as that light and which could teach me that the conclusion is not true. By contrast, I have often judged in the past that I was pushed in the wrong direction by natural impulses in situations of choosing what is good, and I cannot see that I should put more trust in the same natural impulses in other situations.

However, even if these ideas do not depend on my will, that does not prove that they originate from external things. For just as those impulses about which I just spoke seem to be distinct from my will even though they are within me, so likewise it is possible that there is some other faculty, of which I am not yet sufficiently aware and which is the origin of those ideas, in the same way as it always seemed to me up to now that, when I was dreaming, ideas were formed in me without any assistance from external things.

But finally, even if they originated from things that are distinct from me, it does not follow that they must resemble them. In fact, I seem to have found in many cases that there is often a great disparity between them. For example, I find I have two different ideas of the sun. One idea, which seems to have been acquired from the senses and is a paradigm example of an adventitious idea, makes the sun appear very small. The other idea, however, is derived from astronomical reasoning – that is, from certain notions which are either innate in me or are fabricated by me in some way – and it makes the sun appear to be several times greater than the earth. They cannot both be truly similar to the same sun that exists outside me, and reason convinces me that the one that seems to have originated more directly from the sun resembles it the least.

All these considerations are enough to show that, to date, I believed that there are some things outside me which send me their ideas or images through the sense organs or by some other means, as a result of some blind impulse rather than as a result of a judgement that is certain.

But there is also another way to find out if, among the things of which I have ideas, some exist outside me. Insofar as those ideas are simply certain modes of thinking, I do not see any inequality between them and they all seem to originate in me in the same way. But insofar as one idea represents one thing and another represents something else, it is clear that they are very different from each other. For undoubtedly those that represent substances to me are something more and, so to speak, contain more intentional reality than those that represent only modes or non-essential features of substances. Again, the idea by which I understand a supreme God, who is eternal, infinite, all-knowing, omnipotent and the creator of everything that is outside himself, clearly contains more intentional reality than those ideas that represent finite substances.

Now, it is evident by the natural light of reason that there must be at least as much reality in an efficient and total cause as in the effect of that cause. For I ask: where could the effect get its reality from, apart from its cause? And how could the cause give it that reality unless it also possessed it? It follows from this that something cannot be made from nothing and, likewise, that something which is more perfect – in other words, that which contains more reality in itself – cannot be made from that which is less perfect. But this is no less evidently true in the case of effects, the reality of which is actual or formal, than in the case of ideas when only their intentional reality is considered. Thus not only is it impossible, for example, that some stone which previously did not exist could now begin to exist unless it was produced by something which contained, either formally or eminently,[10] all the reality which is produced in the stone; in the same way, heat cannot be produced in something that was not previously hot except by something that is at least of the same order of perfection as heat, and so on for other examples; but it is also true that there cannot be an idea of heat or of a stone in me unless it was put there by some cause in which there is at least as much reality as I conceive in heat or a stone. Although the cause in question does not transfer any of its actual or formal reality to my idea, it should not for that reason be considered as less real, for the reality of the idea is such that, in itself, it requires no more formal reality than what is borrowed from my thought, of which it is a mode. But when an idea contains one particular intentional reality rather than another, it must surely get this from some cause in which there is at least as much formal reality as is contained intentionally in the idea. For if we claimed that an idea contained something that was not in its cause, it would therefore get it from nothing. But however imperfect may be the mode of being by which a thing exists intentionally in the mind by means of an idea, clearly it is still not nothing and therefore it cannot come from nothing.

Nor should I suppose that, because I am considering only the intentional reality of my ideas, it is not necessary for that same reality to be contained formally in the causes of those ideas and that it is enough for it to be found there intentionally. For just as the intentional mode of being belongs to ideas because of their nature, so likewise the formal mode of being belongs naturally to the causes of ideas or, at least, to their principal and primary causes. And although it is possible for one idea to generate another, this does not lead to an infinite regress. Eventually one has to reach some first idea, the cause of which is like an archetype that contains all the formal reality which is found only intentionally in the idea. Thus it is evident to me by the natural light of reason that my ideas are like images of some kind that can easily fall short of the perfection of the things from which they are derived, but they cannot contain something that is greater or more perfect than themselves.

However, I recognize all these things as true more clearly and distinctly as I examine them further and in greater detail. What may I finally conclude from this? It is that, if the intentional reality of any one of my ideas is so great that I am certain that I do not contain this reality in myself either formally or eminently and, therefore, that I myself cannot be its cause, it follows necessarily that I am not alone in the world and that something else also exists, which is the cause of that idea. However, if I find no such idea in myself, then clearly I have no argument that makes me certain of the existence of something distinct from myself because I have examined everything very carefully and, so far, I have not been able to find any other argument.

Now among my ideas – apart from the idea that represents me to myself and about which there can be no question at this point – there is one that represents God, there are some that represent physical and inanimate things, others that represent animals and, finally, there are ideas that represent other people similar to myself.

As regards the ideas that represent other people, animals or angels, I understand easily that they could be fabricated from ideas that I have of myself, of physical things and of God, even if there were no people, animals or angels in existence.

As regards ideas of physical things, there is nothing in them that is so great that it seems incapable of having been derived from myself. For if I look into them further and examine them one by one in the same way as I examined the idea of wax yesterday, I notice that there is very little about them that I perceive clearly and distinctly. There is magnitude, or extension in length, width and depth; there is shape, which results from the termination of magnitude; there is the position that differently shaped things adopt in relation to each other; and there is motion or change of position. To these may be added substance, duration and number. The rest, such as light and colours, sounds, odours, tastes, heat and cold, and other tactile qualities – I think about these only in a very confused and obscure way, with the result that I do not even know if they are true or false, that is, whether the ideas I have of them are or are not ideas of real things.[11]

Although I mentioned a little earlier that falsehood understood in a strict sense, or formal falsehood, can occur only in judgements, there is still clearly some kind of material falsehood in ideas when they represent what is not a thing as if it were a thing. For example, the ideas I have of heat and cold are so lacking in clarity and distinctness that I cannot learn from them whether cold is merely a privation of heat or heat is a privation of cold, or whether both of them are real qualities or whether neither of them is. Since there can be no ideas that do not seem to be ideas of things, if it really is the case that cold is nothing but a privation of heat, then the idea that represents it as if it were a real and positive thing is rightly said to be false and the same applies to other similar ideas. Ideas of this kind are such that it is clearly unnecessary that I assign them some cause apart from myself. For if indeed they are false – that is, they do not represent things of any kind – I know by the natural light of reason that they originate from nothing, that is, that the only reason I have them is that there is something deficient in my nature, because it is obviously imperfect. Even if they are true, they represent such an insubstantial reality to me that I can barely distinguish it from a non-reality and therefore I still do not see why they could not originate from me.

Insofar as some features of our ideas of physical things are clear and distinct, they seem to have been partly borrowed from the idea of myself – for example, from the ideas of substance, duration and number and, possibly, others of the same kind. For when I think that a stone is a substance, that is, the kind of thing that can exist on its own, and when I also think of myself as a substance then, even though I conceive of myself as thinking and not extended but think of the stone as not thinking and extended, and hence there is the greatest difference between the two concepts, they still seem to agree insofar as they are both substances. Likewise, when I perceive that I exist at present and remember that I have existed for some time, and when I have different thoughts and understand how many of them there are, I acquire the ideas of duration and number, which I can subsequently transfer to anything else. All the other features of which the ideas of physical things are constructed, namely extension, shape, position and motion, are not formally contained in me since I am nothing but a thinking thing. However, they are merely modes of a substance, whereas I am a substance, and therefore it seems possible for them to be in me eminently.

Thus the idea of God is the only one left about which to ask the question: does it contain something that could not have originated from me? By the word 'God' I understand some infinite substance, which is independent, supremely intelligent and supremely powerful, and by which both I, and everything else that exists (if anything else exists), were created. All these ideas are surely such that, the more carefully I examine them, the less likely it seems that they could have originated from myself alone. Therefore one should draw the conclusion from what has been said that God necessarily exists. And even though I have an idea of a substance from the very fact that I am a substance myself, it would not, however, be an idea of an infinite substance because I am finite, unless it originated from some substance that is genuinely infinite.

Nor should I think that I do not perceive the infinite by means of a true idea but merely by the negation of the finite, in the way in which I perceive rest and darkness by the negation of motion and light. On the contrary, I understand clearly that there is more reality in an infinite substance than in a finite substance and therefore the perception of the infinite occurs in me in some way prior to that of the finite, that is, the perception of God is prior to the perception of myself. Indeed, how would I understand that I doubt, that I desire – that is, that I lack something and am not completely perfect – if I had no idea of some more perfect being by comparison with which I could recognize my own deficiencies?

Nor can it be said that this idea of God may be materially false and may therefore come from nothing, as I have just observed about the ideas of heat and cold and others like that. On the contrary, since this idea has the highest clarity and distinction and contains more intentional reality than any other idea, there is no other idea which of itself is more true or in which there is less suspicion of falsehood. This idea of a supremely perfect and infinite being is, I claim, true to the highest degree because, although I could perhaps pretend that such a being does not exist, I cannot pretend that the idea of such a being represents nothing real to me, as I claimed earlier about the idea of cold. It is also clear and distinct to the highest degree because whatever I perceive clearly and distinctly as real and true, and as containing some perfection, is completely included in it. Nor does it matter that I do not comprehend the infinite or that there are innumerable other things in God that I do not comprehend and which may be completely outside the scope of my thought.[12] It is the nature of the infinite not to be comprehended by me, who am finite. In order for the idea I have of God to be the most true, and the most clear and distinct of all my ideas, it is enough if I understand it and if I judge that all those things that I perceive clearly and which involve some perfection – and perhaps even innumerable others of which I am ignorant – are in God formally or eminently.

But perhaps I am something greater than I myself understand, and all those perfections that I attribute to God are in me in some way potentially, even if they have not yet appeared and been transformed from potency to act.[13] I already experience the fact that my knowledge increases slightly, and I see nothing to prevent it from thus increasing more and more to infinity. Nor do I see why, with my knowledge thus increased, I could not acquire with its assistance all the other perfections of God nor why, finally, the potentiality for those perfections, if I already have it, would not be enough to produce the corresponding ideas.

But none of this is possible. In the first place, if it were true that my knowledge increased gradually and if there are many things in me in potency which are not yet actualized, none of that is relevant to the idea of God in which there is absolutely nothing in potency. Even this feature – to increase gradually – is a most certain argument for imperfection. Besides, even if my knowledge always increased more and more, nevertheless I understand that it would never be actually infinite because it would never reach a point at which it could not become greater still. I think of God, however, as actually infinite, so that nothing can be added to his perfection. Finally, I perceive that the intentional being of an idea can be produced not by a merely potential being, which, strictly speaking, is nothing, but only by a formal or actual being.

There is evidently nothing in all this that is not evident to whoever examines it carefully by the natural light of reason. However, when I examine it less carefully and when the images of sensible things blind the eye of the mind, I do not easily remember why the idea of a being more perfect than myself originates necessarily from some being which is more perfect in reality; and therefore I would like to inquire further whether I myself, who have this idea, could exist if no such being existed.

From whom, then, would I derive my existence? It would be from myself, or from my parents, or from some other beings which are less perfect than God, for nothing can be thought or imagined that is more perfect than, or even as perfect as, God.

But if I derived my existence from myself, there would be nothing that I would either doubt or wish for, nor would I lack absolutely anything. For I would have given myself every perfection of which I have some idea and thus I would be God himself. Nor should I think that those things which I lack are perhaps more difficult to acquire than those I already possess. On the contrary, it was evidently much more difficult for me – that is, for a thing or substance which thinks – to emerge from nothingness than to acquire knowledge of many things that are unknown to me and that are merely non-essential attributes of that substance. Certainly, if I derived the greater of those two from myself, I would not have denied myself at least those items of knowledge that are easier to acquire, nor even any of those that I perceive are contained in the idea of God, for it does not seem more difficult to do any of that. And if there were some things that were more difficult to do, they would surely also seem to me to be more difficult, at least if I derived whatever else I have from myself, for I would experience the limits of my powers in that situation.

I do not escape the force of these arguments by assuming that I may have always existed as I do now, as if it would follow from that assumption that there is no need to look for the author of my existence. For a lifetime can be divided into innumerable parts that do not depend on each other in any way. The fact that I existed a short while ago does not imply that I must exist at present unless some other cause re-creates me, as it were, in the present moment or, in other words, conserves me. It is clear to anyone who thinks about the nature of time that the same power and action is obviously required to conserve anything during the individual moments of its duration as would be required to create it for the first time, had it not already existed. Thus there is only a distinction of reason between conservation and creation,[14] and this is one of the things that are evident by the natural light of reason.

Therefore, I should now ask myself: have I some power by which I can bring it about that I, who exist at present, will still exist a short time in the future? Since I am only a thinking thing or, at least, I am discussing only those features of that part of me which is specifically a thinking thing, if I had such a power I would undoubtedly be aware of it. But I do not experience any such power, and therefore I know very evidently that I depend on some being which is distinct from me.

However, perhaps that being is not God. Perhaps I was produced either by my parents or by some other causes that are less perfect than God. Hardly. As I have already said, it is clear that there must be at least as much reality in a cause as in its effect. Therefore, since I am a thinking thing and I have some idea of God, whatever cause is eventually assigned to me, it must be agreed that it is a thinking thing and that it includes an idea of all the perfections that I attribute to God. One can ask about that cause in turn: does it derive its existence from itself or from something else? If it derives its existence from itself, it is obvious from what has already been said that it is itself God because, since it derives the power to exist from itself, it undoubtedly also has the power of possessing actually the perfections of which it has an idea, that is, all the perfections that I conceive of in God. If, however, it derives its existence from something else, then the question arises again in the same way about that, whether it derives its existence from itself or from something else, until finally one arrives at the ultimate cause, which is God. It is clear enough that there cannot be an infinite regress here, especially since I am not concerned at this stage with the cause that produced me in the past but much more with the cause that maintains me in existence at present.

Nor is it plausible that there may have been many partial causes which co-operated to produce me, and that I got the idea of one of the perfections that I attribute to God from one cause and, from another, the idea of a second perfection, so that all these perfections occur somewhere in the world although they are not all joined together in the same being, which is God. On the contrary, the unity, simplicity, or the inseparability of all those attributes that are found in God is one of the principal perfections that I understand is present in him. And it is certain that the idea of the unity of all these perfections could not have been produced in me by some other cause unless I had the ideas of his other perfections from the same source; nor could it have made me understand them as joined together and inseparable, unless it also made me understand what those perfections were.

Finally, as regards parents, even if I assume that everything I ever believed about them is true, it would still not mean that they maintain me in existence; nor is there any way in which they have created me insofar as I am a thinking thing. They have only put certain dispositions in the matter in which I – that is, my mind, which is all I mean by 'I' at this point – find myself at present. Thus there can be no question about them in this context. Instead it must absolutely be concluded from the mere fact that I exist and that I have some idea of a most perfect being – that is, of God – that it is very clearly demonstrated that God also exists.

It only remains for me to examine how I received this idea from God. I did not derive it from the senses, nor did it ever arrive unexpectedly as the ideas of sensible things usually do when external objects impinge, or seem to impinge, on the sense organs. Nor was it fabricated by me, for it is clear that I can neither add to it nor subtract anything from it. Thus it follows that it is innate in me, just as the idea of myself is innate in me.

Evidently it is not surprising if God, in creating me, endowed me with this idea so that it would be, as it were, the artisan's trademark imprinted on his work. Nor is it necessary that the mark be distinct from the work itself. From the mere fact that God created me, however, it is very probable that I was made in some way in his image and likeness and that this likeness, in which the idea of God is contained, is perceived in me by means of the same faculty by which I perceive myself. In other words, when I turn my mind's eye towards myself I understand not only that I am an incomplete and dependent being and that I aspire indefinitely towards what is greater or better; I also understand, at the same time, that he on whom I depend is greater than all those things, not just indefinitely and potentially, but that he contains them all to an infinite degree in himself and is thus God. The whole force of this argument consists in the fact that I recognize that it is impossible for me to exist with the kind of nature I have, that is, having in myself the idea of God, if God did not truly exist. I mean the God of whom I have an idea, that is, who has all those perfections that I cannot comprehend but is such that I can reach him in some way through my thought and is clearly immune from all defects. It follows clearly enough that he cannot be a deceiver, since it is evident by the natural light of reason that every fraud and deception results from some defect.

But before I examine this last issue in greater detail and also inquire into other truths that can be derived from it, I should pause here for a brief while to contemplate God himself, to consider his attributes and to contemplate and adore the beauty of this immense light insofar as the eye of my darkened mind can tolerate it. Just as we believe by faith that the greatest happiness of the next life consists simply in the contemplation of this divine majesty, likewise we experience that we derive the greatest joy of which we are capable in this life from the same contemplation, even though it is much less perfect.

FOURTH MEDITATION

Truth and Falsehood

In recent days I have become so used to leading my mind away from the senses and have noted carefully that so little is perceived reliably about physical things, and that much more is known about the human mind and even more again about God, that already I have no difficulty in turning my thoughts away from things that can be imagined to those that are purely intelligible and independent of all matter. Clearly I have a much more distinct idea of the human mind – insofar as it is a thinking thing, is not extended in length, breadth and depth, and includes in itself nothing that is physical – than of any physical thing. When I consider that I doubt or that I am an incomplete and dependent thing, a clear and distinct idea occurs to me of a complete and independent being, that is, of God. And from the fact alone that I have this idea or that I exist while having this idea, I conclude so clearly that God also exists and that each moment of my whole existence depends on him that I do not think that anything can be known by human intelligence more evidently or more clearly. I now seem to see a way by which knowledge of other things can be reached from this contemplation of the true God in whom are hidden all the treasures of the sciences and of wisdom.

First of all, I realize that it is impossible that God would ever deceive me. All deception or fraud involves some imperfection, and although being able to deceive seems to be some kind of evidence in favour of cleverness or power, it is undoubtedly true that the wish to deceive is evidence of malice or foolishness and therefore it cannot belong to God.

Next, I experience a certain faculty of judgement in myself, which, just like everything else that is in me, I received from God. Since God does not wish me to be mistaken he obviously did not give me a faculty such that, when I use it correctly, I could ever be mistaken.

There would be no further doubt about this, except that it seems to follow that I can never be mistaken; for if everything I possess comes from God and if he did not give me a faculty for making mistakes, it seems as if I could never be wrong about anything. And thus, as long as I think only about God and focus completely on him, I find no cause of error or falsehood in myself. But as soon as I turn back to myself, however, I find that I am subject to innumerable errors. When I look for a cause of these errors, I find that I have not only a real and positive idea of God or of a supremely perfect being but I also have, if I may so describe it, a certain negative idea of nothingness or of what is removed as far as possible from every perfection; and I am like some kind of intermediate being between God and nothingness, or I am so constituted between the supreme being and non-being that, insofar as I was created by the supreme being, there is nothing in me by which I can be mistaken or led into error, but insofar as I also participate in some way in nothingness or in non-being – that is, insofar as I myself am not the supreme being and I lack so many things – it is not surprising, then, if I make mistakes. Thus I certainly recognize that error as such is not something real that depends on God but is merely a defect; therefore, in order to be mistaken, I do not need some faculty that God gave me for that purpose but I happen to make mistakes by the mere fact that the faculty of judging truly, which I got from God, is not infinite.

However, that does not satisfy me completely. For error is not a pure negation; it is a privation or lack of some knowledge that somehow I should have. And when I consider the nature of God it does not seem possible that he gave me some faculty that is not perfect in its own right or that lacks some perfection that it should have. If it is true that artisans who are more skilled produce more perfect artifacts, what could have been made by the supreme creator of everything that would not be complete in every way? There is also no doubt that God could have created me so that I am not mistaken, nor is there any doubt either that he always wills what is best. Therefore, is it better for me to be mistaken rather than not mistaken?

As I think more about this, it occurs to me first that I should not be surprised if I do not understand the reason for some things that are done by God, and that I should not doubt his existence because I happen to experience some things and do not comprehend why or how he does them. Since I already know that my nature is very weak and limited and that the nature of God is immense, incomprehensible and infinite, I also know from this that there are innumerable things of which I do not know the causes. For this reason alone, I think there is no role in physics for that whole class of causes which are usually sought in purposes, because I think that I cannot investigate God's purposes without temerity.[15]

It also occurs to me that when we inquire whether God's works are perfect, we should not consider some particular creature on its own but the whole universe of things. For although something may perhaps rightly seem to be very imperfect when it is considered in isolation, it is very perfect when considered as part of the world. Since I decided to doubt everything, I have so far come to know with certainty only that I myself exist and that God exists; however, once I have recognized the immense power of God, I cannot deny that there are many other things created by him or which, at least, could be created by him, so that I acquire the status of a part in the universe of things.

When I come to look at myself more closely and investigate what kinds of mistake I make (which in themselves indicate some kind of imperfection in me), I notice that they depend on two causes acting simultaneously, namely on the faculty of knowing, which I have, and on the faculty of choosing or on freedom of the will – in other words, on the intellect and will together. By using the intellect I merely perceive the ideas about which I can make a judgement, and this can contain no error in the strict sense when it is considered precisely from this point of view. There may exist innumerable things of which I have no idea, but I should be described simply as lacking them in a negative sense rather than as being deprived of them in any strict sense, because I cannot think of any reason to show that God ought to have given me a superior faculty of knowing than the one he gave me. And no matter how skilled I think an artisan may be, I do not think for that reason that they have to put all the perfections into each individual item of work that they are capable of putting into others.

At the same time, I cannot complain that I did not receive from God a sufficiently extensive and perfect will or freedom of choice, for I clearly experience that it is not confined by any limits. What I think is very noteworthy is that there is nothing else in me that is so perfect and so great that I cannot think of it as being even greater still or more perfect. If, for example, I consider my faculty of understanding, I recognize immediately that it is very limited and finite and, at the same time, I form the idea of another similar faculty which is much greater – in fact, the greatest possible, and infinite – and from the mere fact that I can form this idea I perceive that it belongs to the nature of God. Likewise, if I examine the faculty of remembering or imagining, or any other faculty, it is clear to me that I understand all of them as limited and restricted in my own case but as unlimited in God. I experience the will alone, or freedom of choice, as being so extensive in my own case that I conceive the idea of none greater, so that it is principally because of this faculty that I understand myself as being in some sense the image and likeness of God. For although the will is incomparably greater in God than in me – both because of the knowledge and power that accompany it and make it stronger and more efficacious, and because of its object, insofar as it extends to many more things than my will – when it is considered formally and in a strict sense, however, it does not seem to be greater. For the will consists in this alone, that we can either do or not do something (that is, affirm or deny something, seek or avoid it); or rather, it consists in this alone that we bring ourselves to affirm or deny, to seek or avoid, whatever is proposed to us by our intellect in such a way that we feel that we are not determined by any external force. Nor is it true that, in order to be free, I must be capable of moving in either direction; on the contrary, the more I am inclined in one direction the more freely I choose it, either because I clearly recognize it as being true and good or because God so disposes my innermost thoughts. Surely neither divine grace nor natural knowledge ever diminishes freedom; instead, they increase and strengthen it. But the indifference I experience when I am not moved one way or another by any consideration is a lower degree of freedom, and it does not indicate a perfection in our freedom but merely some kind of defect or something lacking in our knowledge. For if I always saw clearly what is true and what is good, I would never deliberate about what judgement to make or what to choose and thus, although I would obviously be free, I could never be indifferent.

I see from these considerations that the cause of my errors is not the power of willing, which I receive from God, when considered on its own, because this power is as extensive as possible and is perfect in its kind. Nor is it the power of understanding because, whatever I understand, it is certain that I understand it correctly, for the ability to understand comes from God and it cannot contain the ability to be mistaken. Where do my errors originate, then? They result from this alone: since the will extends further than the understanding, I do not restrain it within the limits of the understanding but apply it even to things that I do not understand. Given that it is indifferent to those things, it is easily deflected from what is true or good and in that way I make mistaken judgements or bad choices.

For example, when I considered in recent days whether anything in the world exists and when I noticed that, from the fact that I thought about it, it follows clearly that I exist, I still was unable not to judge that whatever I understood so clearly was true. This was not because I was coerced into that conclusion by some external force, but because a strong inclination of the will followed from a great light in the understanding and, as a result, I believed it much more spontaneously and freely insofar as I was less indifferent to it. Now, however, I not only know that I exist, insofar as I am some kind of thinking thing, but I also notice an idea of physical nature; this makes me doubt whether the thinking nature which is in me, or rather which I myself am, is distinct from this physical nature or whether both are identical, and I think that my understanding has not yet any reason to persuade me one way or another. For that reason I am certainly indifferent with respect to affirming or denying either alternative or, indeed, with respect to making no judgement on the question.

This indifference extends not only to things that are not known at all by the understanding but generally to anything that is not understood clearly enough at precisely the time at which the will deliberates about it. Even when probable conjectures lead me in one direction, the mere knowledge that they are only conjectures, and that they are not reasons which are certain and indubitable, is enough to push my assent in the opposite direction. I have experienced enough of this in recent days, when I supposed that all the things were false that I had previously believed to be absolutely true, simply because I realized that it was possible for me somehow to doubt them.

However, when I do not perceive what is true with sufficient clarity and distinction, as long as I refrain from making a judgement it is clear that I act correctly and that I am not mistaken. But if I affirm or deny in those circumstances, then I do not use my freedom of choice correctly. If I opt for the side that is false, I am evidently mistaken; if, however, I choose the opposite, I land on the truth by chance but I do not thereby avoid fault because it is evident by the natural light of reason that the perception of the understanding should always precede the determination of the will. It is this incorrect use of freedom of choice that constitutes the privation which is the essence of error; this privation, I say, is in the use of the will itself insofar as it originates in me, but not in the faculty that I received from God nor even in the use of that faculty insofar as it depends on God.

Nor have I any reason to complain that God has not provided me with a greater power of understanding or that he did not give me a greater natural light than he did, because it is natural for a finite understanding that there are many things which it does not understand and it is natural for a created understanding to be finite. Instead I ought to be grateful to him who never owed me anything for having been so generous to me, rather than think that he failed to give me, or has taken away, those things that he never gave me.

Nor may I complain because he gave me a will that is wider in scope than my understanding. Since the will consists in a single thing that is, as it were, indivisible, it seems as if its nature is such that nothing could be taken away from it. And, clearly, the wider its scope, the more grateful I should be towards the donor.

Finally, I should not complain that God co-operates with me in making those acts of will, or those judgements, in which I am mistaken. Those actions are completely true and good insofar as they depend on God and, as far as I am concerned, it is a greater perfection to be able to perform those acts than not to be able to do so. But a privation, which alone is the essence of falsehood and fault, does not need God's co-operation because it is a non-entity; if it is referred to God as its cause, it should not be called a privation but merely a negation. It is clearly not an imperfection in God that he gave me the freedom to assent or not assent to certain things of which he did not put a clear and distinct perception in my understanding. But it is undoubtedly an imperfection in me that I do not use this freedom well and that I make judgements about things that I do not understand correctly. I see, however, that God could easily have arranged that I would be incapable of ever making a mistake, even though I remain free and have limited knowledge. He could have given my understanding a clear and distinct perception of everything that I would deliberate about, or else he could simply impress on my memory – so firmly that I could never forget it – that I should never make a judgement about anything that I had not understood clearly and distinctly. I readily recognize that, if I were some kind of totality [and if there were nothing else in the world apart from me],[16] I would be more perfect than I am at present, had God made me in that way. But I cannot for that reason deny that, in the whole universe of things, it is in some sense a greater perfection that some of its parts are immune from error while others are not, than if all its parts were exactly similar. I have no right to complain that God chose to give me a role in the world that is not the principal and most perfect of all.

Besides, even if I cannot avoid error by the first strategy, which relies on the clear perception of everything about which I have to deliberate, I can at least do so by the other strategy, which presupposes only that I remember to abstain from making a judgement when the truth about something is not clear. For although I experience in myself the weakness of not being able always to concentrate on one and the same item of knowledge, I can still arrange, by an attentive and frequently repeated meditation, to remember this rule as often as I need it and in that way I could acquire a certain habit of not making mistakes.

Since that is the greatest and principal human perfection, I do not consider that I accomplished little in today's meditation in which I investigated the cause of error and falsehood. If it is clear that there cannot be any other cause than the one I explained, then as long as I restrict the will in such a way that, in making judgements, it extends only to those things that the understanding shows it clearly and distinctly, it is evidently impossible for me to be mistaken because every clear and distinct perception is certainly something and, consequently, cannot come from nothing but necessarily has God for its author – God, I say, the supremely perfect being for whom it is repugnant to be a deceiver – and hence the perception is undoubtedly true. Today I have learned not only what I must avoid in order never to be mistaken, but I have also learned what must be done to reach the truth. I will certainly reach it if I consider only the things that I understand perfectly enough and if I separate them from all other things which I apprehend in a confused and obscure way. I shall do this diligently in future.

FIFTH MEDITATION

The Essence of Material Things. Another Discussion of God's Existence

There are still many things to consider about the attributes of God and about my own nature or my mind. But I will consider them some other time perhaps, because nothing seems more urgent (once I have recognized what should be avoided and what should be done to reach the truth), than to try to emerge from the doubts into which I fell in recent days and to see if I can have any certainty about material things.

In fact, before inquiring whether any such things exist outside me, I should consider their ideas insofar as they are in my thought and see which ideas are distinct and which are confused.

I have a distinct image of quantity, which philosophers usually call continuous quantity, or of its extension or, preferably, of the extension of a quantified thing in length, breadth and depth. I also pick out various parts in it and assign to these parts various magnitudes, shapes, positions and local motions, and I assign various durations to the local motions. All these things, considered in this general way, are not the only things that are clearly perceived and known; by paying attention, I also perceive innumerable particular things about shapes, number, motion and so on, the truth of which is so open and so accommodated to my nature that, when I first discover it, I seem not so much to learn something new as to remember things I already knew or to notice for the first time things that were in my mind for a long time even though I had not previously turned my attention to them.

I think that what deserves most consideration at this stage is that I find I have innumerable ideas of certain things which, even if they do not exist anywhere outside me, still cannot be said to be nothing. Although I think about them to some extent by choice, they are not, however, invented by me and they have their own true and immutable natures. For example, when I imagine a triangle, even if it were true that no such figure exists or has ever existed anywhere outside my thought, it still clearly has some determinate nature or essence or form, immutable and eternal, which was not constructed by me and does not depend on me. This is clear from the fact that various properties of the triangle can be demonstrated; for example, that its three angles are equal to two right angles, that the longest side is subtended by the biggest angle, and similar properties. Even if I never thought of them previously when I imagined a triangle, I now know them clearly independently of whether I wish to or not and therefore they were not invented by me.

If I were to say that the idea of a triangle may have reached me through the sense organs, because I occasionally saw bodies with triangular shapes, that is beside the point. For I can think of innumerable other shapes about which there can be no suggestion that I ever got to know them through the senses and, despite that, I can demonstrate various properties about them just as in the case of the triangle. All these properties are obviously true since they are known clearly by me, and therefore they are something and not simply nothing – for it is obvious that everything that is true is something, and I have already demonstrated above that everything that I know clearly is true. And even had I not demonstrated it, the nature of my mind is certainly such that I still would be incapable of not assenting to them, at least as long as I perceive them clearly. I also remember that, even earlier, when I was completely immersed in the objects of the senses, I always held that the most certain of all were the truths of this type, namely, whatever I knew clearly about shapes or numbers and other truths that pertain to arithmetic or geometry or, in general, to pure and abstract mathematics.

Now if it follows, from the fact alone that I can produce an idea of something from my thought, that everything that I perceive clearly and distinctly as belonging to it does really belong to it, could I not also derive an argument to demonstrate God's existence?[17] Certainly I find in myself an idea of God – that is, of a supremely perfect being – just as much as I find an idea of any shape or number. I understand that it belongs to God's nature that he always exists, as clearly and distinctly as I understand that whatever I demonstrate about any shape or number belongs to the nature of that shape or number. Therefore, even if everything on which I meditated in recent days were not true, I should attribute to God's existence at least the same degree of certainty that I have attributed to mathematical truths until now.

However, it is clear that this is not completely perspicuous at first sight and it seems to be some kind of logical trick. Because I am used to distinguishing existence from essence in everything else, I easily believe that it is also possible to separate existence from the essence of God and, in that way, that one could think about God as not existing. But it is clear to whoever thinks about it more carefully that existence can no more be separated from God's essence than one can separate, from the essence of a triangle, that the three angles are equal to two right angles, or than one could separate the idea of a valley from the idea of a mountain. Thus to think of God (that is, a supremely perfect being) as lacking existence (that is, lacking some perfection) is just as contradictory as to think of a mountain that lacks a valley.

However, even if I can think of God only as existing and of a mountain only with a valley, still the following must surely be true: just as it does not follow that there is any mountain in the world from the fact that I think of a mountain with a valley, likewise from the fact that I think of God as existing it does not seem to follow that God exists. My thought imposes no necessity on things and, since I can think of a horse with wings even though no horse has wings, perhaps I could likewise attribute existence to God even though no God exists.

There is a logical mistake concealed here. From the fact that I cannot think of a mountain without a valley it does not follow that a mountain and valley exist somewhere, but only that mountain and valley, whether they exist or not, cannot be separated from one another. Likewise, from the fact that I can think of God only as existing, it follows that existence is inseparable from God and therefore that he really does exist. It is not that my thought makes this happen or imposes any necessity on any thing; on the contrary, the necessity of the reality itself, namely of God's existence, makes me think this way. I am not free to think of God without existence (that is, of a supremely perfect being without the highest perfection) in the same way that I am free to imagine a horse either with or without wings.

Nor should it be objected at this point that I have to assume that God exists once I have supposed that he has all perfections, but that the first assumption was not necessary, just as it is unnecessary for me to believe that all quadrilateral shapes can be inscribed in a circle; however, if I were to make the latter assumption, then I would have to concede that a rhombus can be inscribed in a circle – which is clearly false. Although it is not necessary that I ever get to thinking about God, whenever I choose to think about the first and highest being and, as it were, to draw out the idea of God from the treasury of my mind, I must necessarily attribute all perfections to him, even if I do not enumerate them all at the time or consider each one of them individually. This necessity is so clear that subsequently, when I realize that existence is a perfection, I must conclude correctly that the first and highest being exists. Likewise, it is not necessary that I ever imagine any triangle but, whenever I decide to think about a rectilinear figure which has only three angles, it is necessary that I attribute to it those properties from which it is correctly deduced that its three angles are not greater than two right angles – even if I do not advert to this at the time. But when I consider which figures are inscribed in a circle, it is not at all necessary to think that they include all quadrilaterals. In fact, I cannot even imagine that, as long as I wish to admit only what I understand clearly and distinctly. Therefore there is a big difference between false propositions like that and the true ideas that are innate in me, among which the idea of God is the primary and principal one. For I clearly understand in many ways that the idea of God is not something fictitious which depends on my thought, but that it is the image of a true and immutable nature. Firstly, for example, because there is nothing else that I can think of, apart from God alone, to the essence of which existence belongs. Secondly, because I cannot understand two or more similar Gods and I assume that one such God exists, I see clearly that it is necessary both that he existed from all eternity and will remain for eternity. Finally, I perceive many other things in God which are such that I cannot change them or take anything away from them.

But whatever argument I eventually use to prove something, I am always brought back to this: the only things that clearly convince me are those that I perceive clearly and distinctly. And even if, among the things that I perceive in this way, some are obvious to everyone while others are discovered only by those who look at them more closely and examine them more carefully, once they are discovered, however, the latter are considered no less certain than the former. For example, even if the fact that the square on the hypotenuse of a right-angled triangle is equal to the squares on the other two sides is not as apparent as the fact that the hypotenuse subtends the largest angle, once it is seen clearly it is not believed any less. In the case of God, however, I would surely know him prior to and more easily than anything else if I were not submerged in prejudices and if the images of sensible things did not besiege my thought from every direction; for what is more clear than this, that the supreme being exists or that God – to whose essence alone existence belongs – exists? Besides, although I had to pay careful attention to perceive this, I am now not only as certain of this as of anything else that seems very certain to me, but I also notice that the certainty of other things depends on this in such a way that, without it, nothing can ever be known perfectly.

Although my nature is such that, as long as I perceive something very clearly and distinctly, I am unable not to believe that it is true, my nature is also such that I cannot fix my mind's eye always on the same thing in order to perceive it clearly, and the memory of an earlier judgement often returns when I am no longer considering the reasons why I made that judgement. Thus other reasons could occur to me, if I were ignorant of God, which would easily make me change my mind and in that way I would never have true and certain knowledge about anything but merely unstable and changeable opinions. Thus, for example, when I think about the nature of a triangle, it seems most evident to me, as someone imbued with the principles of geometry, that its three angles are equal to two right angles, and I am unable not to believe that it is true as long as I think about its demonstration. But as soon as I have turned my mind's eye away, even though I still remember that I perceived it as clearly as possible, it easily happens that I doubt its truth – at least, if I am ignorant of God. For I can convince myself that I was so created by nature that I am sometimes mistaken about things that I think I perceive as clearly as possible, especially when I remember that I have often accepted many things as true and certain that I subsequently judged were false when new considerations were introduced.

But once I perceived that God exists and have also understood, at the same time, that everything else depends on him and that he is not a deceiver, I concluded that all those things that I clearly and distinctly perceive are necessarily true. And even if I no longer consider the reasons on account of which I made that judgement about its truth, no contrary reason can be found – as long as I remember having perceived it clearly and distinctly – that would make me doubt it. Instead, I have a true and certain knowledge of it. Nor does this apply to this one thing alone, but to all the other things that I remember having demonstrated at some time, for example, in geometry and so on. What counter-arguments remain now? That I was made in such a way that I am often mistaken? But I already know that I cannot be mistaken in those things that I understand clearly. Perhaps I formerly accepted many things as true and certain that I subsequently discovered were false? But I did not perceive any of those things clearly and distinctly and, ignorant of this rule of truth, I may have believed them for other reasons that I later found were less reliable. What should be said, then? That I may be dreaming (as I objected to myself a while ago), or that all the things that I am thinking about now are no more true than what occurs to me when I am asleep? But even that does not change anything because surely, if I am dreaming, on condition that something is evident to my understanding it is entirely true.

Thus I see clearly that the certainty and truth of all knowledge depends only on the knowledge of the true God in such a way that, before I knew him, I was incapable of knowing anything else perfectly. But now countless things can be known and be certain for me, both about God and other intellectual things, and also about as much of physical nature as falls within the scope of pure mathematics.

SIXTH MEDITATION

The Existence of Material Things, and the Real Distinction between Mind and Body

I still have to consider whether material things exist. Indeed, I already know that they are at least capable of existing insofar as they are the object of pure mathematics, because I perceive them clearly and distinctly. For there is no doubt that God is capable of producing everything that I am capable of perceiving in this way, and I never thought that there was anything he was incapable of producing unless it was incapable of being perceived distinctly by me. Besides, it seems to follow that they do exist, from the faculty of imagining that I am conscious of using when I turn to such material things. The reason is that, if one considers very carefully what the imagination is, it seems to be nothing but a certain application of the cognitive faculty to a body that is intimately present to that faculty and that therefore exists.

To clarify that, I will first consider the difference between imagination and pure understanding. When I imagine a triangle, for example, I do not merely understand that it is a figure bounded by three lines but, at the same time, I also see those three lines with my mind's eye as if they were present, and that is what I call imagining. However, if I wish to think about a chiliagon, I understand equally well that it is a figure that consists of one thousand sides, just as I understand that a triangle is a figure that consists of three sides; but I cannot imagine a thousand sides in the same way, that is, I cannot see them as if they were present. Even if I represent to myself some very confused figure on that occasion, because of my habit of always imagining something whenever I think of a physical thing, it is clear nevertheless that it is not a chiliagon, because it is not in any way different from what I would also represent to myself if I were to think about a myriagon or any other figure with many sides, and it is useless for knowing the properties by which a chiliagon differs from other polygons. However, if we were discussing a pentagon, I could understand its shape too, just like that of a chiliagon, without the aid of the imagination. But by applying my mind's eye simultaneously to its five sides and to the area they enclose, I am also able to imagine it. I notice clearly in this example that, in order to imagine, I need a characteristic effort of the mind that I do not use in order to understand. This new effort of the mind shows clearly the difference between the imagination and pure understanding.

I also think that the power of imagining which I have, insofar as it differs from the power of understanding, is not required for my essence, that is, for the essence of my mind because, even if I did not have it, I would undoubtedly remain who I am now. It seems to follow that the imagination depends on something that is distinct from me. I understand easily that, if some body existed to which my mind were so united that it could apply itself to it at will as if it were inspecting it, it would be possible to imagine things through that physical body. Thus this way of thinking differs from pure understanding only in the sense that the mind, when it understands, turns back on itself in some way and reflects on one of the ideas that are inside itself; however, when it imagines, it turns towards a body and sees something in it that resembles the idea that had been understood by itself or perceived by sensation. I can easily understand, I say, that the imagination can take place in that way if such a body exists. Since no other equally satisfactory way of explaining it occurs to me, I hypothesize that such a body probably exists. However, it exists only probably and, despite my careful examination, I still do not see how, from the distinct idea of a physical nature which I find in my imagination, I can derive an argument that concludes necessarily that some body exists.

However, I am used to imagining, besides the physical nature which is the object of pure mathematics, many other things, such as colours, sounds, tastes, pain and the like, although none of them distinctly. Since I perceive them better by sensation – from which they seem to come to the imagination with the aid of memory – if I wish to discuss them properly, I have to discuss sensation too and see if, from those things which are perceived in the type of thinking that I call sensation, I can derive an argument for the existence of physical things that is certain.

I shall first remind myself at this point of those things which, having been perceived by sensation, I formerly thought were true, and of the reasons why I thought they were true. I shall then review the reasons why I subsequently raised doubts about them. And finally, I shall consider what I should believe about them now.

First of all, I sensed that I had a head, hands, feet and the other members which compose the body that I considered as a part of myself or, perhaps, as myself in its entirety. I sensed that this body was surrounded by many other bodies by which it could be affected in various beneficial or harmful ways, and I judged the beneficial things by a certain sensation of pleasure and the harmful things by a sensation of pain. Besides pain and pleasure, I also sensed in myself hunger, thirst and other such appetites, and certain bodily inclinations towards happiness, sadness, anger and other similar passions. Outside myself, apart from the extension of bodies, their shapes and motions, I also sensed in them hardness, heat and other tactile qualities. In addition, I had sensations of light, colours, sounds, odours and tastes, by the variety of which I distinguished from one another the sky, the earth, the seas and other bodies.

Given the ideas of all those qualities which were presented to my thought and which were the only things that, strictly speaking, I sensed immediately, it was evidently reasonable to believe that I sensed various things which were clearly distinct from my thought, namely the bodies from which those ideas originated. For I experienced that those ideas would come to me without any consent on my part, so that I was both unable to sense any object, even if I wished to, unless it was present to my sensory organs and I was incapable of not sensing it when it was present. Since the ideas perceived by sensation were much stronger and more vivid and, in their own way, more distinct than any of those that I formed myself, it seemed impossible – when meditating carefully and intentionally on those that I noticed were impressed on my memory – that they originated from myself. Therefore, the only remaining option was that they originated from other things. Because I had no knowledge of those things apart from the very ideas that I got from them, nothing else could have occurred to me except that the ideas resembled the things. And because I also recall that I began using my senses before my reason, and since I saw that the ideas that I formed were not as vivid as those that I perceived by sensation and that, in most cases, they were composed of parts of the latter, I easily convinced myself that I had absolutely nothing in my mind which did not originate in sensation.

It was also reasonable for me to judge that the body which, by some special right, I called my own belongs to me more than any other body. For I was unable ever to be separated from it, as I could be from other bodies; I sensed all my appetites and passions in it and for it; and finally, I was aware of pain and the titillation of pleasure in its parts, but not in other bodies that were situated outside me. Why does a certain sadness of the mind follow from some unknown sensation of pain, and a certain happiness from a sensation of pleasure? Or why does the unknown tightening of the stomach that I call hunger advise me to eat food and a dryness of the throat advise me to take a drink, and so on for all the others? I clearly had no explanation except that I was taught this by nature. There is obviously no other connection (at least, none that I can understand) between the stomach tightening and the decision to take food, or between the sensation of something that causes pain and the thought of sadness that results from it. All the other things that I judged about the objects of the senses seemed to be taught by nature. I was convinced of this before I weighed up any of the reasons that could prove it.

Later, however, many experiences undermined little by little all my faith in the senses. For in some cases towers that seemed round from a distance appeared, close up, to be square, and very high statues standing on top of the towers did not seem tall to an observer on the ground. In countless other similar things I discovered that the judgements of the external senses were mistaken. And not only the judgements of the external senses, but also those of the internal senses. For what can be closer to me than pain? But I once heard, from those who had had a leg or arm amputated, that they still seemed to feel pain in the part of their body that was missing. Likewise, it did not seem certain in my own case that I had a pain in some limb even if I felt a pain in it. I recently added to these reasons for doubting two other much more general ones. The first was that I never believed I sensed anything while awake that I was not also able to think I sensed occasionally while I was asleep; and since I do not believe that the things I seem to sense while asleep come to me from external things, I did not see why I should give any more credence to things that I seem to sense while awake. The second reason was that, as long as I did not know or, at least, as long as I pretended not to know the author of my origin, I saw nothing to prevent me from being so constituted by nature that I was mistaken even about those things that seemed most true to me. As regards the reasons by which I was formerly convinced of the truth of sensible things, it was not difficult for me to reply to them. It seemed as if nature pushed me towards many things from which reason dissuaded me, and therefore I did not think that I should put much faith in what nature taught me. And despite the fact that the perceptions of the senses do not depend on my will, I did not think that I should conclude, for that reason, that they derived from things that are distinct from me; there may perhaps be some faculty in me, even if it is unknown to me, by which they are produced.

However, now that I begin to know better both myself and the author of my origin, I do not think that all the things that I seem to acquire from the senses must be accepted with temerity; but at the same time, it is not necessary that all of them be called into doubt.

Firstly, I know that everything that I understand clearly and distinctly can be made by God in the same way that I understand them; therefore it is enough that I can understand one thing, clearly and distinctly, without another in order to be certain that one thing is distinct from the other, because it is possible for them to be separated, at least by God. It is irrelevant by what power the separation is realized in order for them to be considered distinct. Therefore from the fact alone that I know that I exist and that, at the same time, I notice absolutely nothing else that belongs to my nature apart from the single fact that I am a thinking thing, I correctly conclude that my essence consists in this alone, that I am a thinking thing. And although I may (rather, as I shall say soon: I certainly) have a body that is joined very closely to me, since I have on the one hand a clear and distinct idea of myself insofar as I am a thinking, non-extended thing and, on the other hand, I have a distinct idea of the body insofar as it is merely an extended, non-thinking thing, it is certain that I am really distinct from my body and that I can exist without it.

Besides, I find in myself faculties for thinking in certain special ways, such as faculties for imagining and sensing; I can understand my whole self clearly and distinctly without them but cannot, conversely, understand them without myself, that is, without the intellectual substance in which they inhere, for they include in their formal concept some kind of understanding. I conclude from this that they are distinguishable from me as modes are from a thing. I also acknowledge some other faculties, such as the ability to change place, to assume various shapes, and the like, which cannot be really understood, any more than the previous faculties, without some substance in which they inhere and without which they likewise cannot exist. But it is evident that if they do indeed exist, then these faculties must be in a physical or extended substance and not in an intellectual substance, because the clear and distinct concept of these faculties clearly includes some extension but no intellection.

There is also in me a certain passive faculty for sensing, or for receiving and knowing the ideas of sensible things, but I would not be able to use it in any way unless there also existed an active faculty, either in me or in something else, for producing or causing those ideas. Now it is clear that this cannot be located in me because it evidently presupposes no understanding, whereas those ideas are produced when I am not co-operating and even in spite of me. It follows, therefore, that this faculty must be in some substance which is distinct from me;

and since it must contain as much reality, formally or eminently, as is found intentionally in the ideas produced by that faculty (as I mentioned above), this substance is either a body or a physical nature which formally contains everything that the ideas contain intentionally, or else it obviously must be God or some other creature more noble than a body which contains them eminently. But God is not a deceiver; it is perfectly obvious, therefore, that he does not send these ideas to me directly from himself. Nor does he send them indirectly by means of some creature which contains the intentional reality of the ideas, not formally but only eminently. He obviously gave me no faculty to recognize such an arrangement; on the contrary, he gave me a strong tendency to believe that these ideas are emitted by physical things, and therefore I cannot see how he can be understood as not being a deceiver if they originated from anything except physical things. Therefore, physical things exist. They may not all exist, however, in exactly the same way that I perceive them in sensation, since sensory perception is very obscure and confused in many cases. But at least they include all those things that I understand clearly and distinctly – in other words, all those things that, conceived in a general way, are included in the subject matter of pure mathematics.

As regards other things, which are either only particular things (for example, that the sun has a certain size or shape, etc.) or which are less clearly understood (for example, light, sound, pain and similar things), although they are very doubtful and uncertain, the very fact that God is not a deceiver and therefore that there can be no falsehood in my beliefs, unless I have another faculty provided by God to correct it, provides me with a secure hope of finding the truth even about those things. There is evidently no doubt that everything that I am taught by nature has some truth in it – for by 'nature' in this context, understood in a general way, I understand nothing but God himself or the co-ordinated system of created things that was established by God. Nor do I understand my own nature in particular as anything other than the complex of all those things that were given me by God.

However, there is nothing that my nature teaches me more persuasively than that I have a body that is being harmed when I feel pain, that needs food or drink when I suffer hunger or thirst, and so on. Therefore, I should not doubt that there is some truth in this.

Nature also teaches by means of the sensations of pain, hunger, thirst, etc., that I am not present to my body only in the way that a pilot is present to a ship, but that I am very closely joined to it and almost merged with it to such an extent that, together with it, I compose a single entity. Otherwise, when my body is injured I (who am nothing but a thinking thing) would not feel pain as a result; instead I would perceive such an injury as a pilot perceives by sight if some part of the ship is damaged. Likewise, when my body needs food or drink, I would understand this more clearly and would not have confused sensations of hunger and thirst. For these sensations of thirst, hunger, pain, etc., are undoubtedly mere confused ways of thinking that result from the union and, as it were, the thorough mixing together of mind and body.

Moreover, I am also taught by nature that various other bodies exist in the vicinity of my body, and that I should seek some of them and avoid others. Certainly, from the fact that I perceive very different colours, sounds, odours, tastes, heat, hardness and the like, I conclude correctly that there are some differences between the bodies from which those various sensory perceptions arise that correspond to them, even if they do not, perhaps, resemble them. Besides, from the fact that some of those perceptions are agreeable to me while others are disagreeable it is obviously certain that my body, or preferably, my entire self insofar as I am composed of a body and mind, can be affected by various beneficial or harmful bodies in my environment.

But there are many other things such that, although I seemed to be taught them by nature, I learned them not really from nature but from a certain habit of judging carelessly, and it can easily happen therefore that they are false: for example, that every space is empty, if there is nothing obviously there that would affect my senses; that, for example, there is something in a warm body that resembles exactly the idea of heat that I have; that in something white or green there exists the same whiteness or greenness that I perceive, in something bitter or sweet the same taste, and so on for the others; that stars and towers and all other remote bodies have exactly the same size and shape that they present to my senses, and other similar things.

But in order not to perceive anything here that is not sufficiently distinct, I should define more carefully what exactly I understand when I say that I am taught something by nature. For here I mean nature in a narrower sense than the complexity of everything that I was given by God, for this complexity includes many things that belong only to the mind; for example, I perceive that it is impossible for what was done to be undone, and all the other things that are known by the natural light of reason, and I am not concerned with them at this point.

There are also many things that belong only to the body, for example that it tends downwards and similar things, and I am not concerned with them either. I am concerned here only with those things that were given me by God insofar as I am composed of a mind and body.

Nature in this sense, therefore, teaches me to flee from things that cause a sensation of pain and to seek those that cause a sensation of pleasure, and so on. But it does not seem to teach us to draw any conclusion from these sensory perceptions, without a prior examination by the understanding of the things that are external to us, because it seems that we can learn the truth about them by using the mind alone and not by using the composite of mind and body. Thus although a star does not affect my eye any more than the flame of a small fire, nevertheless that does not provide any real or positive inclination to believe that it is not greater, despite the fact that I have unreasonably judged in this way from my youth. And although I feel heat when I approach the fire, and I also feel pain when I go too near it, there is really no reason to convince me that there is something in the fire that resembles that heat any more than there is something in it that resembles the pain; but there is reason to believe only that there is something in it, whatever it turns out to be, which causes those sensations of heat and pain in us. And although there may be nothing in a given space that affects our senses, it does not follow that there is no body there. But I see in these and many other cases that I have got used to perverting the order of nature. For sensory perceptions, strictly speaking, were given by nature only to signify to the mind what is beneficial or harmful for the composite of which it is a part and, to that extent, they are sufficiently clear and distinct; but I use them as if they were guaranteed rules for the immediate discovery of the essence of external bodies, whereas they provide only very obscure and confused perceptions of them.

However, I have already adequately examined above how, despite God's goodness, it can happen that my judgements are false. But a new difficulty arises at this point about the very things that nature presents as things to be sought or avoided, and even about the internal sensations in which I seem to have detected mistakes – for example, when someone is deluded by the agreeable taste of some food and swallows poison which is concealed in it. But in that case one is urged by nature only to seek whatever has the agreeable taste and not the poison about which nature is completely ignorant. One can draw no conclusion from this, except that this nature is not omniscient. That is not surprising because, since a human being is limited, it deserves only limited perfections.

Still, it is not unusual for us to be mistaken about things to which nature inclines us, for example, in the case of those who are ill and who desire food or drink that very soon afterwards is harmful for them. One could say perhaps, in this case, that they are mistaken because their nature is disordered. But this does not resolve the problem, because someone who is sick is one of God's creatures just as much as someone who is healthy; therefore it seems to be just as objectionable if those who are sick were given a deceptive nature by God. A clock made with wheels and weights observes all the laws of nature just as precisely when it is made poorly and fails to show the correct time as when it satisfies the artisan's intentions in every respect. Likewise, I think of a human body as some kind of machine made from bones, nerves, muscles, veins, blood and skin so that, even if there were no mind in it, it would still have all the motions which it has at present and which do not result from the control of the will and, therefore, from the mind. Consequently, I can easily acknowledge that it would be equally natural for it (if it suffered from dropsy, for example) to experience the same dryness of the throat that the sensation of thirst usually brings to the mind, and for its nerves and other parts of the body to be so affected that it would take a drink which would aggravate its sickness, as to be moved by a similar dryness of the throat to take a drink which is beneficial for it when it is not affected by such a sickness. When I consider the anticipated use of the clock, however, I could say that it deviates from its nature when it does not show the correct time; likewise, considering the machine of the human body as being adapted to the motions that usually occur in it, I could think that it also deviates from its nature if its throat is dry when a drink is not conducive to its conservation. But I am sufficiently aware that this last way of understanding nature is very different from the other one. This latter understanding is simply a name, which results from my thought when I compare someone who is sick and a badly made clock with the idea of someone who is healthy and a clock that is well made, and it is completely extrinsic to the things to which it is applied. But by the former concept of nature I understand something which is really found in things and which, therefore, has some truth in it.

When the nature of a body suffering from dropsy is described as 'corrupted', because it has a dry throat but does not need a drink, this is certainly a case of arbitrarily attaching a name to it. But when it is a question of the composite, or of a mind united with such a body, it is not simply a case of arbitrarily naming something; it is a genuine mistake of nature that it is thirsty when a drink is harmful to it. Therefore, we need to ask here how God's goodness fails to prevent nature, understood in the latter sense, from being deceitful.

First of all, I perceive that there is a big difference between the mind and the body insofar as the body, by its nature, is always divisible whereas the mind is evidently indivisible. When I reflect on the mind (or on myself insofar as I am simply a thinking thing), I certainly cannot distinguish any parts in myself; instead I understand myself to be a completely unified and integral thing. And even though the whole mind seems to be united with the whole body, if however a foot, an arm, or any other part of the body is cut off, I know that nothing is thereby taken away from the mind. Nor can the faculties of willing, sensing, understanding, etc., be said to be parts of the mind, because it is one and the same mind that wills, senses and understands. In contrast, I cannot think of any physical or extended body that I cannot divide easily in my thought; for that reason alone, I understand that it is divisible. That would be enough to teach me that the mind is completely different from the body if I did not already know it adequately from other considerations.

Secondly, I perceive that the mind is not affected immediately by all the parts of the body but only by the brain or, perhaps, only by one small part of the brain, namely the part in which the common sense is said to be.[18] Whenever this part is in the same state, it presents the same thing to the mind even though the other parts of the body may be in different states. This is proved by many experiences that need not be reviewed here.

I also perceive that the nature of the body is such that no part of it can be moved by another part at a certain distance from it, unless it can also be moved in the same way by any of the parts in between, even when the more remote part does nothing. For example, in a cord *ABCD*, if one end of it *D* is pulled, the other end *A* will be moved in the same way as if one of the intermediate parts, *B* or *C*, had been pulled and the end *D* had remained unmoved. In a similar way, when I feel a pain in my foot, physics teaches me that that sensation occurs by means of the nerves that are spread through the foot and are stretched from the foot to the brain like cords; when they are pulled in the foot, they also pull the inner parts of the brain where they terminate, and they stimulate a certain motion there, which was established by nature to affect the mind with a feeling of what seems like a pain in the foot. Since these nerves have to pass through the leg, the thigh, the loins, the back and the neck to reach from the foot to the brain, it can happen that, even if that section of the nerves which is in the foot is not affected but only some other intermediate section, evidently the very same motion occurs in the brain as when the foot is hurt, from which it will necessarily follow that the mind feels the same pain. The same thing must occur in the case of other sensations.

Finally, I perceive that any of the motions that occur in the part of the brain that affects the mind immediately trigger only one particular sensation in it; therefore the best arrangement that could be imagined here would be for it to trigger the specific sensation which, among all the sensations that it could possibly trigger, is conducive most often and to the greatest extent to the conservation of human health. Experience shows, however, that all the sensations with which we are endowed by nature are of this kind; therefore nothing can be found in them that does not bear witness to the power and goodness of God. Thus, for example, when the nerves in the foot are moved violently and more than usual, their motion, passing through the spinal cord to the inner parts of the brain, gives a signal to the mind to sense something, namely a pain that seems to be in the foot, by which it is stimulated to remove its cause, insofar as that is possible, as something harmful to the foot. Human nature could have been so constituted by God that the very same motion in the brain would make the mind aware of something else – for example, the motion itself as it occurs in the brain, in the foot, or in any of the intermediate places between the foot and the brain, or of something completely different. But nothing else would have been as conducive to the conservation of the body. Likewise, when we need a drink, that gives rise to a certain dryness in the throat, which moves its nerves and, as a result, the interior of the brain. This motion affects the mind with a sensation of thirst, because there is nothing in this whole interaction that is more useful for us to know than that we need a drink for the conservation of our health, and likewise for other cases.

It is perfectly clear from these considerations that, despite the immense goodness of God, human nature, insofar as it is composed of a mind and body, cannot avoid being deceptive occasionally. For if some cause that is not in the foot, but in some other part of the body through which the nerves are stretched from the foot to the brain or even in the brain itself, causes the very same motion which is usually caused by a damaged foot, pain will be felt as if it were in the foot. Thus the sense is naturally deceived because, since the same motion in the brain must always trigger the same sensation in the mind and since it results much more frequently from some cause that harms the foot rather than from anything else, it is reasonable that it would always signal to the mind a pain in the foot rather than in any other part of the body. If it happens occasionally that dryness of the throat arises, not as it usually does because a drink is conducive to the health of the body but from some other contrary cause (as happens in the case of dropsy), it is much better that it would mislead in that case rather than always mislead when the body is healthy, and likewise for other examples.

This consideration is extremely helpful, not only for me to notice all the errors to which my nature is subject, but also to enable me to avoid them easily or to correct them. Clearly, I know that all the senses tell me much more frequently what is true rather than false about those things that pertain to the welfare of the body, and I can almost always use more than one of the senses to examine the same thing. I can also use my memory, which links present sensations with previous sensations, as well as my understanding, which has already looked into all the causes of error. Therefore, I should no longer fear that those things are false which my senses reveal to me on a daily basis. The hyperbolic doubts of recent days should be rejected as ridiculous, especially the extreme doubt that arose from my failure to distinguish between being asleep and being awake. I realize now that there is a very big difference between them, because dreams are never joined by memory with all the other activities of life, as happens with those that occur while we are awake. Evidently if, while I am awake, someone appeared to me suddenly and then immediately disappeared, as happens in dreams, in such a way that I did not see either where they came from or where they went to, I would reasonably judge that they were a ghost or an image depicted on my brain and not a genuine human being. But when things occur in such a way that I see distinctly where they come from, where and when they occur, and when the perception of them is linked with the rest of my life without any interruption, then I am perfectly certain that they occur to me while I am awake and not while asleep. Nor should I have even the slightest doubt about their truth if, having called upon all my senses, my memory and my understanding to examine them, I get no report from any of them which conflicts with the others. For from the fact that God is not a deceiver it follows that, in such cases, I am completely free from error. But the urgency of things to be done does not always allow us time for such a careful examination; it must be granted, therefore, that human life is often subject to mistakes about particular things, and the weakness of our nature must be acknowledged.

OBJECTIONS AND REPLIES (SELECTIONS)

First Objections[19]

(a) What cause, I ask, does an idea require? Or what is an idea? Is it the thing itself which is thought about, insofar as it is in the intellect intentionally? What does it mean to be in the intellect intentionally? One time I learned that it means: to determine an intellectual act itself by means of an object. That is evidently nothing in the thing itself but involves naming it by reference to something outside it. Just as for something to be seen is nothing more than an act of seeing, which is located in me, so likewise being thought or being in the intellect intentionally is having a thought of the mind that remains in and terminates in itself. This can occur even if the thing in question is not changed or moved, and even if it does not exist. I am asking, then: what is the cause of something which does not actually exist and which is nothing but a mere name?

However, our great author says: 'When an idea contains one particular intentional reality rather than another, it must surely get this from some cause.' On the contrary, from no cause! For intentional reality is merely a name, and does not actually exist. A cause has a real and actual influence on something: but that which does not actually exist does not receive that influence, and therefore it neither receives nor needs the real influence of a cause. Thus I have ideas, but not their cause – much less one that is greater than me and is infinite.

(b) Even if it is granted that a supremely perfect being, by its very nature, implies existence, it still does not follow that such an existence is something that is actually present in the nature of things, but only that the concept of existence is inseparably linked with the concept of a supreme being. You cannot deduce from this that the existence of God is something actual, unless you presuppose that God is a supreme being who actually exists. If that were true, it would actually include all perfections, including the perfection of real existence.

Replies

(a) What I wrote, however, was: an idea is the thing itself which is thought, insofar as it is in the intellect intentionally. He pretends to understand these words in a way that is obviously different from the way I understand them, in order to give me an opportunity of explaining them more clearly. He says: 'To be in the intellect intentionally is to determine an intellectual act itself by means of an object, which is nothing in the thing itself but involves naming it by reference to something outside it.' One should notice that he refers here to the thing itself as if it were located outside the intellect; that is why saying that it is in the intellect intentionally merely involves naming an object by reference to something outside it. But I was speaking about an idea that is never outside the intellect and, consequently, 'intentional being' means simply to be in the intellect in the way in which objects are usually there. Thus, for example, if anyone asks what happens to the sun as a result of being in my intellect intentionally, it is best to reply that nothing happens to it apart from its being named by reference to something outside itself, that is, that, as an object, it directs an operation of the intellect. But if someone asks about the *idea* of the sun, what is it? and if the reply is that it is the thing thought about insofar as it is in the intellect intentionally, no one will understand that to be the sun itself insofar as it is named after something outside itself. 'To be in the intellect intentionally' will not mean, in that case, to direct the intellect's operations as an object, but to be in it in the way in which objects of the intellect usually are there, so that the idea of the sun is the sun itself existing in the intellect – not, however, formally, as it does in the heavens, but intentionally, that is, in the way in which objects are usually in the intellect. This mode of existing is evidently much less perfect than that by which things exist outside the intellect but, clearly, it is not nothing as a result, as I have already written.

When the very learned theologian says that these words involve an equivocation, it seems as if he wants to warn me about something that

I have just noted, lest I happen to forget it. He says, in the first place, that a thing existing in this way in the intellect by means of an idea is not an actual entity, that is, it is not something which is located outside the intellect. And that is true. Then he also says that it is 'not something fictitious, or a being of reason,[20] but something real which is understood distinctly'. In these words he concedes everything that I assumed. He adds, however, 'that it is only conceived and does not actually exist (that is, because it is only an idea, and not something located outside the intellect); it can be conceived but cannot in any way be caused'. In other words, it does not require a cause in order to exist outside the intellect. I agree with that, but it obviously requires a cause in order to be conceived and that is the only issue at stake here.

For example, if someone had in their intellect the idea of some machine that had been thought with great artifice, it would be appropriate to ask right away: what is the cause of this idea? It would not be enough to say that the machine does not exist outside the intellect and, therefore, that it cannot be caused and can only be conceived. For the only question being asked is: what is the cause of its being conceived? Nor would it be enough to answer that the intellect itself is its cause, namely as the cause of its own operation. There is no disagreement about that here; the only point in contention concerns the cause of the intentional artifice which the idea contains because, in order for this idea of a machine to contain one intentional artifice rather than another, it must derive it from some cause. The same issue arises with respect to the intentional artifice of this idea and the intentional reality of the idea of God. There are various possible causes of the intentional artifice of this machine. The cause may be some actual machine, similar to this one, which was previously seen, as a result of which the idea resembling it was formed; or it may be an extensive knowledge of mechanics that is present in the intellect; or it may be a great intellectual creativity by which the intellect can invent such an idea even without prior knowledge of mechanics. It should also be noted that all the artifice, which is merely intentional in the idea, must necessarily be in its cause, whatever that turns out to be, either formally or eminently. The intentional reality which is in the idea of God should be understood in the same way. But where will this be, except in a really existing God?

But my acute reader sees all this and therefore concedes that it is legitimate to ask: why does this idea contain this particular intentional reality rather than some other? And he replies to this question, firstly: 'What I wrote about the idea of a triangle applies in the same way to all ideas; that is, even if a triangle did not exist anywhere, it still has some determinate nature or essence, or an immutable and eternal form.' But, he says, 'that is not to postulate a cause'. However, he well realizes that this is unsatisfactory; for if the nature of a triangle is also immutable and eternal, we are still just as entitled to ask the question why we have the idea of a triangle. For that reason, he added: 'if you persist in demanding an explanation, it is located in the imperfection of our intellect, etc.'. In answering in that way he seems to mean only that those who choose to disagree with me have no plausible answer to the question. For it is obviously no more probable that the imperfection of our intellect is the cause of our having an idea of God, than that a lack of expert knowledge of mechanics is the cause of our imagining some very complicated machine rather than some other machine which is less perfect. On the contrary, it is obvious that if someone has an idea of a machine that contains every conceivable artifice, one can conclude much more reasonably that the idea derives from some cause in which every conceivable artifice really existed, even if it exists only intentionally in the idea. For the same reason, since we have an idea of God that contains every conceivable perfection, one can conclude very evidently that the idea depends on some cause in which all that perfection is also found, namely, in God who really exists.

(b) My argument was as follows: whatever we understand clearly and distinctly as belonging to the true and immutable nature, essence, or form of something, can be truly predicated of it. But when we have examined with sufficient care what God is, we understand clearly and distinctly that it belongs to his true and immutable nature that he exists. Therefore, we can then truly predicate of him that he exists. The conclusion at least follows correctly, in this case, from the premises. Now the major premise cannot be denied either, since it was already agreed earlier that 'everything that we understand clearly and distinctly is true'. Only the minor premise remains, and I agree that there is a significant difficulty in this. In the first place, we are so used to making a distinction in everything else between existence and essence that we do not realize adequately the extent to which existence belongs to the essence of God more than in the case of other things. Secondly, if we do not distinguish what belongs to the true and immutable essence of something from what can be predicated of it only by a figment of the intellect, then even if we realize adequately that existence belongs to the essence of God, we fail to draw the conclusion that God exists because we do not know whether his essence is immutable and true or merely one of our figments.

But in order to remove the first part of this difficulty, we need to distinguish between possible existence and necessary existence, and we should note that possible existence is contained in the concept or idea of everything that is clearly and distinctly understood. However, necessary existence is contained only in the idea of God. Whoever is careful in paying attention to this difference between the idea of God and all other ideas will undoubtedly realize that, although we understand all other things only as if they existed, it does not follow that they exist but simply that they are capable of existing. For we understand that it is not necessary for actual existence to be combined with their other properties. But from the fact that we understand actual existence to be combined necessarily and always with the other attributes of God, it certainly does follow that God exists.

To remove the second part of the difficulty, it should be noted that ideas that do not contain true and immutable natures – but are merely fictitious natures which are invented by the intellect – are capable of being divided by that same intellect, not only by abstraction but by a clear and distinct mental operation. Thus any idea that cannot be divided in this way by the intellect was certainly not composed by it in the first place. For example, when I think about a winged horse, an actually existing lion or a triangle drawn inside a square, I easily understand that I can also think, conversely, about a horse without wings, a non-existing lion, or a triangle without a square, and so on, and therefore these ideas do not have true and immutable natures. However, if I think about a triangle or a square (I will not use the examples of a lion or a horse, because their natures are not completely clear to us), then certainly I can assert truthfully of the triangle whatever I understand as being contained in the idea of a triangle – for example, that its three angles are equal to two right angles, etc. Likewise, I can claim that whatever I find contained in the idea of a square is true. And even though I am able to understand a triangle while abstracting from the fact that its three angles are equal to two right angles, I still cannot deny, by means of a clear and distinct operation, that it has that property – that is, if I understand correctly what I am saying. Besides, if I think about a triangle drawn inside a square and avoid attributing to the square what belongs only to the triangle, or to the triangle what belongs to the square, and if I examine only those properties which result from the combination of the two figures, its nature would not be any less true and immutable than the nature of a triangle or a square considered separately. Thus it would be appropriate to claim that the square is not less than twice the area of the triangle drawn inside it, and other similar things, which belong to the nature of this composite figure.

However, if I thought that existence is contained in the idea of a supremely perfect body, because to exist both in reality and in the intellect is a greater perfection than to exist only in the intellect, I could not thereby conclude that such a supremely perfect body exists but only that it is capable of existing. For I am well able to recognize that such an idea was constructed by my own intellect, by combining together all physical perfections at the same time, and that existence does not result from those other perfections; on the contrary, one can just as easily affirm or deny the existence of them. Indeed, while examining the idea of a body I perceive no power in it by which it can produce itself or conserve itself in existence; from this I conclude validly that necessary existence, about which alone there is a question here, no more belongs to the nature of a body, no matter how perfect it is, than it belongs to the nature of a mountain that it does not have a valley or to the nature of a triangle that it has angles which together are greater than two right angles.

However, if we now ask not about a body but about something else (whatever it happens to be) that possesses all possible perfections at the same time, whether existence should be included among them, we shall initially have doubts about it. Our mind, which is finite, is used to thinking about those perfections only separately and therefore it may not notice immediately how they are necessarily combined together. But if we examine carefully whether existence – and what kind of existence – belongs to a supremely perfect being, we shall be able to perceive the following clearly and distinctly. Firstly, that at least possible existence belongs to it just as it belongs to all other things of which we have distinct ideas, even to those which are invented by a figment of our intellect. Then if we acknowledge its immense power, we cannot think that its existence is possible unless, at the same time, we acknowledge that it can exist by its own power, and we shall conclude from this that it really exists and that it existed from eternity. For it is very well known by the natural light of reason that anything which is capable of existing by its own power always exists. We shall thus understand that necessary existence is contained in the idea of a supremely powerful being, not by a figment of our intellect, but because it belongs to the true and immutable nature of such a being that it exists. We shall also easily perceive that such a supremely powerful being is incapable of not having in itself all the other perfections that are contained in the idea of God and, therefore, without any figment of our intellect and by their own nature, they are combined together and they exist in God.

Second Objections[21]

(a) So far, you acknowledge that you are a thinking thing but you do not know what this thinking thing is. What if it were a body, which, by its various movements and interactions, produces what we call thought? Although you think you have excluded every kind of body, you may have been mistaken because you hardly excluded yourself and you may be a body. How do you demonstrate that a body cannot think or that bodily movements are not that thought? But the whole system of your body, which you think you have excluded, or some parts of it – for example, the brain – could co-operate to produce those movements that we call thought. I am a thinking thing, you say; but do you know that you are not a bodily movement or a body that is moved?

(b) Since you are not yet certain of the existence of God, and since you cannot say that you are certain of anything or that you know anything clearly and distinctly unless you first know certainly and clearly that God exists, it follows that you cannot yet know clearly and distinctly that you are a thinking thing since, according to you, such knowledge depends on a clear knowledge of God's existence, which you have not yet proved at the point where you conclude that you know clearly what you are.

Besides, an atheist knows clearly and distinctly that the three angles of a triangle are equal to two right angles. However, they are so far from supposing God's existence that they openly deny it because, they argue, if God existed he would be the supreme being, the supreme good, that is, he would be infinite. But in every class, the infinite excludes every other perfection, that is, every entity and good and, even more, every non-entity and evil; since there are many things, beings, goods, non-beings and evils, we think you should answer this objection properly so that the impious have nothing left to rely on.

(c) But how do you know you are certain that you are not deceived, and that you cannot be deceived, about things that you think you know clearly and distinctly? How often have we found someone deceived about things that they believed they knew more clearly than the sun? Thus this principle of clear and distinct knowledge ought to be so clearly and distinctly explained that no one of sound mind could ever be deceived about things that they believe they know clearly and distinctly.

(d) When you reply to the theologian,[22] you seem to go astray in the conclusion, which you express as follows: 'Whatever we understand clearly and distinctly as belonging to the true and immutable nature of something can be truly predicated of it. But when we have examined with enough care what God is, we understand clearly and distinctly that it belongs to his nature that he exists.' You should conclude:

'therefore when we have investigated carefully enough what God is, we can assert truthfully that it belongs to the nature of God that he exists'. It does not follow from this that God truly exists, but only that he must exist if his nature is possible or if it is not self-contradictory. In other words, the nature or essence of God cannot be conceived without existence and therefore, given his essence, he truly exists. This is equivalent to the argument that others have expressed as follows: 'If it is consistent to claim that there is a God, then it is certain that he exists. But it is consistent to claim that he exists.' However, there is a question about the minor premise, which is: 'But it is consistent for him to exist.' Those who disagree claim either to doubt or to deny that.

(e) Besides, it does not seem to follow from the distinction of the mind from the body that the mind is incorruptible and immortal. What if its nature were limited by the duration of the life of the body, and if God granted it only enough strength and existence to coincide with the life of the body?

Replies

(a) You also ask: how do I demonstrate that a body cannot think? But forgive me if I reply that this question does not arise at that stage, for the first occasion on which I dealt with it was in the Sixth Meditation, in the following words: 'it is enough that I can understand one thing, clearly and distinctly, without another in order to be certain that one thing is distinct from the other' and so on. And a little later:

> Although I have a body that is joined very closely to me, since I have on the one hand a clear and distinct idea of myself insofar as I am a thinking, non-extended thing and, on the other hand, I have a distinct idea of the body insofar as it is merely an extended, non-thinking thing, it is certain that I (that is, a mind) am really distinct from my body and that I can exist without it.

It is easy to add to this: 'Anything that can think is a mind or is called a mind; but since mind and body are really distinct, no body is a mind. Therefore it is impossible for a body to think.'

I do not see what you can deny in this. Is it that it is not enough that we understand one thing clearly without another in order to recognize that they are really distinct? In that case, you should provide some more certain criterion of a real distinction, for I am confident that it is impossible to produce one. What will you say, then? Are two things really distinct if each can exist without the other? But I ask in reply: how do you know that one thing can exist without the other? If this is to be a criterion for a distinction, it must be knowable. Perhaps you will say that this can be known by using the senses because you can see or touch one thing when the other is absent, and so on. But the testimony of the senses is less reliable than that of the intellect, and it can happen in various ways that one and the same thing appears in different forms or in several places in different ways and, as a result, it is taken for two things. Also, if you remember what was said about the wax towards the end of the Second Meditation, you will realize that even bodies are not, strictly speaking, perceived by the senses but only by the intellect, so that to sense one thing without another is nothing other than to have an idea of one thing and to understand that that idea is not identical with the idea of the other thing. This can be understood only from the fact that one thing is perceived without the other, and it cannot be understood clearly unless the idea of each thing is clear and distinct. Thus, if your criterion for a real distinction provides any certainty, it is reducible to mine.

(b) When I said that we are unable to have knowledge that is certain unless we first know that God exists, I explicitly claimed that I was speaking only about knowledge of those conclusions that we can remember when we no longer consider the premises from which we deduced them.[23] But knowledge of principles is not usually called 'scientific knowledge' by logicians.[24] However, when we advert to the fact that we are thinking things, that is a primary notion, which is not deduced from a syllogism. Even if someone says, 'I think, therefore I am or I exist,' they do not deduce existence from thinking by using a syllogism, but they recognize it by means of a simple mental insight as something that is self-evident. This is evident from the fact that, if they deduced it by using a syllogism, they would first have to have known the major premise, 'that everything which thinks is or exists'. But they learn that much more from the fact that they experience, in themselves, that it is impossible to think without existing. The nature of our mind is such that it generates general propositions from its knowledge of particulars.

(c) Once we think that something is perceived correctly by us, we are spontaneously convinced that it is true. If this conviction is so strong that we could never have any reason to doubt what we are convinced of in this way, then there is nothing further to inquire about; we have everything that we could reasonably hope for. Why should we be concerned if someone happens to pretend that the very thing, about the truth of which we are so firmly convinced, appears false to God or to an angel and therefore that it is false, absolutely speaking? Why should we care about such an absolute falsehood, for we do not believe in it at all and have not the slightest evidence to support it? We are assuming a conviction that is so firm that it cannot be changed in any way, and such a conviction is evidently the same thing as the most perfect certainty.

But there may be a doubt whether anyone has such a degree of certainty, or such a firm and unchangeable conviction.

It is clear that such certainty is not available in the case of things that we perceive (even to the slightest extent) obscurely and confusedly; for such obscurity, of whatever kind, is a sufficient reason to doubt them. Nor is it available in the case of things which, however clear, are perceived only by sense; for we have often noticed that mistakes can arise in sensations – for example, when a person with dropsy drinks, or when snow appears yellow to someone with dropsy and they do not see it less clearly and distinctly than we do when it looks white to us. It follows then that this degree of certainty, if it is achieved at all, is realized only in the case of those things that are perceived clearly by the mind.

Among the latter, however, some are so clear and simple that we can never think about them without believing that they are true; for example, that while I am thinking, I exist; that those things which have once been done cannot be undone; and similar things about which it is manifestly possible to have such certainty. For we cannot have any doubt about them unless we think about them, but we cannot think about the very same things without believing that they are true, which is what was supposed. Therefore, we cannot doubt them without at the same time believing that they are true; in other words, we can never doubt them.

Nor is this an objection, that we have often found that others 'were deceived about things that they believed they knew more clearly than the sun'. For we have never seen this happen, nor could anyone see it happen, to those who derived the clarity of their perception from the intellect alone; we saw it happen only to those who derived their certainty either from the senses or from some false prejudice.

Likewise it is no objection if someone pretends that those things appear false to God or an angel, because the evidence of our perception does not allow us to believe whoever pretends such things.

There are other things that are perceived very clearly by our intellect when we consider adequately the reasons on which our knowledge of them depends and are such that we are consequently unable to doubt them at the time. However, we are capable of forgetting those reasons and, meanwhile, remembering the conclusions drawn from them and the question arises whether we still have a firm and unchangeable conviction about those conclusions when we remember that they were derived from evident principles; for we have to assume such a recollection in order for them to be called conclusions. I reply that such certainty is available only to those who know God in such a way that they understand that it is impossible for him to have given them a faculty of understanding that would not lead towards the truth. But it is not possible for others to have the same certainty.

(d) You seem to make a mistake yourself when you criticize the conclusion of the syllogism that I constructed. In order to get the conclusion that you want, the major premise would have to be formulated as follows: 'Whatever we understand clearly as belonging to the nature of something can be affirmed truthfully to belong to its nature.' However, in this form it contains nothing more than a useless tautology.[25] But my major premise was as follows: 'Whatever we understand clearly as belonging to the nature of something can be affirmed truthfully of that thing.' Thus if being an animal belongs to the nature of a human being, then a human being can be said to be an animal. If having three angles equal to two right angles belongs to the nature of a triangle, then it can be affirmed that a triangle has three angles equal to two right angles. If existing belongs to the nature of God, then it can be affirmed that God exists, and so on. The minor premise, however, was as follows: 'But it belongs to the nature of God that he exists.' From which it follows evidently, 'Therefore, it can be affirmed truthfully of God that he exists', and not, as you wished, 'Therefore, we can truthfully affirm that it belongs to the nature of God that he exists.'

Thus, in order to use the qualification that you introduce, you would have to deny the major premise and say: 'Whatever we understand clearly as belonging to the nature of something may not therefore be affirmed of that thing unless its nature is possible or is not inconsistent.' But I suggest that you notice how weak this qualification is. Either you understand the term 'possible', as everyone commonly does, to mean 'what is not inconsistent with human conceptions' and, in that sense of the term, it is evident that the nature of God as I have described it is possible; for I assumed that there was nothing in it that we did not perceive clearly and distinctly should belong to it, and thus it could not be inconsistent with our conceptions. Alternatively, you may well imagine that there is some other kind of possibility on the part of the object itself; if that is not consistent with the previous meaning, it cannot in any way be known by the human intellect and therefore it is just as capable of overthrowing everything else that is known to human beings as of contradicting the nature or existence of God. If we can deny that the nature of God is possible even though we find no impossibility on the part of the concepts – on the contrary, all the things that are contained in the concept of that divine nature are so interconnected that to deny that any of them belongs to God seems confused; if that were so, we could deny by a similar argument that the three angles of a triangle are equal to two right angles or that someone who is actually thinking exists. And it would be even more justifiable to deny that anything we have learned through the senses is true. Thus all human knowledge would be removed but without any justification.

(e) I confess that I cannot refute your supplementary objection, that the immortality of the soul does not follow from the distinction of the soul from the body, because one could say that the soul was made by God in such a way that its duration is terminated at the same time as that of the body. Nor do I assume so much that I could try to determine by the power of human reason any of those things that depend on the free will of God. Our natural knowledge teaches that the mind is distinct from the body and that it is itself a substance; that the human body, insofar as it differs from other bodies, is composed only of the configuration of its parts and other similar non-essential features; and finally, that the death of the body depends merely on some division or change of shape. We have no reason or precedent to convince us that the death or annihilation of a substance, such as the mind, must follow such a trivial cause as a change of shape, which is nothing more than a mode; indeed, it is not a mode of a mind but of a body, which is really distinct from the mind. Nor have we any reason or precedent to convince us that any substance can perish. That is enough to conclude that the mind, insofar as it can be known by natural philosophy, is immortal.

But if you were asking about the absolute power of God, whether he may have decreed that human souls would be limited to the same length of time within which the bodies to which he united them are destroyed, God alone can reply to that.

* * *

There are two kinds of demonstration, namely, by analysis and by synthesis.

Analysis shows the true way by which a thing was discovered methodically and, as it were, *a priori*, so that if the reader wishes to follow it and to pay enough attention to everything, they will understand the thing as perfectly and will make it their own as if they had discovered it themselves. It includes nothing, however, by which a less attentive or resistant reader would be compelled to believe, for if they fail to pay attention to even the slightest detail of what is involved, the necessity of the conclusion will escape them.

In contrast, synthesis operates in the opposite and, as it were, an *a posteriori* manner (although the proof itself is often more *a priori* in this than in the former method), and demonstrates the conclusion clearly and uses a long series of definitions, postulates, axioms, theorems and problems, so that if any one of the consequences is denied, it shows immediately that it was contained in the antecedents and in this way it compels assent from the reader no matter how resistant or stubborn they may be. But it is not as satisfactory as analysis, nor does it satisfy the minds of those who are anxious to learn because it does not teach the way in which something was discovered.

* * *

Reasons which prove the existence of God,
and the distinction of the soul from the body,
arranged in a geometrical format.

I. By the term 'thought', I mean everything which is in us in such a way that we are immediately conscious of it. Thus all operations of the will, intellect, imagination, and the senses are thoughts. But I added the word 'immediately' to exclude whatever follows from thoughts; for example, although a voluntary motion has some thought as its principle, it is not itself a thought.

II. By the word 'idea', I understand the form of any thought by the immediate perception of which I am conscious of the thought itself. Hence I cannot express anything in words and understand what I am saying without, by that very fact, being certain that I have an idea of whatever is meant by those words. Thus I do not apply the term 'ideas' only to the images which are depicted in the imagination; in fact, I do not call them ideas at all here, insofar as they are depicted in the bodily imagination, that is, in some part of the brain, but only insofar as they inform the mind itself when it turns towards that part of the brain.

III. By 'the intentional reality of an idea', I understand the reality of a thing that is represented by an idea insofar as it is in the idea. In the same way one can talk about an intentional perfection, or an intentional artifice, and so on. For anything that we perceive in the objects of our ideas is in the ideas themselves intentionally.

IV. Things are said to be *formally* in the objects of our ideas when they occur there in the same way that they are perceived; and they are said to exist *eminently* in the objects when they do not occur there in the same way, but in a way which is so great that it can provide a substitute for the way in which we perceive them.

V. Something is called a *substance* if it is a subject in which resides, or by which exists, everything that we perceive, that is, every property, quality or attribute of which we have a real idea. Nor do we have any idea of the substance itself in a strict sense, except that it is the thing in which whatever we perceive exists either formally or eminently, or whatever is present intentionally in one of our ideas, for it is known by the natural light of reason that no real attribute can belong to nothing.

VI. The substance in which thought inheres immediately is called 'mind'; I speak here of a mind rather than a soul, because the term 'soul' is equivocal and is often used in reference to a physical thing.

VII. The substance that is the immediate subject of local extension and of the non-essential features that presuppose extension – such as shape, position, local motion, etc. – is called a 'body'. But whether it is one and the same substance that is called mind and body, or whether they are two different substances, will be investigated later.

VIII. The substance that we understand as supremely perfect, and in which we conceive of nothing that involves any defect or limitation of perfection, is called God.

IX. When we say that something is contained in the nature of something or in its concept, that is the same as saying that it is true of that thing or that we can affirm it of that thing.

X. Two substances are said to be really distinct when each of them can exist without the other.

Third Objections[26]

Objection[27]

Now from the fact that I think or that I have an image, when I am either awake or dreaming, it follows that I am a thinking being; for 'I think' and 'I am thinking' mean the same thing. From the fact that I am a thinking thing it follows that I exist, because that which thinks is not nothing. But when the text goes on to add, 'that is, a mind, soul, intellect or reason',[28] a doubt arises. It does not seem to be sound reasoning to say, I am thinking, therefore I am a thought; nor, I am understanding, therefore I am an understanding. For in the same way I could say, I am walking, therefore I am the act of walking. Thus Mr Descartes is taking the thing that understands as if it were identical with understanding, which is an act of the intellect, or at least he is identifying the thing that understands with the understanding, which is a faculty of the intellect. But all philosophers distinguish a subject from its faculties and acts, that is, from its properties and its essences; an entity is one thing, its essence is something else. It is possible therefore that a thinking thing is the subject of the mind, of reasoning, or of understanding, and therefore is something physical. The opposite is assumed but not proved. But this inference is the basis of the conclusion which, it seems, Mr Descartes wishes to establish.

In the same place he says, I know that I exist, and asks what is this 'I' whom I know? It is very certain that knowledge of this, understood in this precise way, does not depend on things that I do not yet know.[29]

It is very certain that knowledge of this proposition, 'I exist', depends on this one, 'I think', as he correctly taught us. But what is the source of our knowledge of the proposition 'I think'? Certainly not anything other than this, that we are incapable of thinking of any act whatsoever without its subject; for example, of dancing without a dancer, or knowing without a knower, of thinking without a thinker . . .

Reply

When I said, 'that is, a mind, soul, intellect or reason, etc.', I did not understand those words as referring to mere faculties but to the things that were endowed with a faculty of thinking. This is what everyone understands by the first two terms and what is often understood by the second two. I explained this so explicitly, in so many places, that it seemed as if there was no room for doubt.

Nor is there any equivalence here between walking and thinking. For walking is usually taken to be only the action itself, whereas thought is sometimes understood as an action, sometimes as a faculty and sometimes as the thing in which it is a faculty.

Besides, I do not claim that the understanding and the thing that understands are identical or indeed that the thing that understands is the same as the intellect, if the word 'intellect' is used to refer to the faculty, but only if it refers to the thing itself that understands. I admit that I used the most abstract words I could find in order to signify the thing or substance that I wanted to strip of everything that does not belong to it, in the same way as, in contrast with me, this philosopher uses the most concrete words possible, 'subject', 'matter' and 'body', to signify the thinking thing itself so that it is not separated from the body.

I am not afraid that his method of combining many things together may appear to many people to be more appropriate for discovering the truth than mine, in which I distinguish particular things as much as I can. But let us stop talking about words and concentrate on the reality.

'It may be,' he says, 'that the thinking thing is something physical; the opposite is assumed, not proved.' But I did not assume the opposite nor did I use it in any way as a premise; instead I explicitly left it undecided until the Sixth Meditation, where it was proved.

He then says, correctly, that we cannot conceive of any act without its subject; for example, we cannot conceive of thought without a thinking thing because whatever thinks is not nothing. But then, without any reason and contrary to all logic and the standard use of language, he adds: it seems to follow from this that the thinking thing is physical. The subjects of all actions are indeed understood under the category of substance (or even, if he wishes, under the category of 'matter', that is, metaphysical matter), but they are not therefore understood under the category of 'body'.

Objection

Besides, when Descartes says that the ideas of God and of our soul are innate in us, I want to know if the souls of those who are fast asleep and not dreaming are thinking. If they are not, then they have no ideas during that time. Therefore no idea is innate because whatever is innate is always present.

Reply

When we say that some idea is innate in us, we do not think that it is always present to us; in that sense no idea would be innate. We mean only that we have within us a power to produce the idea in question.

Fourth Objections[30]

(a) If someone is certain that they know that the angle in a semicircle is a right angle and therefore that the triangle formed by this angle and the diameter of a semicircle is a right-angled triangle, they may, nonetheless, doubt or may not have grasped with certainty that the square on the base of the triangle is equal to the squares on the sides, and they may even deny it because they are misled by some fallacy. If they use the same reasoning as that proposed by our illustrious author, it seems as if they are confirmed in their false conviction. For example, someone says: I clearly and distinctly perceive that this triangle is right-angled, but I still doubt whether the square on the base is equal to the squares on the sides. Therefore it is not essential to the triangle that the square on the base is equal to the squares on the sides.

Besides, even if I deny that the square on the base is equal to the squares on the sides, I am still certain that it is a right-angled triangle, and the knowledge that one of its angles is a right angle remains clear and distinct in my mind. Since that is the case, even God cannot bring it about that it is not right-angled.

Therefore anything that I can doubt, and that can even be removed while I retain the idea of the triangle, does not belong to its essence.

Moreover, since I know that everything that I understand clearly and distinctly can be made by God in the way in which I understand it, it is enough for me to be able to understand clearly and distinctly one thing without another to be certain that one is distinct from the other, because they could be separated by God. But I understand clearly and distinctly that this triangle is right-angled, without understanding that the square on the base is equal to the squares on the sides. Therefore it is at least possible for God to make a right-angled triangle in which the square of the base is not equal to the squares of the sides.

I do not see what can be said in reply to this, except that the speaker in question does not perceive the right-angled triangle clearly and distinctly. But how do I succeed in perceiving my own mind more clearly and distinctly than they perceive the nature of a triangle? For they are just as certain that the triangle in the semicircle has one right angle, which is the definition of a right-angled triangle, as I am certain, from the fact that I am thinking, that I exist.

However, they are mistaken in thinking that it does not belong to the nature of this triangle, which they know clearly and distinctly is right-angled, that the square on its base, etc. Likewise, why may I not be mistaken in thinking that nothing else belongs to my nature, which I know clearly and distinctly is a thinking thing, apart from the fact that I am a thinking thing? It may perhaps belong to my nature that I am an extended thing.

(b) I have one more difficulty. How does he avoid committing the fallacy of a vicious circle when he says that we are certain that what is perceived clearly and distinctly is true only because God exists? But we can be certain that God exists only because we perceive it clearly and distinctly. Therefore before we are certain that God exists we have to be certain that whatever we perceive clearly and distinctly is true.

There is something else that I forgot. It seems false to me – something that our illustrious author claims as certain – that there can be nothing in him insofar as he is a thinking thing of which he is not aware. However, he understands the phrase 'himself, insofar as he is a thinking thing' to mean only his mind insofar as it is distinct from his body. But is there anyone who does not see that there may be things in the mind of which the mind is not aware? The mind of an infant in its mother's womb has the power of thinking; but it is not aware of it. There are innumerable similar examples, which I will not mention.

Replies

(a) However, our learned friend argues at this point: even though I am capable of having some knowledge of myself without any knowledge of the body, it does not follow that this knowledge is complete and adequate, so that I could be certain of not being mistaken when I exclude the body from my essence. He explains the argument by reference to a triangle inscribed in a semicircle. We can understand clearly and distinctly that it is a right-angled triangle even if we are unaware, or even if we deny, that the square on its base is equal to the squares on its sides but we cannot infer that it is possible to have a [right-angled][31] triangle in which the square on the base is not equal to the squares on the sides.

However, this example differs in many ways from what I proposed. First of all, although a triangle might be taken concretely to be a substance, the property of having the square on the base equal to the squares on the sides is certainly not a substance. Therefore neither of these may be understood as complete things in the same sense in which the mind and body are complete; nor can either of them be called a thing in the sense in which I said, 'It is enough that I can understand one thing (that is, a complete thing) without another . . . etc.,'[32] and this is clear from the words which follow: 'besides, I find in myself faculties, etc.'[33] I did not call these faculties things, but I distinguished them carefully from things or substances.

Secondly, although we can understand clearly and distinctly that a triangle in a semicircle is right-angled without realizing that the square on its base is equal to the squares on its sides, we cannot, however, understand clearly, in a similar way, a triangle in which the square on the base is equal to the squares on the sides without realizing, at the same time, that it is right-angled. In contrast, we are capable of perceiving clearly and distinctly the mind without the body and the body without the mind.

Thirdly, although it is possible to have a concept of a triangle inscribed in a semicircle in such a way that the equality between the square on the base and the squares on the sides is not included in the concept, it is not possible to have this concept in such a way that one does not understand that there is some relation between the square on the base and the squares on the sides in this triangle. Therefore, as long as one does not know what that relation is, one cannot deny anything about it except whatever we understand clearly as not belonging to the triangle. This could never include the relation of equality. However, there is nothing at all included in the concept of a body that belongs to the mind, and there is nothing in the concept of the mind that belongs to the body.

Thus, although I said that 'it is enough that I understand clearly and distinctly one thing without another, etc.,' it is not possible to continue as follows: 'But I clearly and distinctly understand this triangle,' and so on. The reason is, first of all, that the relation between the square on the base and the squares on the sides is not a complete thing. Secondly, the relation of equality is understood clearly only in a right-angled triangle. Thirdly, no one can understand the triangle distinctly if they deny the relation between the squares on the base and the sides.

(b) I did not use a vicious circle when I said that we are certain that what we perceive clearly and distinctly is true only because God exists, and that we are certain that God exists only because we perceive it clearly. I have explained this adequately in my reply to the Second Objections, . . . by distinguishing between what we actually perceive clearly and what we remember having perceived clearly some time earlier. For we are certain, initially, that God exists because we consider the reasons that prove it. Subsequently, however, it is enough that we remember that we perceived something clearly in order to be certain that it is true. That would not be enough unless we knew that God exists and that he does not deceive.

As regards the claim that there can be nothing within the mind insofar as it is a thinking thing of which it is not aware; that seems to be self-evident to me, because we cannot understand anything in the mind, understood in this way, which is not a thought or which does not depend on thought. Otherwise it would not belong to the mind insofar as it is a thinking thing, and we cannot have any thought in us of which we are not aware at the time we have it. For this reason I do not doubt that the mind begins to think and, at the same time, to be aware of its thinking as soon as it is put into the body of an infant, even if subsequently it does not remember it because the impressions of those thoughts do not survive in its memory.

But it should be noted that, although we are always actually aware of the acts or operations of our mind, we are not always aware of our mental faculties or powers, except potentially. Thus, for example, when we are engaged in using some faculty, we are actually aware of the faculty immediately if the faculty in question is in the mind. It follows that, if we fail to become aware of it, we can deny that it is in our mind.

Fifth Objections[34]

(a) You establish that this claim, 'I am, I exist,' is true whenever you assert it or think about it. But I do not see why you need so much complexity since you had other reasons for being certain, and it was true, that you exist. You could have concluded the same thing from any of your other actions, since we know by the natural light of reason that whatever acts must exist.

(b) When you say, later on, that the universe of things is in some way more perfect if some of its parts are liable to error than if they are all alike,[35] that is the same as claiming that the perfection of a republic would be somehow greater if some of its citizens were evil than if they were all good. It follows that, just as it seems obvious that a ruler should prefer if all the citizens were good, it likewise seems as if the author of the universe should have arranged that all its parts would be created immune to error and would be so. Although you can say that the perfection of those who are immune to error appears greater in comparison with those who are liable to error, that is true only by accident. Likewise, the virtue of good people, although it shines out in some way in comparison with those who are evil, shines out only by accident. Thus, just as it is not desirable that some citizens should be evil in order to show up those who are good, it seems, likewise, that it ought not to have been arranged that some parts of the universe would be subject to error so that those who are immune to error would appear better.

You say that you have no right to complain if God chose a certain role for you in the world which was not the most perfect or the primary one of all. But that does not resolve the doubt about why it was not enough for him to give you the lowest role among those which were perfect, rather than one which was imperfect. For although it does not seem wrong if a ruler does not appoint all citizens to the highest offices and, instead, has some in middle-rank offices and others again in lower offices, a ruler would still be criticized if they not only assigned some citizens to the lowest offices but also assigned depraved functions to others.

(c) As regards your idea of yourself, there is nothing to add to what I have already said, especially about the Second Meditation.[36] For it becomes clear there that, far from having a clear and distinct idea of yourself, you seem to have none at all. The reason is this: although you recognize that you are thinking, you do not know what kind of thing you, who are thinking, are. Since this operation alone is known, the most important thing, namely the substance that operates, is still hidden from you. Hence the following comparison comes to mind: you could be said to resemble a blind person who, when they feel heat and are advised that it comes from the sun, think they have a clear and distinct idea of the sun in the sense that, if anyone asks what the sun is, they can reply: it is a thing that produces heat.

But you go on to add that, not only are you a thinking thing, but you are not an extended thing. However, I shall overlook the fact that this was said without proof when it was still in question and I shall ask, firstly: do you then have a clear and distinct idea of yourself? You say you are not extended; you say what you are not, rather than what you are. In order to have a clear and distinct idea or, what amounts to the same thing, to have a true and genuine idea of something, is it not necessary to know the thing positively and, as I would say, affirmatively, and is it enough to know that it is not something else? Thus, would it be a clear and distinct idea of Bucephalus if someone knew only that Bucephalus is not a fly?[37]

But rather than insist on this point, I prefer to ask: as a thing which is not extended, then, are you not spread thoughout the body? I do not know what your answer might be because, even though I acknowledged from the beginning that you were only in the brain, I discovered that by conjecture rather than by following your views directly. I based my conjecture on the following phrase, which is found later, where you say that you are not affected by all parts of the body but only by the brain or by one small part of it.[38] It was not at all clear whether you were therefore only in one part of the brain or whether you were in the whole body but were affected only by one part of it, in the same way as we commonly say that the soul is spread throughout the body but, despite that, it sees only through the eye.

(d) I make the same claim about the animal spirits that you have to transmit in order to feel, to receive messages, or to move. Let us leave aside the fact that we cannot understand – if you yourself are at a particular point – how you are able to impress a motion on them unless you are a body or unless you have a body with which you could touch them and at the same time start them moving. For if you say that they move themselves and that you merely direct their motion, remember that you denied elsewhere that a body can move itself;[39] one could therefore conclude that you are the cause of their motion. You would also have to explain to us how such direction works without some exertion and therefore some motion on your part. How can there be any pressure on something and on its motion, without mutual contact between the mover and what is moved? How can we have contact without a body (something which is so clear by the natural light of reason), since 'nothing can touch or be touched without a body'.[40]

Replies

(a) When you say that I could have concluded the same thing from any of my other actions apart from thinking, you depart a long way from the truth because the only action of which I am completely certain (with the metaphysical certainty that is at issue here) is my thinking. For example, I cannot argue: I walk, therefore I exist, except to the extent that being conscious of my walking is a thought. The inference is certain only when applied to thought but not when applied to the motion of the body, which is something non-existent in dreams during which, nonetheless, it seems to me that I am walking. Thus from the fact that I think I am walking, I infer most properly the existence of the mind that thinks this thought but not the existence of the body that walks. The same applies to other actions.

(b) You assume here and elsewhere that the fact that we are subject to error is a positive imperfection when (especially with respect to God) it is merely the negation of a greater perfection in creatures. Nor is the analogy appropriate between the citizens of a republic and the parts of the universe. The evil of its citizens, when referred to a republic, is something positive; but the fact that human beings are subject to error or that they do not have every perfection is not something positive when referred to the good of the universe. It would be more appropriate to suggest an analogy between someone who wanted to have the whole human body covered with eyes so that it would appear more beautiful (because it seems to them that the eye is the most beautiful part of the body), and someone who thinks that there should be no creatures in the universe who are subject to error, that is, who are not completely perfect.

(c) It is easy to refute what you say about the idea of the sun that a blind person gets from its heat alone. For the blind person can have a clear and distinct idea of the sun as something that heats, even if they do not have a similar idea of the sun as a thing that illuminates. Nor is the comparison valid between me and the blind person. In the first place, knowledge of a thing that thinks is much more extensive than knowledge of anything that heats and, in fact, it is much more extensive than what we know about anything else, as was shown in the appropriate place. Secondly, no one can argue that the idea of the sun that the blind person acquires does not contain everything that can be perceived about the sun except those who, endowed with sight, are also aware of its light and shape. But not only do you not know more about the mind than me – you do not even know what I know; in this context, therefore, you are more like the blind person and I, together with the whole human race, could at most be said to be one-eyed.

(d) Even if the mind were united to the whole body it would not necessarily follow that it is extended throughout the body, because it is not essential to it to be extended but only to think . . . Nor, therefore, is it necessary for it to be a body, even if it has the power to move a body.

Sixth Objections[41]

(a) The sixth difficulty arises from the indifference attributed to judgement and liberty. You deny that indifference belongs to the perfection of the will and claim that it belongs only to its imperfection, so that there is no indifference whenever the mind perceives clearly what should be believed, or what should or should not be done. If this is accepted, do you not see that you destroy God's freedom by taking away the indifference of his freedom when he creates this particular world rather than some other world or none at all? However, it is an article of faith that God was eternally indifferent about creating one particular world, or many worlds, or no world at all. At the same time, who would doubt that God always perceived what was to be done or not done with the clearest understanding? Therefore, a very clear perception and understanding does not remove the indifference of the will.

(b) We do not understand why, as you claim, there are no real accidents[42] in any body or substance that could exist by God's power without any subject and that, in fact, do exist in that way in the Eucharist. However, there is no reason for our professors to be upset until they see whether that is demonstrated in your physics, which we look forward to seeing. They are reluctant to believe that this question will be presented there so clearly that they will be both enabled and obliged to accept it, and to reject the traditional view.

(c) How is it possible for the truths of geometry and metaphysics, such as those you mention, to be immutable and eternal but not be independent of God? What kind of causality is involved in their dependence on God? Could he not then have arranged things so that the nature of a triangle did not exist? And I would like to know: how could he have arranged eternally that it is not true that twice four is eight, or that a triangle does not have three angles? Either these truths depend completely on an intellect while it is thinking them or on things that exist; or else they are independent, since God does not seem capable of having arranged that any of those essences or truths did not exist eternally.

(d) The ninth difficulty concerns us greatly, when you claim that we should distrust the operations of the senses, and that intellectual certainty is much greater than the certainty of sensation. What happens, however, if the intellect has no certainty unless it got it originally from well-disposed senses and if, indeed, it cannot correct the error of any sense unless some other sense first corrects that error? A stick in water seems to be bent as a result of refraction, despite the fact that it is straight. What corrects that mistake? Is it the intellect? Not at all – it is the sense of touch. The same applies to other cases. Thus if you employ all the senses when they are appropriately disposed and if they always report the same thing, you will achieve the highest certainty of which human beings are capable; but this will often escape you if you put your trust in the operation of the mind, because it is often mistaken about things that it believed were completely indubitable.

(e) Could you also provide us with a reliable rule, and with criteria which are certain, that would make us certain when we understand one thing without another so completely that it is certain that one is so distinct from the other that it is capable of subsisting separately, at least by the power of God? In other words, how can we know certainly, clearly and distinctly, that an intellectual distinction was not made by the intellect itself but that it derives from the things themselves? For when we think about the immensity of God without thinking about his justice or when we think about his existence without thinking about the Son and the Holy Spirit, do we not perceive that existence, or that God exists, completely without the other persons of the Trinity? Someone who has no faith could deny the existence of the Son or the Holy Spirit in the same way as you deny that mind or thought belong to the body. Just as it is invalid to conclude that the Son or Holy Spirit is essentially distinct from God or could exist apart from God so, likewise, no one will concede to you that human thought or the human mind is distinct from the body even though you conceive of one without the other or deny one of the other, even though you do not think that this results from any mental abstraction on your part . . .

Finally, as long as we do not know what bodies and their motions can do, and since you confess that no one can know everything that God was able to give and what he gave to a particular subject unless God himself reveals it to us, who could know that God has not placed in certain bodies a power and property of doubting, thinking, etc.?

Replies

(a) As regards freedom of the will, the kind of freedom that God has is very different from ours. It is self-contradictory to claim that God's will was not eternally indifferent with respect to everything that has happened or that will ever happen, because one cannot imagine any good or truth, anything to be believed or to be done or omitted, the idea of which was in the mind of God prior to his will determining that it should be such. Nor am I speaking here of temporal priority; it was not even prior in order or in nature, or in what is called 'reasoned reason'[43] in such a way that the idea of good would impel God to choose one thing rather than another. For example, he did not choose to create the world in time because he saw that this would be better than creating it eternally; nor did he will that the three angles of a triangle should be equal to two right angles because he knew that it was impossible to have it otherwise, and so on. On the contrary, it was because he decided to create the world in time that this is better than if it had been created eternally; and it was because he willed that the three angles of a triangle should be necessarily equal to two right angles that this is consequently true and that it is impossible for it to be otherwise. And so on for other examples . . . Thus the supreme indifference of God is the strongest evidence for his omnipotence. But in the case of human beings, since they find that the nature of every good and every truth has already been determined by God and that their wills cannot tend towards anything else, it is clear that they will embrace what is good or true more willingly and therefore more freely insofar as they perceive it clearly, and that they are never indifferent except when they do not know what is better or more true or when they do not see the distinction between them so clearly that they are unable to have any doubt. Thus the indifference that applies to human freedom is very different from that which applies to divine freedom. Nor is it relevant here that the essences of things are said to be indivisible because, firstly, no essence can apply univocally to God and to human beings. Secondly, indifference is not essential to human freedom, for we are not free only when ignorance of what is right makes us indifferent; we are much more free when a clear perception impels us to pursue something.

(b) In order to reject the reality of accidents it seems to me unnecessary to look for any reasons apart from those that I have already presented. Firstly, every sensation occurs through touch and therefore nothing can be sensed apart from the surface of bodies. But if there were real accidents, they would have to be something other than the surface of bodies (which is nothing but a mode). Therefore, if there are any such accidents, they cannot be sensed.

Secondly, it is completely contradictory to claim that there are real accidents, because whatever is real can exist apart from any other subject and whatever is capable of existing separately in this way is a substance rather than an accident. Nor is it relevant that real accidents are said to be incapable of being separated from their subjects 'naturally', and that this can happen only by God's power. For something to happen naturally is the same as happening by the ordinary power of God, and this does not differ in any way from his extraordinary power and does not add anything extra to things. Thus if everything that can exist naturally without a subject is a substance, it follows that anything that can exist without a subject even by the extraordinary power of God, however great it is, must also be called a substance. I acknowledge that one substance can be related to another substance in an accidental way; however, when this happens, it is not the substance itself which has the form of an accident but it is merely the manner in which it is related to the other substance. For example, when clothing is accidentally related to a human being, it is not the clothing itself, but being clothed, which is an accident. However, the main reason that motivated philosophers to postulate real accidents was that they thought that, without them, sensory perception could not be explained. For that reason I promised, in my physics, to provide a detailed exposition of each of the senses. Not that I wish anyone to believe me about any of these things; rather, given what I had already written in the *Dioptrics*, I thought that careful readers would easily be able to anticipate what I can offer about the other senses.[44]

(c) It is evident to those who consider the immensity of God that there cannot be anything at all that does not depend on him, not only anything that subsists but even any order or law, or any reason for what is good or true. Otherwise, as indicated a little earlier, God would not have been completely indifferent in creating what he created. For if there had been some essence of goodness prior to his creative command, that would have determined God to do what is best; instead, he determined himself with respect to what should be done at that time and it is for that reason, as it says in Genesis, that 'they are very good'.[45] In other words, the reason why they are good depends on the fact that he chose to make them in that way. Nor is there any reason to inquire about what type of cause is involved in the way in which this goodness and other truths, both mathematical and metaphysical, depend on God. Given that the classification of causes was established by those who may not have considered this type of cause, it would hardly be surprising if they failed to give it a special name. Despite that, however, they did provide a name for it; it can be called an efficient cause in the same way in which a king can be the efficient cause of a law, even though the law is not something physical but is only what is called a moral entity. Nor is there any need to ask how God could have brought it about that, from eternity, twice four would not be equal to eight, and so on. I confess that we cannot understand that. But, since I do understand well that there cannot be any kind of entity that does not depend on God and that it is easy for God to arrange certain things so that we human beings cannot understand how they could be other than they are, it would be unreasonable for us to doubt something that we understand well simply because we do not understand something else that we know is beyond our comprehension. Therefore, it should not be thought that eternal truths depend on the human intellect or on other existing things; they depend on God alone who, as the supreme legislator, instituted them from eternity.

(d) In order to understand the certainty of sensation properly, one must distinguish three levels, as it were, of sensation. When the bodily organ is merely affected by external objects, that belongs to the first level; and this can be nothing more than the motion of particles of that sensory organ and the change in shape or position which results from that motion. The second level includes everything that follows immediately in the mind from the fact that it is united with this bodily organ; this includes perceptions of pain, pleasure, thirst, hunger, colours, sound, taste, smell, heat, cold and so on, which in the Sixth Meditation were said to arise from the union and, as it were, the merging of the mind with the body. The third level includes all the judgements that we have been accustomed to make about external things since our earliest years, on the occasion of motions in a bodily organ.

For example, when I see a stick one should not imagine that various 'intentional species' fly from the stick to my eye,[46] but simply that rays of light are reflected from the stick and trigger certain motions in the optic nerve and, as a result, in the brain (as I explained at sufficient length in the *Dioptrics*).[47] The first level of sensation consists in this motion of the brain, which we have in common with brute animals. The second level follows from this, and includes only the perception of the colour or light which is reflected from the stick; this arises from the fact that the mind is so closely joined with the brain that it is affected by motions that occur in the brain. Nothing more than this should be included in sensation if we wish to distinguish it carefully from the intellect. However, if I judge that the stick, which is located outside me, is coloured as a result of the sensation of colour by which I am affected; likewise, if from the extension of the colour, and from its boundary and its position in relation to parts of my brain, I reason about the size of the stick, its shape and its distance from me; even though this is commonly attributed to sensation and I have classified it under the third level of sensation, it is evident that it depends on the intellect alone. And I have demonstrated in the *Dioptrics* that size, distance and shape can be perceived only by reasoning from one of these properties to another. The only difference is that we attribute to the intellect the things that we now judge for the first time as a result of some new observation, whereas we refer to sensation the judgements that we have made since our earliest years, in exactly the same way as we still do, about things that affected our senses or whatever we have concluded from them by inference. The reason for this is that we reason and judge so quickly, as a result of habit or, rather, we remember judgements that we made earlier about similar things, that we fail to distinguish these operations from a simple sensory perception.

It is clear from this that when we say that 'intellectual certainty is much greater than the certainty of sensation', that means simply that the judgements which we make in our maturity as a result of new observations are more certain than those we made uncritically in our earliest years; and that is undoubtedly true. It is obvious that the first or second levels of sensation are not at issue in this context, because there can be no falsehood in those. When it is said, then, that a stick appears bent in water as a result of refraction, that is the same as saying that it appears to us in such a way that an infant would judge that it is bent and that we ourselves would judge likewise if we followed the prejudices that we acquired from our earliest years.[48] But if one adds here that this mistake is corrected not by the intellect but by the sense of touch, I cannot accept that. For even though we judge that the stick is straight by touching it, and thus by judging in the manner to which we have become accustomed since childhood and which is consequently called 'sensation', that is not sufficient to correct the visual mistake. We also need some reason to decide to believe the judgement based on touch rather than the judgement based on sight and, since this reason was not present in our infancy, it is attributed to the intellect rather than to sensation. Thus even in this very example, it is only the intellect that corrects the mistake of sensation, nor can anyone identify any other case in which error arises from trusting our intellect rather than sensation.

(e) In fact, I have never seen or perceived human bodies thinking; all I have perceived is that the same human beings are endowed with both a body and with thought. I saw clearly that this is realized by the composition of a thinking thing with a bodily thing, as follows: by examining the thinking thing in isolation, I discover nothing in it that pertains to a body, in the same way that no thought is found in a body when considered on its own. On the contrary, by examining all the modes of body and mind I found no mode the concept of which does not depend on the concept of the thing of which it is a mode. From the fact that we often see two things joined together, it does not follow that they are one and the same thing; however, from the fact that we sometimes observe one of them without the other, it certainly does follow that they are distinct. The power of God should not prevent us from making this inference, for it is just as conceptually impossible for things that are perceived clearly as two distinct things to become one and the same, intrinsically and without any composition, as for things to become separated that are in no way distinct. Therefore, if God gave the power of thinking to certain bodies (and he surely did so in the case of human bodies), then he is able to separate that power from those bodies and thus it is still really distinct from them.

The Principles of Philosophy

1644

NOTE ON THE TEXT

The first edition of this text was published in Latin by Elzevier, Amsterdam, in 1644 under the title: *Principia Philosophiae* (*The Principles of Philosophy*). It included the Dedication to Princess Elizabeth, followed by a detailed Index, which listed the titles of all the articles. The first French edition appeared three years later, under the title: *Les principes de la philosophie, escrits en Latin par René Des-Cartes et traduits en François par un de ses amis* (*The Principles of Philosophy, written in Latin by René Descartes and translated into French by one of his friends*) (Paris: Henry le Gras, 1647). The French translation was rather free and it introduced many additional new sentences and phrases into the original text. One may assume that many of these changes were either written by Descartes or had his approval but, to the extent that they were significant, they represented changes in his views or later efforts to express them more clearly.

In preparing the present translation I have followed the 1644 Latin text. In a few cases, where a significant change in the French text could be included as an addition rather than an alternative to the original text, I have added a translation of the French edition in square brackets.

The subtitles of the articles appeared in the 1644 text as brief marginal summaries of the contents of each article. This was easier to achieve in compact Latin phrases than in either an English or French translation. Rather than attempt to duplicate the format of the first Latin editions, I have followed the practice adopted from the earliest translations by inserting the marginal headings as subtitles in the text. The reader might bear in mind, however, that the original text appeared as a series of consecutive paragraphs, one following directly after the other without any extra spacing between articles and without subtitles in the body of the text.

The Principles of Philosophy was divided into four parts. Part One was a summary statement of Descartes' metaphysics, and Parts Two, Three and Four were entitled, respectively: 'The Principles of Material Things', 'The Visible Universe' and 'The Earth'. Since these three parts were primarily an exposition of Descartes' natural philosophy, this edition includes only Part One (unabridged).

LETTER TO PRINCESS ELIZABETH

To Her Most Serene Highness Princess Elizabeth,
eldest daughter of King Frederick of Bohemia, Count Palatine
and Elector of the Holy Roman Empire

Most Serene Highness:

The most rewarding result of my previously published writings was that you deigned to read them and that, by making your acquaintance in this way, I discovered that your natural gifts were such that I was convinced that it would benefit the human race if I publicized them as an example for future generations. It would be inappropriate if I were either to flatter you or make unwarranted claims, especially here where I am trying to establish the foundations of truth, and I know that the unadorned and simple judgement of a philosopher would be more acceptable to your generous modesty than the ornate praise of flatterers. Therefore, I will write only what I know by reason or experience to be true and I will philosophize here, in the introduction, in the same way as in the remainder of the book.

There is a significant distinction between genuine virtues and apparent virtues and, even among the former, between those that result from an accurate knowledge of things and those that involve a certain degree of ignorance. By 'apparent virtues' I mean certain relatively uncommon vices which contrast with other notorious vices and are such that, because they differ from these vices more than the intermediate virtues do, they are more frequently admired as a result. For example, there are more people who timidly flee from danger than those who rashly become involved in it; consequently, the vice of timidity is contrasted with temerity as if it were a virtue and is commonly valued more highly than genuine courage. Likewise, those who are prodigal are often esteemed more than those who are liberal, and no one acquires a reputation for great piety more easily than those who are superstitious or hypocritical.

However, as regards genuine virtues, many result not only from knowledge of what is right but also from some error. For example, goodness often arises from simplicity, piety from fear, and courage from desperation. These are so distinct from each other that they are designated by different names, but those pure and sincere virtues, which result exclusively from knowledge of what is right, all have the very same nature and are included under the one name of wisdom. A person is genuinely wise (insofar as their nature allows) if they have a firm and efficacious will to use their reason correctly at all times as much as possible, and to do what they know is best. By this alone they will possess justice, fortitude, temperance and all the other virtues, but combined together in such a way that none is distinguished from all the others. Thus although these virtues are very much superior to those that include some element of vice, they are not usually praised as much, because they are less well known to most people.

Besides, wisdom described in this way requires two things, namely, perception by the intellect and a propensity in the will. No one is incapable of that which depends on the will, but some people have a much more acute intellect than others. Although it should be enough for those who are naturally less gifted that, as long as they have a firm and constant will to omit nothing by which they could acquire knowledge of what is right and to do everything that they judge is right, even those who are ignorant of many things can be wise in their own measure and on that account they may be very pleasing to God. But those in whom a very firm will to act rightly is combined with a very acute intelligence and the greatest devotion to discovering the truth are much more eminent.

It is obvious that Your Highness possesses such great devotion, because neither the distractions of the court nor the customary education that normally condemns young women to ignorance was able to prevent you from studying all the worthwhile arts and sciences. Besides, the supreme and incomparable acuteness of your intelligence is apparent from the fact that you have examined in depth the mysteries of all those sciences and learned them accurately in such a short time. I have even greater evidence, which I alone possess, in support of that claim because I have found that you alone have understood perfectly all the work that I have published to date. My publications seem to be very obscure to many other people, including those who are very learned and gifted; and for most people it is true that, if they are well versed in metaphysics, they hate geometry, whereas if they are trained in geometry they do not understand what I wrote about first philosophy. I recognize that your intelligence is the only one to which all these disciplines are equally clear, and for that reason I describe it as incomparable. And when I consider that such a varied and perfect knowledge of everything is found not in some professor who is already old and has spent many years in contemplation but in a young princess, who in beauty and age is more like one of the Graces than an ageing Minerva or one of the Muses, I cannot avoid being lost in the greatest admiration.

I also recognize that there is nothing required for absolute and sublime wisdom which is not apparent in your actions, both from the point of view of knowledge and of the will. Your actions display a certain eminent and majestic kindness and gentleness, challenged by continual misfortunes but never diminished or broken. I am so impressed by this that I think that not only should this my philosophy be offered and dedicated to the wisdom that I respect in you – since philosophy is nothing but the study of wisdom – but I am equally anxious to be recognized as a philosopher and most devoted servant of Your Serene Highness, Descartes.

THE PRINCIPLES OF PHILOSOPHY

PART ONE:

The Principles of Human Knowledge

1. *Insofar as it is possible, everything should be doubted once in a lifetime by whoever is searching for the truth.*

Since we were born as infants and made various judgements about observable things before we had full use of our reason, we are diverted from knowledge of the truth by many prejudices. It seems that we can be liberated from these only if, once during our life, we try to doubt everything in which we find the slightest reason for doubt.

2. *Things which are doubtful should be considered as if they were false.*

It will be helpful to consider as if they were false all the things that we will doubt, so that we will discover much more clearly what is most certain and easy to know.

3. *Meanwhile, this doubting should not be extended to our daily lives.*

But this doubt should be restricted, in the mean time, only to the contemplation of the truth. For, as regards our daily lives, the opportunity to do something would very often pass us by before we were able to free ourselves from all our doubts, and therefore we often have to accept what is merely probable or even, sometimes, to choose one of two alternatives even though neither one seems to be more probable than the other.

4. *Why we can doubt observable things.*

Now, therefore, since we are concerned merely with seeking the truth, we shall doubt initially whether any observable or imaginable things exist; firstly, because we have found that the senses sometimes err and it is prudent never to trust too much those who have deceived us even once; secondly, because while we are asleep we daily seem to sense or imagine innumerable things that do not exist at all, and there seem to be no criteria by which we could distinguish between being asleep and being awake once we have agreed to doubt in this way.

5. *Why we can doubt even mathematical demonstrations.*

We shall doubt even other things that we previously accepted as most certain – even mathematical demonstrations and even those principles which, up to now, we thought were self-evident – both because we have occasionally seen people err in such matters and accept as most certain and self-evident what seemed false to us, and especially because we have learned about God, who is omnipotent and by whom we were all created. For we do not know if he may have wished to create us so that we are always mistaken, even about things that appear to be most well-known to us, for this seems to have been just as possible as creating us so that we are occasionally mistaken – something that we have already recognized happens. And if we suppose that we owe our existence not to a most powerful God but to ourselves or to some other being, then the less powerful the author that we assign to our origin the more credible it is that we are so imperfect that we are always mistaken.

6. *That we have a free will which enables us to withhold our assent from doubtful things and thereby to avoid error.*

Meanwhile whoever eventually happens to be the source of our being, and however powerful and deceptive they are, we still experience in ourselves a freedom such that we can always refrain from believing things that are not fully investigated and certain, and thereby we can take care that we are never mistaken.

7. *As long as we are doubting, we cannot doubt that we exist; and this is the first thing we know when philosophizing methodically.*

Thus by rejecting all those things that we can in any way doubt and even pretending that they are false, we easily suppose that there is no God, that there are no heavens or bodies, and that we ourselves have no hands or feet, nor indeed any body at all – but not, however, in such a way that we, who think these thoughts, are nothing. For it is impossible for us to think that whatever thinks does not exist during the very time that it thinks. Therefore [despite the most extravagant assumptions, we cannot prevent ourselves from believing that this inference] this knowledge, 'I am thinking, therefore I exist', is the foremost and most certain that occurs to anyone who philosophizes methodically.

8. *In this way we discover the distinction between soul and body, or between a thinking thing and a physical thing.*

This is the best way to discover the nature of the mind and its distinction from the body. Since we are supposing that everything which is distinct from us is non-existent, if we examine what we are we see clearly that no extension, shape, local motion, or anything similar which should be attributed to the body pertains to our nature apart from thought alone. Therefore, thought is known prior to and more certainly than anything physical, because we have already perceived our thought while we are still doubting other things.

9. *What is thought?*

By the word 'thought' I understand all the things that we are aware of as occurring in us, insofar as we are aware of them. Thus not only understanding, willing and imagining but even sensing is the same as thinking in this context. For if I say 'I see or I walk, therefore I exist', and if I understand this as referring to the seeing or walking that is done by the body, the conclusion is not absolutely certain because, as often happens during sleep, I can think I see or walk even if I do not open my eyes and do not move from where I am and even if, perhaps, I had no body. But if I understand it as the sensation or awareness of seeing or walking, since it then refers to the mind which alone senses or thinks that it sees or walks, it is obviously certain.

10. *Logical definitions obscure what is most simple and self-evident: the latter should not be included among the kinds of knowledge that are acquired by study.*

I shall not explain here many of the other words that I have already used, or that I shall use below, because they seem to me to be sufficiently known in themselves. I have often noticed that philosophers go astray by trying to explain in logical definitions things that are very simple and self-evident, and in doing so they make them more obscure. And when I said that the proposition 'I am thinking, therefore I exist' is the foremost and most certain of all those that could occur to anyone who is philosophizing methodically, I did not thereby deny that, prior to that, one needs to know what thought is, what existence is and what certainty is; also, 'that it is impossible that that which thinks does not exist', and similar things. But because these are very simple notions and, on their own, provide no knowledge of anything that exists, I therefore did not think that they should be mentioned.

11. *How our mind is known better than our body.*

Now, in order to explain how our mind can be known not only prior to and more certainly than our body but also more evidently than our body, it should be noted that it is very well known by the natural light of reason that nothingness has no attributes or qualities and that nothing can happen to it. Therefore, whenever we encounter some qualities, there is necessarily some thing or substance to which they belong, and the more qualities we find in some thing or substance the more clearly we know it. That we find more qualities in our mind than in anything else that we know is obvious from the fact that nothing can make us understand anything other than ourselves, without at the same time bringing us a much more certain knowledge of our own mind. Thus if I judge that the earth exists from the fact that I touch or see it, it follows that I am already much more certain of judging that my own mind exists; for it is possible for me to judge that I touch the earth even though the earth does not exist at all, but it is impossible for me to make that judgement if my mind, which makes the judgement, does not exist. And likewise for other cases [which come into our thoughts because we, who think them, exist even if they happen to be false or have no existence].

12. *Why this is not equally well known by everyone.*

The only reason why this seemed otherwise to those who have not philosophized methodically is that they never distinguished the mind from the body with sufficient clarity. Although they thought that they were more certain that they themselves existed than of anything else, they still did not realize that, in this context, 'they themselves' should be understood as their minds alone. Instead they preferred to understand it as referring to their bodies, which they saw with their eyes and touched with their hands and to which they wrongly attributed the power of sensing. This is what prevented them from perceiving the nature of the mind.

13. *In what sense knowledge of other things depends on knowledge of God.*

However, when the mind, which knows itself and is still in doubt about everything else, looks about in order to extend its knowledge further, it initially finds in itself ideas of many things; as long as it merely contemplates these ideas and neither affirms nor denies that there is anything external to itself that resembles them, it cannot be mistaken. It also finds some common notions and constructs various demonstrations from them; as long as it thinks about these, it is completely convinced that they are true. Thus, for example, it has in itself ideas of numbers and figures, and it also includes among its common notions 'that if equals are added to equals, the result will be equal', and others like that. It is easily demonstrated from these that the three angles of a triangle are equal to two right angles, etc. Thus the mind is convinced that this and similar conclusions are true as long as it thinks about the premises from which it deduced them. But it cannot think about them all the time; therefore, when at a later time [it remembers some conclusion without reference to the way in which it can be demonstrated and] it is conscious of the fact that it does not yet know if it may have been created in such a way that it is mistaken even with respect to things which seem most evident, it seems reasonable to doubt such conclusions and believe that it cannot have knowledge which is certain before it discovers the author of its origin.

14. *The existence of God is implied by the fact that necessary existence is included in our concept of God.*

When it considers that, among its various ideas, there is an idea of a supremely intelligent, perfect and powerful being, which is by far the most important of all its ideas [it judges without difficulty from what it perceives in this idea that God, who is this completely perfect being, is or exists; for although it has distinct ideas of many other things, it does not notice anything in them that convinces the mind of their existence], the mind recognizes in this idea an existence that is not simply possible or contingent, as in the ideas of all other things that it perceives distinctly, but an existence that is absolutely necessary and eternal. The mind perceives, for example, that having three angles equal to two right angles is necessarily contained in the idea of a triangle and, consequently, it is completely convinced that a triangle has three angles which are equal to two right angles. In the same way, the mind ought to conclude clearly that a supremely perfect being exists from the fact alone that necessary and eternal existence is included in the idea of a supremely perfect being.

15. *Necessary existence is not contained in the same way in the ideas of other things, but merely contingent existence.*

The mind will be all the more convinced of this if it realizes that it finds no idea of any other thing in itself in which it notices that necessary existence is contained in the same way. From this it understands that this idea of a supremely perfect being was not invented by itself nor does it represent some kind of fictional reality, but that it has a true and immutable nature, which is incapable of not existing since it includes necessary existence in itself.

16. *Prejudices prevent this necessity of God's existence from being clearly known by everyone.*

Our mind will easily believe this, I claim, if it first liberates itself completely from prejudices. But since we are used to distinguishing essence from existence in everything else and since we even arbitrarily invent the idea of various things that do not exist and never existed anywhere, it can easily happen, when we are not clearly focused on the contemplation of the supremely perfect being, that we can doubt whether this idea may be one of those that we invented arbitrarily or, at least, one to which the distinction of essence and existence applies.

17. *To the extent that the intentional perfection of an idea is greater, its cause must be greater.*

When we consider further the ideas we have, we see that some of them do not differ much from one another insofar as they are simply modes of thinking; but insofar as one idea represents one thing and another represents something else, they are very different from each other, and their causes must be correspondingly more perfect to the extent that the ideas contain more intentional perfection in themselves. For if someone has an idea of some very complex machine, it is appropriate to ask: what is the cause from which they got that idea? For example, did they see such a machine made by someone else, or did they learn the mechanical sciences very well, or do they have so much natural ability that they could have invented it themselves without having seen it anywhere? For the whole artifice, which is contained merely intentionally or as in an image in the idea, must be contained in its cause, whatever kind it is, not only intentionally or representatively but formally or eminently, at least in the case of the primary and principal cause.

18. *Hence we may construct a second proof of God's existence.*

Thus since we have an idea of God or of a supreme being, we are right to ask about the cause from which we derive this idea. We find such immensity in it that we are completely certain, for that reason, that it could have been given to us only by some entity which really contains the sum of all perfections, that is, by a really existing God. For it is very evident by the natural light of reason not only that nothing is caused by nothing, and that what is more perfect cannot be produced by something which is less perfect as its total and efficient cause, but that there cannot be in us even an idea or image of something of which there is not some archetype – either in ourselves or outside us – that really contains all its perfections. And since we do not in any way find all those supreme perfections of which we have an idea in ourselves, we correctly infer from that alone that they are, or that they certainly were, in some reality distinct from us, namely in God. It follows evidently from this that they are still there.

19. *Although we do not comprehend the nature of God, his perfections are nonetheless known to us more clearly than anything else.*

This is sufficiently certain and evident to those who are used to contemplating the idea of God and considering his supreme perfections. Although we do not comprehend them – because it follows from the nature of the infinite that it is not comprehended by us, who are finite – nevertheless we can understand them more clearly and distinctly than any physical thing, because they fill our thought better and are simpler, and because they are not obscured by any limitations. [Besides, there is no speculation which could better help our understanding to improve and which is more important, because the consideration of an object which has no limits in its perfections fills us with satisfaction and conviction.]

20. *We were not made by ourselves but by God; and therefore God exists.*

Not everyone is aware of this;[49] besides, when people have an idea of some complex machine they usually know the source of that idea, but we do not similarly remember that the idea of God came to us at some stage from God, because we have always possessed it; therefore, we still have to inquire where we ourselves came from, we who have in ourselves an idea of the supreme perfections of God. For it is certainly most evident by the natural light of reason that that entity which knows something more perfect than itself does not derive its existence from itself – because it would have given itself all the perfections of which it has an idea, and hence it cannot derive its existence from anything that does not have all those perfections in itself, that is, from an entity that is not God.

21. *The duration of our existence is sufficient to prove God's existence.*

Nothing can obscure the evidence of this demonstration on condition that we acknowledge the nature of time or of the duration of things, which is such that its parts do not depend on one another and never exist simultaneously. Therefore, from the fact that we exist now it does not follow that we shall exist even in the very next moment unless some cause – namely the same cause that first produced us – continually reproduces us, as it were, that is, conserves us. We understand easily that we have no power to conserve ourselves and that he who has so much power that he conserves us who are distinct from him also conserves himself much more or, rather, that he does not need any conservation of any kind and therefore is God.

22. *All God's attributes which can be known by the natural power of the mind can also be known from our way of knowing God's existence.*

The great benefit in this way of proving God's existence by means of the idea of God is that we come to know at the same time what he is like, insofar as the weakness of our nature allows. When we reflect on the idea of God, which is innate in us, we see that he is eternal, omniscient, omnipotent, the source of all goodness and truth, the creator of all things, and finally that he possesses in himself all those things in which we can recognize clearly any infinite perfection or which are limited by no imperfection.

23. *God is not physical, nor does God have sensations as we do, nor does he will the evil of sin.*

There are clearly many things in which we recognize some perfection but also notice some element of imperfection or limitation, and therefore they are not applicable to God. Thus it is certain that God is not a body because divisibility is included in the nature of a body together with local extension, and it is an imperfection to be divisible. Although it is a perfection of some kind in us that we sense, still every sense involves being acted on, and to be acted on is to depend on something else. Therefore, God may not in any way be thought to sense but only to understand and will. Even the latter do not resemble our understanding and will by involving operations that are somehow distinct, but they are such that, always by one and the same simple action, God understands, wills and realizes everything simultaneously. I say everything, that is, all things; God does not will the evil of sin, since it is not a thing.

24. *We can arrive at knowledge of creatures from knowledge of God, remembering that he is infinite and that we are finite.*

Now, since God alone is the true cause of everything that exists or that can exist, it is obvious that the best way for us to philosophize is to try to deduce an explanation of the things created by him from our knowledge of God himself and thereby acquire the most perfect science, which is knowledge of effects through causes. To make progress safely enough, without fear of straying, we should use the precaution of always remembering as much as possible that God, the author of things, is infinite and that we are completely finite.

25. *We should believe everything that was revealed by God, even if it transcends our comprehension.*

Thus if God reveals anything to us about himself or about other things that surpass the natural powers of our intelligence – such as the mysteries of the Incarnation and the Trinity – we shall not refuse to believe them even if we do not understand them clearly. Nor shall we be in any way surprised that there are many things both in his immense nature and also in things created by him that transcend our comprehension.

26. *We should never dispute about the infinite; however, things in which we notice no limits, such as the extension of the world, the divisibility of parts of matter, the number of the stars, etc., should be considered merely as indefinite.*

Thus we shall never tire ourselves in disputes about the infinite. For since we are finite, it would obviously be absurd for us to determine anything about the infinite and in that way to try, as it were, to make it finite and to comprehend it. Therefore, we will take care not to reply to those who ask whether half of an infinite line is also infinite, or whether an infinite number is odd or even, and such like; for it seems that no one should think about those things except people who think their own mind is infinite. However, in the case of all those things in which we cannot, from some point of view, find any limit, we will not claim that they are infinite but will regard them as indefinite. Thus since we cannot imagine an extension so great that we do not understand that an even greater one is possible, we will say that the magnitude of possible things is indefinite. And since it is impossible to divide any body into so many parts that we do not understand that these individual parts are even further divisible, we will think of quantity as indefinitely divisible. And since it is impossible to imagine so many stars that we would not believe that even more could be created by God, we will suppose their number is also indefinite. And so on for the rest.

27. *The difference between 'indefinite' and 'infinite'.*

We say that these things are indefinite rather than infinite, both because we reserve the term 'infinite' for God alone – since, in him alone, not only do we not recognize any limits in any sense but we understand positively that there are no limits; and also because we do not understand positively that other things lack limits in some sense, but we merely acknowledge negatively that, if they have any limits, we cannot find them.

28. *We should not examine the final causes of created things, but only their efficient causes.*

Thus we shall never find any explanation of natural things in the purpose which God or nature intended in making them [and we shall banish completely from our philosophy the search for final causes], because we should not be so arrogant as to believe that we can know God's purposes. We should think of him instead as the efficient cause of all things and, using the natural light of reason with which he endowed us, we shall see what conclusions we should draw – concerning those of his attributes about which he wishes us to know something – about the effects which are observable to our senses; [we shall also be assured that whatever we have once seen clearly and distinctly as belonging to the nature of these things has the perfection of being true,] being mindful, as already indicated, that this natural light should be believed only as long as it is not inconsistent with God's revelation.

29. *God is not the cause of errors.*

The first of God's attributes that is considered here is that he is supremely truthful and the source of all light. Therefore, it is clearly inconsistent that he would deceive us or that he would be the positive and proper cause of the errors to which we find ourselves subject. The reason is that, although the ability to deceive might seem like a sign of intelligence among us human beings, the will to deceive certainly results only from malice or fear and stupidity, and therefore it cannot be found in God.

30. *It follows that everything that we perceive clearly is true and that the doubts mentioned earlier can be removed.*

It follows from this that the light of nature or the faculty for knowing given us by God can never perceive any object that is not true insofar as it is perceived by that faculty, that is, insofar as it is clearly and distinctly perceived. God would be rightly called a deceiver if he gave us a perverted faculty that mistakes what is false for the truth [when we use the faculty properly]. In this way is removed that most serious doubt, which results from not knowing if our nature might be such that we are mistaken even about things that seem most evident to us. Indeed, all the other sources of doubt, which were mentioned above, are easily removed by this principle. Mathematical truths should no longer be doubtful for us, because they are very clear. If we notice something by means of the senses then, whether we are awake or asleep, as long as it is clear and distinct and we distinguish it from what is confused and obscure, we shall easily see what should be accepted as true in anything. There is no need to pursue that question here at great length, because I have already discussed it in the *Metaphysical Meditations* and a more detailed explanation presupposes knowledge of what follows below.

31. *Our errors are mere negations when referred to God and, when referred to ourselves, they are privations.*

Although God is not a deceiver, nevertheless it often happens that we are mistaken. To investigate the source and cause of our mistakes and to learn how to avoid them, it should be noted that they do not depend on the intellect as much as on the will, nor are they things which require a real co-operation by God for their production. For they are mere negations when referred to God and, when referred to us, they are privations.

32. *There are only two modes of thinking in us, namely, the perception of the intellect and the operation of the will.*

Thus all the modes of thinking that we experience in ourselves can be referred to two general types, one of which is perception or the operation of the intellect, and the other is willing or the operation of the will. For to sense, imagine and understand purely are only different kinds of perception, just as to desire, avoid, affirm, deny and doubt are different types of willing.

33. *We make mistakes only when we make a judgement about something that is not adequately perceived.*

However, when we perceive something, it is obvious that we are not mistaken as long as we do not affirm or deny anything about it. The same is true also when we affirm or deny only what we perceive clearly and distinctly should be affirmed or denied. Error arises only when we make a judgement about something even though we do not perceive it properly.

34. *Judging requires not only the intellect but also the will.*

The intellect is indeed required for making a judgement because we are unable to make any judgement about something that we do not perceive in any way. However, the will is also required in order to give assent to something that is perceived in some way. But a full and comprehensive perception of a thing is not required in order to make at least some kind of judgement, for we are capable of assenting to many things that we know only in an obscure and confused manner.

35. *The scope of the will extends further than the intellect, and this is the cause of errors.*

Now, the perception of the intellect extends only to the few things that are accessible to it and it is always very limited. But the will may be said to be infinite, in some sense, because we never notice anything that can be the object of someone else's will, or even of the immense will of God, which is outside the scope of our will. Thus we easily extend our will beyond the things that we perceive clearly and, when we do this, it is not surprising if we happen to be mistaken.

36. *Our errors cannot be attributed to God.*

However, God cannot in any way be thought to be the author of our mistakes merely because he did not give us an omniscient intellect. For it is the very nature of a created intellect to be finite, and it is the nature of a finite intellect not to extend to everything.

37. *The highest human perfection is to act freely or voluntarily, and thereby to be worthy of praise or blame.*

It is consistent with its nature for the will to extend very widely, and it is in a sense the highest perfection for human beings to act through the will, that is freely, and thus in a certain special way to become the author of their own actions and to merit praise for them. Automata, however, are not praised if they display exactly all the movements for which they were designed, because they do so out of necessity. Instead their designer is praised for having made them so precisely, because the designer constructed them freely and not out of necessity. For the same reason, when we embrace the truth we are praised for doing so, much more because we embrace it voluntarily than if we were incapable of not embracing it.

38. *The fact that we err is a defect in our action rather than in our nature; and the faults of subordinates may often be attributed to their superiors, but never to God.*

That we fall into error is indeed a defect in our action or in our use of freedom, but not in our nature since this is the same whether we judge correctly or incorrectly. Although God could have given such insight to our intellect that we would never be mistaken, we have no right to demand this from God. In the case of human beings, if someone has the power to prevent some evil and if, despite that, they do not prevent it, we say that they are the cause of it; but it is not the case that, because God could have arranged that we are never mistaken, he should therefore be thought to be the cause of our errors. For the power that human beings have over one another was established so that it would be used to protect them from evils, but the power that God has over everything is supremely absolute and free. Therefore, we ought to be extremely grateful to him for the goods that he bestowed on us, but we have no right to complain that he did not lavish on us everything that we know he could have lavished on us.

39. *Freedom of the will is self-evident.*

That there is freedom in our will and that we are able to assent or not assent, in many cases arbitrarily, is so evident that it should be counted among the first and most common notions that are innate in us. This was most evident above when, attempting to doubt everything, we reached a point at which we imagined some most powerful author of our origin who tried to deceive us in every way. Despite that, we experienced such freedom in ourselves that we were able to refrain from believing whatever was not fully examined and certain. Nor could there be any other things that are more self-evident and clear than what seemed to be beyond doubt at that time.

40. *It is certain that everything is pre-ordained by God.*

Since we already acknowledge God, we perceive that he has such immense power that we believe it is criminal to think that there is anything we could ever do that was not pre-ordained by him. We can easily involve ourselves in great difficulties if we try to reconcile this pre-ordination by God with the freedom of our will and if we attempt to comprehend both at the same time.

41. *How freedom of our will and God's pre-ordination may be reconciled.*

We shall avoid these difficulties if we remember that our mind is finite, and that the power of God – by which he not only knew eternally everything that exists or could exist, but also willed and pre-ordained them – is infinite. Therefore this power is sufficiently accessible to us to enable us to perceive clearly and distinctly that God possesses it; but it cannot be comprehended by us sufficiently to enable us to see how it leaves human actions free and undetermined. We are so conscious of our freedom and indifference that there is nothing that we comprehend more perfectly or evidently, and it would be absurd just because we do not comprehend one thing which, of its very nature, we know should be incomprehensible to us, to doubt something else of which we have a profound understanding and which we experience in ourselves.

42. *How we are mistaken by using our will, despite not choosing to be mistaken.*

Since we know that all our mistakes depend on our will it might seem surprising that anyone is ever mistaken, because no one chooses to be mistaken. But there is a big difference between choosing to be mistaken and choosing to assent to the things in which mistakes can occur. Although it is true that there is no one who explicitly chooses to be mistaken, there is hardly anyone who does not frequently choose to assent to things in which mistakes occur without their being aware of it. The very desire to seek the truth often causes people, who do not know how it should be sought correctly, to make judgements about things that they do not perceive and in that way they make mistakes.

43. *We are never mistaken when we assent only to what is clearly and distinctly perceived.*

It is certain, however, that we shall never accept what is false as if it were true if we give our assent only to things that we perceive clearly and distinctly. It is certain, I claim, because God is not a deceiver and therefore the faculty of perception that he gave us is incapable of tending towards what is false; the same applies to the faculty of assenting, as long as it applies itself only to what is clearly perceived. Even if there were no argument to prove this, nature has so impressed it on the minds of everyone that, whenever we perceive something clearly, we spontaneously assent to it and we cannot in any way doubt that it is true.

44. *We always judge badly when we assent to something that is not clearly perceived, even if we land on the truth by chance; that may happen when we believe that the things in question were adequately perceived previously.*

It is also certain that when we assent to some belief that we do not perceive, either we fall into error or we find the truth by chance and, as a result, we do not know that we are not mistaken. But evidently it happens rarely that we assent to things that we recognize as not having been perceived by us, for the light of nature tells us that one should never judge anything unless it is known. However, we are often mistaken in thinking that many things were formerly perceived by us and, once they are entrusted to memory, we assent to them as if they were fully perceived even though, in fact, we never perceived them.

45. *What is meant by a clear perception or a distinct perception.*

There are very many people who, in their whole lives, never perceive anything accurately enough to lead them to a judgement that is certain. For a perception has to be not only clear but also distinct, if a certain and indubitable perception can be based on it. I call a perception clear when it is present and accessible to an attentive mind, in the same way as we say that we see things clearly when they are present to our eye when it is looking and, while it is open, they strike it strongly enough. However, I call a perception distinct which, when it is clear, is so separated and so disconnected from all other perceptions that it evidently contains nothing that is not clear.

46. *The example of pain shows that a perception may be clear without being distinct; however, it cannot be distinct unless it is clear.*

When someone feels a great pain, for example, that perception of pain is very clear but it is not always distinct; for people commonly confuse this perception with their obscure judgement about the nature of something that, they think, is in the painful part of the body and resembles the sensation of pain, which is the only thing they perceive clearly. Thus a perception can be clear without being distinct, but no perception can be distinct unless it is clear.

47. *To correct our childhood prejudices, we should examine the simple notions and see what is clear in each of them.*

The mind was so immersed in the body during our childhood that, although it perceived many things clearly, it never perceived anything distinctly. Despite that, it made judgements about many things and thereby we acquired many prejudices, which, subsequently, are never given up by most people. However, to enable us to liberate ourselves from them, I shall briefly list here all the simple notions from which our thoughts are composed and shall distinguish in each of them what is clear from what is obscure or from what can be a source of error.

48. *All the things that we can perceive can be considered as things or as states of things, or as eternal truths. A list of things.*

We think of whatever falls within our perception either as things or states of things, or as eternal truths, which have no existence outside our minds. The most general [notions with which we think of] things are 'substance', 'duration', 'order', 'number' and others of the same kind that apply to every class of thing.[50] However, I recognize no more than two most general classes of things: one is intellectual or thinking things, that is, those that pertain to the mind or a thinking substance; the other is material things or what pertains to extended substance, that is, to body. Perception, volition, and all modes of perceiving and willing are referred to thinking substance, whereas magnitude or extension in length, breadth and depth, shape, motion, position, the divisibility of its parts and such like are referred to extended substance. But we also experience some others in ourselves that should not be referred exclusively either to the mind or the body and that arise, as will be shown below in the appropriate place,[51] from the close and intimate union of our mind and body. These include the appetites of hunger and thirst, etc.; likewise, the emotions or passions of the soul that do not consist in thought alone – for example, the passion of anger, joy, sadness, love, etc. – and also all the sensations, such as those of pain, pleasure, light, colour, sounds, odours, tastes, heat, hardness and other tactile qualities.

49. *Eternal truths cannot be listed in a similar way, nor is it necessary to do so.*

Now we consider all the above as things or as qualities or modes of things. When, however, we recognize that it cannot happen that something is made from nothing, then the proposition 'nothing is made from nothing' is considered, not as if it were some thing that exists or even as a mode of a thing, but as some kind of eternal truth that is present in our mind, and it is called a common notion or an axiom. Among the axioms are the following: 'It is impossible for the same thing to be and not to be at the same time', 'whatever was done cannot be undone', 'whoever thinks is incapable of not existing while thinking', and innumerable others. It is not easy to list all of them, but it is also impossible not to know them when we have an opportunity to think about them and are not blinded by prejudices.

50. *They can be clearly perceived but not all by everyone, as a result of prejudices.*

As regards these common notions, there is no doubt that they can be perceived clearly and distinctly. Otherwise they would not have been called common notions, although some of them do not deserve the name equally for all people because they are not perceived equally by all. I think this is not, however, because one person's faculty of knowing extends wider than that of another but because those common notions are opposed to the prejudiced opinions of some people who, consequently, cannot easily grasp them, even though other people who have been liberated from those prejudices perceive them very clearly.

51. *What is a substance, and that the term 'substance' does not apply univocally to God and to creatures.*

However, as regards those entities that we perceive either as things or as modes of things, it is worth the effort involved to consider each of these types separately. By the term 'substance' we understand only a thing that exists in such a way that it needs nothing else in order to exist. [There can be some obscurity in explaining this phrase, 'it needs nothing else'.] 'A substance that needs absolutely nothing else' can be understood as referring to one thing alone, namely to God. We perceive that all other substances are able to exist merely with the assistance of God's conservation. For that reason the term 'substance' does not apply to God and to other substances univocally, as they say in the schools;[52] that is, there is no meaning of the term that can be understood distinctly and that is common to God and to creatures. [But, among created entities, there are some that are of such a nature that they cannot exist without some other things; therefore, we distinguish them from these others that need only the ordinary conservation of God, by naming the latter substances and the former qualities or attributes of the substances.]

52. *The term 'substance' applies univocally to the mind and the body, and how a substance can be known.*

Physical substance and mind (or created, thinking substance) can both be understood under this common concept, insofar as they are things that need only God's conservation in order to exist. However, a substance cannot be recognized initially from the mere fact that it is an existing thing because, on its own, that does not itself impinge on us. But we recognize it easily from one of its attributes, by using the common notion that there are no attributes, or no properties or qualities, in nothingness. Thus from the fact that we recognize the presence of some attribute, we conclude that some existing thing or substance to which it can be attributed also necessarily exists.

53. *There is one principal attribute of every substance, such as thought for mind and extension for body.*

While a substance can be known from any one of its attributes, there is still one principal property of every substance, which contains its nature and essence and to which all the other properties are referred. Extension in length, width and depth constitutes the nature of physical substance, and thought constitutes the nature of thinking substance. For everything else that can be attributed to a body presupposes extension, and is merely a certain mode of an extended thing; likewise, all the things that we find in the mind are merely different modes of thinking. Thus, for example, we cannot understand shape except in an extended thing, or motion except in an extended space; likewise, we cannot understand imagination, or sensation, or willing except in a thinking thing. However, in contrast, extension can be understood without shape or motion, and thought can be understood without imagination or sensation, and so on for the rest, as will be evident to anyone who examines them.

54. *How we can have clear and distinct notions of thinking substance and of physical substance, and also of God.*

Thus we can easily have two clear and distinct notions or ideas, one of a created thinking substance and the other of physical substance, if we distinguish carefully all the attributes of thought from all the attributes of extension. And we can also have a clear and distinct idea of an uncreated and independent thinking substance, that is, of God, on condition that we do not suppose that it represents adequately everything which is in God, and that we do not imagine anything else in it but consider only those features that are genuinely contained in it, and that we perceive as belonging clearly to the nature of a supremely perfect entity. Certainly no one can deny that we have such an idea of God in ourselves unless they think that there is no knowledge at all of God in human minds.

55. *How duration, order and number are also understood distinctly.*

We also understand distinctly duration, order and number if we do not assign the concept of a substance to them; instead we should think of the duration of anything as merely a mode in which we conceive of it insofar as it continues to exist. Likewise, we should not think of order or number as something that is distinct from things that are ordered or numbered, but merely as modes in which we think about them.

56. *What are modes, qualities and attributes?*

We understand the term 'modes' here in exactly the same way as the terms 'attributes' or 'qualities' are understood elsewhere. However, when we think of a substance as being changed or modified, we call them 'modes'; when a substance can be distinguished by a particular modification, we use the term 'quality'; finally, when in a more general way we see that they exist only in a substance, we call them 'attributes'. Therefore, we say that there are no modes or qualities in a strict sense in God, but only attributes, because any change in God is unintelligible. Even in the case of created things, whatever remains unchanged in them – for example, existence and duration in a thing that exists or endures – should be called an attribute rather than a quality or mode.

57. *Some attributes are in things, others in thought. What are duration and time?*

Some are in the things themselves, of which they are said to be attributes or modes, whereas others are only in our thought. Thus when we distinguish time from duration, as the latter is usually understood, and call it the measure of motion, it is only a mode of thinking; for we do not understand that there is any real duration in motion that is absent in bodies that are not in motion. This is evident from the fact that, if two bodies move for an hour, one slowly and the other quickly, we do not count more time in one than in the other even if it moves much more. But to measure the duration of anything, we compare it with the duration of the greatest and most regular motions from which years and days originate and we call this duration 'time'. Thus time adds only a mode of thinking to duration as it is generally understood.

58. *Number and all universals are merely modes of thinking.*

Likewise, when number is considered, not in any created things but abstractly or in general, it is merely a mode of thinking, as are all the others that we call universals.

59. *How universals originate, and what are the five common universals: genus, species, difference, property and accident.*

These universals originate simply from the fact that we use one and the same idea for thinking about all the individual things that resemble each other, just as we also apply one and the same term to all the things that are represented by that idea, and this term is universal. Thus when we see two stones and when we focus not on their nature but merely on the fact that there are two of them, we form the idea of their number, which we call 'two'. When we subsequently see two birds or two trees and consider not their nature but simply the fact that there are two of them, we recall the same idea that we had earlier. This idea, then, is universal, and we always designate this same number by the same universal term 'two'. Likewise, when we see a shape enclosed by three lines, we form a certain idea of it that we call the idea of a triangle, and we subsequently use this as a universal idea to represent to our mind all other shapes that are enclosed by three lines. When we notice that some triangles have one right angle and others do not, we form the universal idea of a right-angled triangle which, in relation to the former which is more general, is called a species. The rightness of the angle is the universal difference by which all right-angled triangles are distinguished from other triangles. The fact that the square of the hypotenuse is equal to the squares on the other two sides is a property which is characteristic of those triangles alone and of no others. Finally, if we were to suppose that some of these angles moved and that others were not in motion, this would be a universal accident in them. Hence we get five universals, as they are usually called: genus, species, difference, property and accident.

60. *Distinctions: and firstly, what is a real distinction?*

Number, insofar as it is in things themselves, arises from the distinction between things. And there are three kinds of distinction, namely, a real distinction, a modal distinction, and a distinction of reason. There is a real distinction, in a strict sense, only between two or more substances. We perceive that substances are really distinct from each other simply from the fact that we are able to understand, clearly and distinctly, one substance without the other. Since we acknowledge God, we are certain that he can give effect to anything that we understand clearly. Thus, for example, from the fact alone that we already have an idea of an extended or physical substance, although we do not yet know for certain if any such substance ever existed, we are nevertheless certain that it could exist; and if it did exist, every part of it that is defined by us in thought is really distinct from the other parts of the same substance. Likewise, from the fact alone that every person understands themselves to be a thinking thing and can exclude in thought from themselves every other substance, both thinking and extended, it is certain that each person, seen from this perspective, can be really distinguished from every other thinking substance and from every physical substance. And even if we suppose that God has joined a physical substance to some such thinking substance so closely that they could not be more closely joined, and that he formed a single entity from the two substances, they are still really distinct. The reason is that, no matter how closely he joined them, he cannot lose the power that he had previously to separate them or to conserve one in existence without the other, and those things that can be separated by God or can be conserved in existence separately are really distinct.

61. *Modal distinctions.*

There are two kinds of modal distinction. One is between a mode, in the strict sense, and the substance of which it is a mode; the other is between two modes of the same substance. The first type of distinction can be recognized from the fact that we can perceive a particular substance clearly without the mode which is said to be distinct from it whereas, conversely, we cannot understand the mode without the substance. Thus shape and motion are distinguished modally from the physical substance in which they inhere; likewise, affirmation and recollection are distinct from the mind. The second type of modal distinction is known from the fact that we can recognize one mode without the other, and vice versa, but we cannot get to know either of them without the single substance in which they both inhere. Thus, if a stone is square and is in motion, I can understand its square shape without motion and, conversely, I can understand its motion without a square shape, but I cannot understand either the motion or the shape without the substance of the stone. However, the distinction by which the mode of one substance differs from another substance, or from a mode of another substance – for example, the motion of one body from another body or from the mind, or the distinction of motion from doubt – seems as if it should be called real rather than modal, because those modes are not clearly understood without the really distinct substances of which they are modes.

62. *Distinction of reason.*

Finally, there is a distinction of reason between a substance and any one of its attributes without which the substance cannot be understood, or between two such attributes of any particular substance. This distinction is recognized from the fact that we cannot form a clear and distinct idea of the substance if we exclude the attribute from it, or that we cannot perceive clearly the idea of one of the attributes if we separate it from the other attribute. For example, since any substance ceases to exist if it ceases to endure, a substance is distinguished from its duration only by a distinction of reason; and all modes of thinking, when considered as they exist in objects, are distinguished only by reason both from the objects about which they are thought and from each other when they are in one and the same object. I realize that elsewhere I identified this type of distinction with a modal distinction, towards the end of my replies to the first objections in the *Meditations on First Philosophy*.[53] But there was no opportunity for distinguishing them accurately in that place, and it was enough for my purposes that I distinguished both of them from a real distinction.

63. *How thought and extension may be known distinctly, as constituting the nature of mind and body.*

Thought and extension can be seen as constituting the natures of intelligent substance and physical substance. Therefore they should not be conceived as anything other than thinking substance itself and extended substance itself, that is, as anything other than mind and body. In that way, they are understood very clearly and distinctly. In fact, we understand extended substance or thinking substance more easily than substance on its own – which involves omitting the fact that a substance thinks or is extended. For there is some difficulty in abstracting the notion of substance from the notions of thought and extension because there is only a distinction of reason between them and the notion of a substance, and a concept does not become more distinct by including less in it but only by distinguishing carefully what is included in it from everything else.

64. *How thought and extension can also be known as modes of a substance.*

Thought and extension can also be taken as modes of a substance insofar as one and the same mind may have many different thoughts, just as one and the same body, without changing its quantity, may be extended in many different ways. For example, at one time a body may be greater in length and smaller in width and depth while a short time later, in contrast, it may be greater in width and shorter in length. Thus thought and extension are modally distinguished from substance and they can be understood just as clearly and distinctly as the substance can be, on condition that they are seen not as substances or as things that are separated from others but merely as modes of things. From the fact that we think of them in the substances of which they are modes, we distinguish them from those substances and recognize them as they really are. In contrast, if we wished to think of them apart from the substances in which they inhere, we would thereby look on them as subsisting things and in that way we would confuse the ideas of mode and substance.

65. *How the modes of thought and extension are likewise knowable.*

For the same reason we shall best perceive the various modes of thought, such as understanding, imagination, memory, volition, etc., and likewise, the various modes of extension or those that pertain to extension, such as all shapes, or the position and movements of parts, if we regard them simply as modes of the things in which they occur; and as regards motion, it is best perceived if we consider nothing but local motion and do not inquire into the force by which it is produced (which, however, I shall try to explain in its proper place).[54]

66. *How sensations, emotions and appetites are known clearly, although we often make incorrect judgements about them.*

There remain sensations, emotions and appetites, which may also be perceived clearly if we are very careful not to make any judgements about them apart from what is included precisely in our perception and of which we are inwardly aware. But this is very difficult to do, at least in the case of sensations, for all of us have judged from our childhood that all the things that we sense are things existing outside our minds and are exactly similar to our sensations, that is, to the perceptions that we have of them. Thus, for example, when we saw a colour we thought we saw something that existed outside us and that was exactly similar to the idea of the colour that we experienced in ourselves on that occasion. Because of the habit of making such judgements, it seemed as if we saw it so clearly and distinctly that we took it as certain and indubitable.

67. *We are often mistaken, even in our judgements about pain.*

The same applies to all other things that are sensed, even to pleasure and pain. Although we do not think that these exist outside ourselves, they are nevertheless usually seen not as if they were in the mind alone or in our perception but as if they were in the hand or the foot, or in some other part of our body. When, for example, we perceive a pain as if it were in our foot, it is not certain that the pain is something that exists outside our mind, in our foot, any more than when we see a light in the sun, the light exists outside us in the sun. Both are prejudices of our childhood, as will be apparent below.

68. *How to distinguish in such matters what we know clearly from what can provide an occasion for error.*

In order to distinguish what is clear from what is obscure in this context, it must be very carefully noted that pain, colour and other similar things are perceived clearly and distinctly when they are considered simply as sensations or as thoughts. But when they are judged to be things existing outside the mind, it is impossible to understand in any way what kind of things they are. Obviously, if we say that we see a colour in some body or feel a pain in some limb, that is the same as saying that we see or feel something there, but it is a something of which we are completely ignorant – in other words, we do not know what we see or feel. However, if we are not as careful, we may easily convince ourselves that we have some knowledge of it because we assume that it is something that resembles the sensation of colour or pain which we experience in ourselves. However, if we examine what is represented by the sensation of colour or of pain as if it existed in the coloured body or the painful limb, we will realize that we are completely ignorant about it.

69. *Magnitude, shape, etc., are known in a very different way from colours, pains, etc.*

If someone considers that they know in a very different way what is the size of a body that is perceived, or its shape or motion (at least, its local motion, because philosophers, by imagining that there are other kinds of motion apart from local motion, have made the nature of motion much less intelligible for themselves), its position, duration or number, and such like, which were already said to be perceived clearly in bodies, they know these in a very different way from the fact that, in some body, there is a colour or odour or taste, or any of the other things that I said should be referred to the senses. Despite the fact that when we see a body, we are just as certain that it exists because it appears as shaped as we are because it appears coloured, we acknowledge that what it means for it to be shaped is much more evident than what it means for it to be coloured.

70. *We can make judgements about things that we can sense in two ways: in one way, we can avoid error and, in the other, we fall into error.*

It is clear, therefore, that to say that we perceive colours in objects is the same as saying that we perceive something in objects of which we are ignorant but by which is caused in ourselves a certain sensation that is very clear and evident and that is called a sensation of colour. There is, however, a great difference between these two ways in which we make judgements. For when we judge simply that there is something in objects (that is, in the things from which we get sensations, whatever those things happen to be) but that we do not know what it is, we are so far removed from making a mistake that we can avoid error, because we are aware of the fact that there is something we do not know and are therefore less inclined to make a rash judgement about it. However, when we think that we perceive colours in objects even though, in reality, we do not know what we are applying the word 'colour' to, nor can we understand any resemblance between the colour that we suppose in objects and the colour that we experience in our sensation; and when we do not advert to this, while at the same time there are many other things such as magnitude, shape, number, etc., which we clearly understand are perceived or understood by us as they are or, at least, as they may be in objects; we easily fall into the mistake of judging that what we call 'colour' in objects is something which is exactly similar to the colour that we sense, and consequently we think that something is perceived clearly by us although we do not perceive it at all.

71. *The principal cause of error results from the prejudices of childhood.*

The first and principal cause of all errors can be identified as follows. During our childhood, our mind was so closely joined with the body that it had no time for any other thoughts apart from those by which it sensed things that affected the body. Nor did it refer those thoughts to anything existing outside itself; rather, it simply felt pain when something harmful happened to the body and felt pleasure when something beneficial happened to it. And when the body was affected without any great harm or benefit, then – depending on the various parts affected and the ways in which they were affected – the mind had different sensations, namely those that we call the sensations of taste, smell, sound, heat, cold, light, colour and such like, which did not represent anything located outside these thoughts. At the same time the mind perceived magnitudes, shapes, movements and so on; these were presented to the mind not as sensations but as things of a certain kind or as modes of things that existed (or, at least, were capable of existing) outside thought, although the mind was not yet aware of the difference between the two kinds of thought. But the machine of the body was so constructed by nature that it could move in various ways by its own force, and when it began to turn itself blindly and tried to seek what was beneficial and to avoid what was harmful, the mind that was present in it began to notice that what it sought or avoided in this way existed outside itself. It attributed to the externally existing things not only magnitudes, shapes, movements and such like, which it perceived as things or as modes of things, but it also attributed to them tastes, smells, and so on, the sensations of which it realized were produced in itself by the external objects. However, the mind also considered each thing only from the point of view of its usefulness to the body in which it was immersed, and it thought that there was more or less reality in each object by which it was affected in proportion to whether it affected it more or less. As a result, it thought that there was much more substance or bodiliness in rocks and metals than in water or air because it sensed much more hardness or heaviness in them. In contrast, it thought of the air as nothing as long as it experienced no wind, cold or heat from it. And since it was not illuminated by any more light from the stars than from the faintest flames of a lamp, it imagined that no star was any greater than such flames. Since it did not notice that the earth turned on its axis or that its surface was curved like a globe, it was consequently more inclined to believe that the earth was immobile and that its surface was flat. Our mind was imbued with a thousand other similar prejudices from our childhood. In early youth the mind did not remember that they were adopted without sufficient consideration; instead it accepted them as very evident and true, as if they were known through sensation or implanted in the mind by nature.

72. *The second cause of error is that we cannot forget these prejudices.*

Despite the fact that the mind, in its mature years, is no longer completely subject to the body and does not refer everything to it, but inquires into the truth of things as they are in themselves and discovers that many of the things it previously judged are false, it does not thereby easily erase those prejudices from its memory and, as long as they remain there, they can be the causes of many errors. Thus, for example, we imagined from our childhood that the stars were very small; however, even though astronomical reasons show us clearly that they are very large, our prejudice is still so strong that it is very difficult for us to imagine them other than as we formerly did.

73. *The third cause of error is that we become fatigued by thinking of things that are not presented to our senses; as a result, we are inclined to make judgements about them on the basis not of our current perceptions but of a preconceived opinion.*

Our mind, moreover, is not able to think about other things without a certain amount of difficulty and fatigue, and it finds the greatest difficulty of all in thinking about things that are not present either to the senses or the imagination, either because it has such a nature as a result of being joined with the body, or because it was so occupied with sensations and images in its earliest years that it acquired more practice and a greater facility in thinking about those than about other things. As a result, many people do not understand any substance unless it is imaginable and physical, and even unless it is capable of being sensed. Nor do they realize that the only things that are imaginable are those that involve extension, motion and shape, even though there are many other things that are intelligible. They also think that nothing can exist unless it is physical and that there is nothing physical that cannot be sensed. Since we do not perceive anything as it really is by sense alone – as will be shown clearly below – it follows from this that most people, during their whole lives, perceive everything in a confused way.

74. *The fourth cause of error is that we link our concepts with words which do not correspond accurately to things.*

Finally, because of the use of language, we link all our concepts with the words by which we express them and we store them in our memory only at the same time as the words. Since it is easier subsequently to remember the words than the things, we hardly ever have a concept of anything that is so distinct that we separate it from every concept of the words, and the thoughts of almost all people are much more concerned with words than with things. Thus people often assent to words that they do not understand, because they think that they once understood them or that they learned them from other people who understood them properly. All these things – although they cannot be dealt with here in detail because the nature of the human body has not yet been explained, nor has the existence of any body even been proved – seem as if they could be understood enough to assist in distinguishing clear and distinct concepts from obscure and confused concepts.

75. *Summary of what needs to be observed in order to philosophize correctly.*

Thus in order to philosophize seriously and to seek the truth about all things that can be known, all prejudices should first be set aside or we should watch carefully that we do not believe any of the opinions that we formerly accepted unless we find that they are true when we subject them to a new test. Then, we must consider in an orderly way all the notions that we have in ourselves, and all and only those should be judged to be true which, considering them in this way, we know clearly and distinctly. Having done this, we shall first of all realize that we exist, insofar as we have a thinking nature. We shall also realize, at the same time, both that God exists and that we depend on him and that, from a consideration of his attributes, it is possible to seek the truth about other things since he is their cause. Finally, apart from the notions of God and of our mind, we find in ourselves knowledge of many propositions of eternal truth, such as: that nothing comes from nothing, etc., and also of a certain physical or extended nature, which is divisible, mobile, etc., and of certain sensations that affect us, such as pain, colour, tastes, etc., even though we do not yet know what is the cause of our being affected in this way. When we compare this with what we previously thought in a confused way, we shall acquire a habit of forming clear and distinct concepts of everything that is knowable. The main principles of human knowledge seem to me to be included in these few things.

76. *Divine authority is to be preferred to our perception; but apart from that, it is inappropriate for philosophers to assent to anything except their perceptions.*

Above all else, however, we should impress on our memory as a supreme rule that whatever was revealed to us by God should be believed as most certain. Although the light of reason, however clear and evident it is, may seem to suggest something different to us, we should put our faith exclusively in divine authority rather than in our own judgement. However, in the case of things about which divine faith does not teach us anything, it is very inappropriate for a philosopher to accept anything as true that they have never perceived as true; and it is even more inappropriate to trust in the senses, that is, in the uncritical judgements of their childhood, than in their mature reason.

Descartes' Correspondence: Selections, 1643–9

NOTE ON THE TEXT

Descartes left behind a large body of correspondence. A first edition of selected letters was prepared by Claude Clerselier and published posthumously in three volumes, under the title *Lettres de Mr Descartes* (Paris: 1657, 1659 and 1667). Many of the letters were replies to scientific and mathematical queries from correspondents, especially from Marin Mersenne. In contrast the correspondence with Princess Elizabeth (1618–80), which began after publication of the *Meditations*, raised some of the central questions about mind–body dualism that have occurred to readers of Descartes ever since. They also included questions from Elizabeth about her health and the effect of bad health on her ability to concentrate on philosophical questions. In replying to such questions, Descartes was further encouraged to think through the implications of mind–body dualism for the reciprocal interaction of body and mind and this in turn resulted in his discussion of the passions.

Henry More (1614–87) was a leading member of the group known as the Cambridge Platonists and was both sympathetic to Descartes' dualism and critical of some of the philosophical difficulties it seemed to generate. Descartes acknowledged that he was among the most perceptive of his many correspondents and he took particular care to answer the questions raised by More.

These selections from the correspondence with Princess Elizabeth were translated from the French texts; in most cases the introductory paragraphs and concluding greetings have been omitted, and the central body of the letter, which includes the main objections or replies, is translated in its entirety. The letters to More were originally written in Latin and are translated from the Latin text, which is found in volume five of the Adam and Tannery edition of Descartes' works.

Princess Elizabeth to Descartes, 16 May 1643

. . . how can the human soul, which is only a thinking substance, determine the movement of the animal spirits in order to perform a voluntary action?[55] It seems as if every determination of movement results from the following three factors: the pushing of the thing that is moved, the manner in which it is pushed by the body that moves it, and the quality and shape of the latter's surface. The first two presuppose that the bodies touch, while the third presupposes extension. You exclude extension completely from your concept of the soul and, it seems to me, it is incompatible with being an immaterial thing. That is why I am asking for a definition of the soul which is more specific than what is provided in your *Metaphysics*, that is, of the substance of the soul when it is separated from its action of thinking. For even though we assume that the substance and its thinking are inseparable, just like God's attributes – however, it is difficult to establish their inseparability in the mother's womb or in cases of serious fainting – we can get a better idea of them by considering them separately.

Descartes to Elizabeth, 21 May 1643

I can truthfully say that the question asked by Your Highness seems to me to be the one that can most justifiably be put to me as a result of the writings I published. For there are two things about the human soul on which depends all the knowledge we can acquire about its nature: one is that it thinks and the other is that, since it is united with the body, it can act and be acted on in conjunction with the body. I have said almost nothing about the second of these, and I tried to provide a good explanation only of the first one because my main aim was to prove the distinction between the soul and the body; only the first feature could help in this, whereas the second one would not have been helpful. But since Your Highness sees things so clearly that no one can conceal anything from you, I will now try to explain how I conceive the union of the soul with the body and how the soul has the power to move the body.

In the first place, I think that there are certain primitive notions in us which are like originals, on the model of which we construct all our other knowledge. There are very few such notions. For apart from the most general notions of being, number, duration, etc., which apply to everything that we can conceive, we have only the notion of extension that is specifically for the body, and from that follow the notions of shape and movement; and for the soul on its own we have only the concept of thought, which includes perceptions of the understanding and inclinations of the will. Finally, for the soul and body together, we have only the concept of their union, on which depends the notion of the soul's power to move the body and the body's power to act on the soul by causing its sensations and passions.

I also think that all our knowledge of human beings consists only in distinguishing these notions carefully and in not applying any of them to things to which they do not belong. For if we try to resolve a particular difficulty by using some notion that does not apply to it, we cannot fail to go wrong. The same thing happens if we try to explain one of these notions by reference to another; since they are primitive notions, each of them can be understood only through itself. Insofar as the use of our senses has made the notions of extension, shape and movement more familiar than other notions, the main cause of our errors is that we try to use these notions to explain things to which they do not apply – for example, when someone uses the imagination to conceive of the nature of the soul, or tries to conceive of the way in which the soul moves the body by using the concept of how one body moves another.

That is why in the *Meditations*, which you deigned to read, I tried to provide a conception of the notions that apply to the soul on its own by distinguishing them from those that apply to the body on its own. The next thing I need to explain is how to conceive of the notions that apply to the union of the soul with the body, without reference to those that apply to the body or the soul on their own. What I wrote at the end of my Replies to the Sixth Objections may be useful here, for we can examine these notions only in our own soul. By its nature, our soul possesses all of them but does not always distinguish them adequately from each other or, perhaps, does not attribute them to the objects to which they should be applied.

Thus I think that, up to now, we have confused the notion of the soul's power to act on the body with the power by which one body acts on another; and we attributed both of them not to the soul (because we did not know it yet) but to various qualities of bodies such as weight, heat and others that we imagined as real, that is, as having an existence which is distinct from that of the body and, consequently, as being substances even though we called them mere qualities. And to conceive of these powers, we sometimes used the notions that we have for knowing the body and sometimes those we have for knowing the soul, depending on whether what we attributed to them was either material or immaterial. For example, by assuming that weight is a real quality of which we know nothing apart from the fact that it is the power to move a body in which it is present towards the centre of the earth, we have no difficulty in conceiving how it moves the body nor how it is joined to it. And we never think that this occurs by a real contact between two surfaces, for we experience in ourselves that we have a specific notion with which to conceive it. I think that we use this notion badly when we apply it to weight, which is something that is not really distinct from the body – something which I hope to show in my Physics – and that it was given us instead to conceive of the way in which the soul moves the body.

Elizabeth to Descartes, 20 June 1643

Sometimes my domestic duties, which I ought not to neglect, and sometimes engagements and social duties that I cannot avoid overwhelm this feeble mind so much with interruptions and boredom that, for a long time afterwards, it is useless for anything else. I hope I can use that as an excuse for my stupidity in not being able to understand the idea by which we are supposed to decide how the mind (which is neither extended nor material) can move the body, by comparison with the idea you formerly had of heaviness. Nor can I understand why this power to move a body towards the centre of the earth, which you falsely attributed to it in the past as a quality, should convince us that a body could be pushed by something immaterial, no more than a demonstration of the contrary truth (which you promise in your Physics) could confirm us in believing that it is impossible. The main reason is that this idea (which cannot equal the perfection or intentional reality of the idea of God) may be false, because of ignorance of whatever really moves these bodies towards the earth's centre. And since there is no observable material cause, this motion would have been attributed to its opposite, an immaterial cause – something that I have never been able to conceive except by the negation of what is material – even though there can be no communication between an immaterial cause and the motion.

I confess that it would be easier for me to attribute matter and extension to the soul than to attribute the ability to move a body, and to be moved by a body, to an immaterial being. For if the former were accomplished by information, it would have to be the case that the minds that cause the movement are intelligent – something you do not attribute to anything which is physical. And although you show the possibility of the second option in your *Metaphysical Meditations*, it is still very difficult to understand how a soul such as you described it, which had the faculty and habit of reasoning correctly, could lose all that as a result of a few vapours and how, despite being able to subsist without the body and having nothing in common with it, it would be ruled by it in such a way.

But since you agreed to instruct me, I entertain these thoughts as if they were friends whom I do not believe I can keep, while reassuring myself that you will explain to me both the nature of an immaterial substance and the way in which it acts on, and is acted on by, the body and all the other things that you wished to teach.

Descartes to Elizabeth, 28 June 1643

I am very much obliged to Your Highness because, when you realized that I explained myself poorly in my recent letter about the question which you were kind enough to raise, you deigned to have the patience to listen to me again on the same subject and to give me an opportunity to mention the things that I omitted. The main omissions seem to have been that, having distinguished three kinds of idea or primitive notion – namely, our notions of the soul, of the body, and of the union of soul and body – each of which is known in a distinctive way and not by comparing one idea with another, I should have explained the difference between these three kinds of notion and between the operations of the soul by which we have these notions. I should also have described how each of them could become familiar and easy for us. Then, having explained why I used the analogy with heaviness, I should have shown how, even if one wished to conceive of the soul as material (which is, strictly speaking, to conceive of its union with the body), one still recognizes later that it is separable from the body. These are, I think, all the issues that Your Highness prescribes for me here.

In the first place, then, I notice a great difference between these three kinds of notion because the soul is conceivable only by pure understanding; the body, that is, extension, shapes and movements, may also be conceived by pure understanding on its own, but it can be conceived much better by the understanding assisted by the imagination; and finally, things that pertain to the union of the soul and body are known only obscurely by the understanding on its own or even by the understanding assisted by the imagination, but they are known very clearly by the senses. That is why those who never philosophize and use only their senses have no doubt that the soul moves the body and the body acts on the soul. But they think that both the body and soul are the same thing; in other words, they conceive of their union. For to conceive of the union of two things is to conceive of them as one thing. Metaphysical thoughts that exercise the pure understanding make the notion of the soul familiar to us; and the study of mathematics, which exercises primarily the imagination in thinking about shapes and movements, gets us accustomed to forming very distinct notions of body. Finally, it is only by using our lived experience and ordinary interactions, and by abstaining both from meditation and from studying things that use the imagination, that one learns to conceive the union of the soul and the body.

I am almost afraid that Your Highness may think that I am not speaking seriously here; but that would be contrary to the respect I owe you, which I would never fail to show. I can also say truthfully that the main rule that I followed in my study – and the rule that I believe has helped me most to acquire some knowledge – is that I never gave more than very few hours a day to thoughts that occupy the imagination, and very few hours a year to thoughts that occupy the understanding on its own; I spent all the rest of my time in relaxing the senses and reposing my mind. I even include, among the uses of the imagination, all serious conversations and everything that requires attention. That is what made me retire to the country; for although, in the busiest city of the world, I could have had as many hours' study as I currently enjoy, I could not spend them as usefully if my mind was distracted by the attention required by the ordinary business of daily life. I take the liberty of writing to Your Highness here that I genuinely admire the fact that, among the cares and business which are never absent in the case of people who, simultaneously, are of noble birth and have great minds, you have been able to find time for the meditations that are required to know the distinction between mind and body.

But I thought that, more than thoughts that require less attention, these meditations were responsible for making you find obscure the notion we have of the union of mind and body, because it seemed to me that the human mind is incapable of conceiving very distinctly, and simultaneously, both the distinction and union of body and soul. The reason is that, in order to do so, it would be necessary to conceive of them as one single thing and, at the same time, to conceive of them as two things – which is self-contradictory. Assuming that Your Highness still retains a vivid memory of the reasons that prove the distinction of the soul and body, and not wishing to ask you to get rid of them in order to conceive of the union that everyone constantly experiences in themselves without philosophizing – viz. of being a single person who has a body and thought together, and being of such a nature that thought can move the body and can sense the changes that occur in it – I therefore used an analogy above with heaviness and with the other qualities that we commonly imagine are united with certain bodies, for the way in which thought is united with our body. I was not worried that this analogy might be defective on account of the fact that these qualities are not real, as they are imagined to be, because Your Highness was already completely convinced that the soul is a substance which is distinct from the body.

However, since Your Highness suggested that it is easier to attribute matter and extension to the soul than to attribute to the soul the ability to move, and to be moved by, a body without having any matter itself, I beseech you to take the liberty to attribute this matter and extension to the soul, for that is nothing more than conceiving of its union with the body. Having conceived of that union properly and having experienced it in yourself, you will find it easy to think that the matter that you have attributed to this thought is not the thought itself and that the extension of this matter has a different nature from the extension of thought, in this sense: the former is determined to a certain place from which it excludes every other bodily extension, whereas this does not apply in the latter case. In this way Your Highness will easily recover your knowledge of the distinction between the soul and the body, despite the fact that you conceive of their union.

Finally, although I think that it is very necessary to have understood well, once in a lifetime, the principles of metaphysics because they provide us with knowledge of God and our soul, I also think that it would be very harmful to occupy one's understanding frequently in thinking about them because the understanding would find it difficult to leave itself free for using the imagination and the senses. It is best to be satisfied with retaining in one's memory and one's belief the conclusions that have once been drawn from the principles of metaphysics, and to devote one's remaining study time to those thoughts in which the understanding acts together with the imagination and the senses.

Elizabeth to Descartes, 1 July 1643

I also find that my senses show me that the mind moves the body but they do not teach me (any more than the understanding or the imagination) the way in which it happens. To explain that, I think there are properties in the soul that are unknown to us and that might perhaps overturn what your *Metaphysical Meditations* convinced me of, with such sound reasons, about the extension of the soul. This doubt seems to be based on the rule that you provide there, when speaking about truth and falsehood, that all our errors arise from making judgements about things that we have not adequately perceived. Even if extension is not necessary for thought, it is not incompatible with it either and it may contribute to some other function of the soul that is no less essential to it. At the very least, it defeats the scholastic contradiction that the whole soul is in the whole body and in each part of the body. I do not apologize for confusing the notion of the soul with that of the body by reasoning in the same way as uneducated people; but that does not remove the first doubt, and I would despair of finding any certainty in the world if you did not provide it, since you alone have prevented me from adopting scepticism, which is where my initial reasoning led me.

Descartes to Elizabeth, May or June 1645

It seems to me that we can easily notice the difference between the understanding, and the imagination or the senses, in the following situation. Imagine someone who otherwise had every reason to be happy but who sees constantly represented before them tragedies in which every act involves death; they are preoccupied in thinking only about sad and pitiful things, but they know that they are fictions or fables so that they merely draw tears from their eyes and stimulate their imagination without affecting their understanding. I believe that that alone would be enough to accustom their hearts to contracting and to make them sigh; as a result, their blood circulation would be obstructed and slowed down and the largest particles of blood, by clotting together, could easily block the spleen if they got caught in its pores and stop. The more subtle parts of the blood, by retaining their motion, could affect the lungs and cause a cough, which in due course would be dangerous. In contrast, consider someone who has very many reasons for being sad but makes a great effort to turn their imagination away from them – never thinking about them except when forced to do so by the immediate demands of daily life – and who uses the rest of their time for thinking only of things that could bring them happiness and joy; apart from the fact that it would be very useful for them in making better judgements about important things (because they would think about them dispassionately), I have no doubt that that alone would be able to restore their health even if their spleen and lungs were already badly affected by the poor condition of the blood that is caused by sadness, especially if they also used medical remedies to thin the part of the blood that causes obstructions. I think the waters of Spa[56] are very good for this purpose, particularly if Your Highness follows the usual suggestions of physicians in taking them, namely: to rid one's mind completely of all kinds of sad thoughts and even of all serious meditations about the sciences, and to apply oneself exclusively to imitating those who, in looking at the greenery of a wood, the colours of a flower or the flight of a bird, and other similar things that require no concentration, convince themselves that they are not thinking of anything at all. This is not a case of wasting time, but of using it well; for one could be satisfied in the hope that, in this way, one might recover complete health, which is the basis of all the other goods one can enjoy in this life.

Elizabeth to Descartes, 30 September 1645

Knowledge of God's existence and of his attributes can console us for the misfortunes to which we are exposed in the ordinary course of nature and the order that God has established, such as losing our goods in a storm, losing our health as a result of some airborne infection, or losing our friends through death. But it cannot console us for those misfortunes that are imposed on us by other human beings whose will seems to be completely free, because only faith can convince us that God takes care to control wills and that he determined the destiny of every person before the creation of the world.

The immortality of the soul, and the knowledge that it is much more noble than the body, is capable of making us seek death and also despise it; for one cannot doubt that we shall live much more happily when we are free from the infirmities and passions of the body. I am surprised that those who claim to be convinced of this truth and live without revelation prefer a painful life to a beneficial death.

The vast expanse of the universe, which you have demonstrated in the third book of your *Principles*, serves to detach our affections from what we see; but it also separates this particular providence, which is the foundation of theology, from the idea we have of God.

Descartes to Elizabeth, *6 October 1645*

It is easy to prove that the pleasure of the soul, which constitutes happiness, is not inseparable from the pleasure and comfort of the body, either by reference to tragedies that please us more in proportion to the amount of sadness they excite in us, or by reference to bodily exercises – such as hunting, tennis and so on – which are pleasant despite being very painful. One even sees that it is often the fatigue and pain which increase the pleasure they cause. The source of the pleasure that the soul gets from these exercises consists in the fact that they make it aware of the strength, skill, or some other perfection of the body with which it is united. But the pleasure it gets from crying when watching some sad or tragic play in a theatre derives principally from the fact that the soul seems to perform a virtuous action by having compassion for the afflicted. Generally, the soul is pleased when it feels passions arise in itself, no matter what passions they are, on condition that it remains in control of them.

But I have to examine these passions in greater detail in order to be able to define them. I shall find that easier to do here than if I had written to someone else, because Your Highness has taken the trouble to read the treatise that I had earlier drafted on the nature of animals,[57] and you already know how I conceive the formation of various impressions in their brain, some of which result from external objects that move the senses while others result from the internal dispositions of the body or from traces of previous impressions or, in the case of human beings, from the action of the soul, which has the power to change impressions in the brain just as these impressions, reciprocally, have the power to excite in the soul thoughts that do not depend on its will. Thus, in general, one can apply the term 'passion' to all those thoughts that are excited in this way in the soul without the influence of any action from the soul itself, but simply as a result of the impressions that occur in the brain; for everything that is not an action is a passion.

However, one usually restricts the term 'passion' to those thoughts that are caused by a specific movement of the animal spirits. Thoughts that result from external objects, or from internal dispositions of the body, such as the perception of colours, sounds, odours, hunger, thirst, pain and so on, are called sensations, some of which are external and others internal. Thoughts that depend only on traces left by previous impressions in the memory and by the normal movement of the animal spirits are dreams, whether they arise during sleep or when we are awake as the mind follows idly the impressions it finds in the brain and does not determine itself by anything that it initiates itself. But when the soul uses its will to determine itself to some thought that is not only intelligible but also imaginable, this thought makes a new impression on the brain and this is not a passion in the soul but an action, which is, properly speaking, the imagination. Finally, when the normal flow of animal spirits is such that it usually excites sad or happy thoughts, or other similar thoughts, they are not attributed to passions but to the nature or humour of the person in whom they arise and, for that reason, one person is said to have a sad nature and another is said to be of a cheerful disposition, and so on. Thus there remain only the thoughts that result from a specific movement of the animal spirits, the effects of which are experienced as if they were in the soul itself and these are, strictly speaking, passions.

It is true that we hardly ever have any thoughts that do not depend on more than one of the causes just mentioned. But they are named after their principal cause or after the cause with which we are primarily concerned. Thus many people confuse the sensation of pain with the passion of sadness, a pleasant sensation with the passion of joy (which they also call pleasure or delight), or the sensations of hunger and thirst with the desire to eat and drink (which are passions). The reason is that, usually, the causes that bring about pain also move the animal spirits in the way required to excite sadness, and those causes that make us feel some pleasure move the spirits in the way required to excite joy, and so on for the other cases.

Sometimes the inclinations or habits that dispose someone to a particular passion are confused with the passion itself, even though it is easy to distinguish between the two. For example, if it is announced in a city that its enemies are coming to lay siege to it, the initial judgement made by the citizens about the harm they may suffer is an act of their minds and not a passion. Even though the same judgement may be made by many different people, they are not all equally moved by it; some are moved more or less than others, depending on whether they are more or less habitually inclined to fear. Before their minds are affected by the emotion, which alone constitutes the passion in question, they must at least conceive of the danger and impress an image of it on their brain (which happens by means of another action which is called imagination) and, in this way, they determine the animal spirits that flow from the brain, through the nerves to the muscles and enter the muscles that are used to constrict the openings of the heart. This has the result of inhibiting blood circulation and, as a result, the whole body becomes pale, cold and trembling and other animal spirits that flow from the heart towards the brain are moved in such a way that they cannot help form any images in the brain except those that excite the passion of fear in the soul. All these things follow each other so quickly that they all seem to be only a single operation. Likewise, in all other passions, there is a specific movement of the animal spirits that originate in the heart.

That is what I was thinking of writing to Your Highness eight days ago, and my plan had been to provide a specific explanation of each of the passions. But I found it difficult to list them all and I had to let the messenger depart without my letter. Meanwhile, I received the letter that Your Highness was kind enough to write to me. Thus I have an extra reason for replying and this forces me to defer a discussion of the passions to another occasion. I want to say here that all the reasons that prove that God exists and that he is the primary and immutable cause of all the effects that do not depend on human free will seem to prove, in the same way, that he is also the cause of all those that do depend on human free will. For one could not prove that God exists without thinking of him as a supremely perfect being. And he would not be supremely perfect if anything could occur in the world that does not result completely from him. It is true that it is by faith alone that we are taught about the grace by which God raises us up to supernatural beatitude. But philosophy alone teaches us that it is impossible for the least thought to enter the human mind unless God wills it and unless he has willed from eternity that it enter there. The scholastic distinction between universal and particular causes is irrelevant here. For example, although the sun is the universal cause of all flowers, it is not for that reason the cause of the difference between tulips and roses; that depends on the fact that the production of tulips also results from other particular causes, which are not subordinate to the sun. But God is the universal cause of everything in such a way that, at the same time, he is their total cause and therefore nothing can occur without his will.

It is also true that knowledge of the immortality of the soul, and of the joys of which it will be capable when it is no longer in this life, could provide a reason for dying for those who are tired of this life if they were certain of having all these joys in the afterlife. But there is no reason to assure them of this and there is only the false philosophy of Hegesias[58] (whose book was banned by Ptolemy, because many people took their own lives after reading it), which tries to convince us that this life is bad. True philosophy teaches exactly the opposite: that, even among the saddest occurrences and the most persistent pains, one can always be content in this life as long as one knows how to use one's reason.

As regards the vastness of the universe, I cannot see, in thinking about it, how one can be asked to separate particular providence from the idea that we have of God. For finite powers are completely different from God: they can be exhausted, and therefore, when we see them used for many magnificent effects, we have reason to think that it is unlikely that they are also used for various insignificant effects. However, the more magnificent we judge the works of God the more we notice the infinity of his power and, the better we know this infinity, the more convinced we are that it extends to the most insignificant human actions.

When Your Highness claimed that this particular providence is the foundation of theology, I do not believe that you understood it as some change which occurs in God's decrees on the occasion of actions that result from our free will. For theology does not accept any such change; and when it obliges us to pray to God, that is not so that we can inform God of whatever we need or try to ask him to change something in the order established by his providence from eternity. Either one of those would be wrong. It is merely so that we can get what he decreed, from eternity, should be obtained by our prayers. I think that all the theologians agree about this, even the Arminians,[59] who seem to be the ones who put most emphasis on free will.

Elizabeth to Descartes, 28 October 1645

I would not dare ask you this if I did not know that you do not leave a task unfinished and that, in undertaking to instruct a stupid person like me, you prepared yourself for the inconveniences involved.

That is what makes me continue to tell you that I am not convinced by the reasons that prove that God exists and that he is not only the immutable cause of all the effects that do not depend on human free will but is also the cause of all those that do so depend. It follows from his supreme perfection that he could be such a cause, that is, that he was able not to give human beings a free will; but since we experience that we have a free will, it seems to me to contradict common sense to believe that the will depends on God in its operations as it does for its existence.

Descartes to Elizabeth, 3 November 1645

As regards free will I confess that, when we think exclusively about free will in ourselves, we cannot avoid thinking that it is independent. But when we think of the infinite power of God, we cannot avoid believing that all things depend on him and, consequently, that our free will is no exception. For it involves a contradiction to say that God created human beings with such a nature that their acts of will do not depend on his will. That is the same as saying that his power is, at one and the same time, both finite and infinite; finite, because there is something that does not depend on it, and infinite, because he was able to create such an independent thing. However, just as knowledge of God's existence should not prevent us from being certain of our own free will, because we experience it and feel it in ourselves, in the same way knowledge of our free will should not make us doubt the existence of God. For the independence that we experience and feel in ourselves, and which is sufficient to make our actions praiseworthy or blameworthy, is not incompatible with a different kind of dependence by which all things are subject to God.

Elizabeth to Descartes, 30 November 1645

I also admit that, even though I do not understand how the independence of free will is no more incompatible with our idea of God than its dependence would be incompatible with its liberty, it is impossible for me to put the two of them together, since it is just as impossible for the will to be at one and the same time both free and bound by the decrees of providence as it is impossible for God's power to be both finite and infinite at once. I do not understand the compatibility that you speak about, nor how this dependence of the will could be different in nature from its liberty, unless you take the trouble to explain it to me.

Descartes to Elizabeth, January 1646

I turn to the problem that Your Highness raised about free will, and I shall try to explain its dependence and its freedom by an analogy. If a king prohibited duels and if he knew for certain that two gentlemen in his kingdom who lived in different towns were involved in a controversy and were so angry with one another that nothing could stop them from attacking each other if they ever met; if, I say, this king gives one of them an errand to go one day to the other town where the second man lives, and gives an errand to the other to go, on the same day, to the town where the first one is, he knows surely enough that they will not fail to meet and to attack each other and thus disobey his prohibition. But he does not force them to do so. His knowledge and even his will to determine them in this way does not prevent it from being equally voluntary and free that they fight when they meet each other, just as they would have done even if he knew nothing about it and they had met each other on some other occasion. They are also equally deserving of punishment for having disobeyed the king's prohibition. Now what a king can do in this way in respect of some free actions of his subjects, God (who has infinite foreknowledge and power) does infallibly in respect of free human actions. Before he sent us into the world, he knew exactly what all the inclinations of our wills would be. It was God himself who put those inclinations in us and it was God who arranged all external things so that such and such objects would appear to our senses at such and such times, on the occasion of which he knew that our free will would determine us to one thing or another. He willed this, but he did not thereby decide that our will should be limited to whatever we choose. One can distinguish in the king two distinct levels in his will: one by which he willed the two gentlemen to fight, because he arranged things so that they would meet, and the other by which he did not will it because he forbade duels. In a similar way theologians distinguish in God an absolute and independent will by which he wills that all things happen as they do, and another will that is relative and refers to the merits or demerits of human beings, according to which he wills that his laws should be obeyed.

Elizabeth to Descartes, 25 April 1646 [60]

Since the physical part is not as clear to the untutored, I do not see how one can know the various movements of the blood that cause the five basic passions because they never occur alone. For example, love is always accompanied by desire and joy, or by desire and sadness, and the more love increases the more the other passions increase accordingly. How is it possible, then, to notice the difference in the beat of the pulse, the digestion of food and other changes in the body that are used to identify these movements? Besides, the motion you noted in each of these passions is not the same in all temperaments. In my own case sadness always takes away my appetite even when it is not mixed with any hatred and arises simply from the death of some friend.

When you speak about external signs of these passions, you say that admiration joined with joy makes the lungs expand with various intermittent movements so as to cause laughter. I would ask you to explain, please, how admiration (which, according to your description, seems to affect only the brain) could so promptly open the orifices of the heart in order to cause this effect.

Descartes to Elizabeth, May 1646

I did not include [in the *Treatise on the Passions*] all the principles of Physics that I used to distinguish the movements of blood that accompany each passion, because I would not have been able to deduce them properly without explaining the formation of all parts of the human body. That is something so difficult that I would not dare to undertake it yet, even though I have almost satisfied myself about the truth of the principles that I used in that work. The primary ones are as follows: that the function of the liver and spleen is to contain permanently a reserve of blood that is less purified than what is in the veins; that the fire in the heart needs to be maintained continually, either by the juice from nourishment that comes directly from the stomach or else, if that is not available, by the reserve blood, because the other blood which is in the veins expands too easily; and that there is a link between our soul and body such that the thoughts that accompanied some movements of the body from the beginning of our lives continue to accompany them at present. Thus if the same movements are triggered again by some external cause, they will also trigger in the mind the same thoughts and, reciprocally, if we have the same thoughts again, they produce the same bodily movements. Finally, the machine of our body is made in such a way that one single thought of joy, of love or of something similar is enough to send the animal spirits through the nerves into all the muscles that are required to cause the various movements of the blood, which I claimed accompany the passions. It is true that I had difficulty in distinguishing the relevant movements for each passion, because they never occur alone. However, since the same passions do not always occur together, I tried to notice the changes that take place in the body when they occur in different combinations. Thus, for example, if love were always joined with joy, I could not know which of them to associate with the heat and dilation that they cause us to feel around the heart. But because love is sometimes joined with sadness and, in that case, one still feels the warmth but no longer the dilation, I judged that the heat belongs to love and the dilation to joy. Although desire almost always accompanies love, they are not always together to the same extent because, even if one loves greatly, one desires little as long as one has little hope. And since one does not then have the diligence and promptness one would have if our desire had been greater, one can judge that they arise from desire and not from love.

I quite agree that, for many people, sadness takes away their appetite. However, since I always found in my own case that it increased my appetite, I based my explanation on that. I think the differences which occur here arise as follows: the first thing that triggered sadness for some people, near the beginning of their lives, was that they did not receive enough nourishment whereas for others it arose from the fact that their nourishment was harmful. For the latter group, the movement of animal spirits that takes away their appetite has always remained linked, since their childhood, with the passion of sadness. We also see that the movements that accompany other passions are not exactly the same in everyone, and this could be explained by similar causes.

As for admiration, it has its origin in the brain and therefore the condition of the blood alone could not cause it, although it can often do so in the case of joy or sadness. However, by means of the impression which it makes on the brain, it can affect the body just as much as any other passion or it may even, in some sense, have a greater effect because the surprise it involves causes the most prompt movements of all. And just as we can move our hand or foot at almost the same instant as we think of moving them, because the idea of this movement which is formed in the brain sends the animal spirits into the muscles which are used for this effect, likewise, the idea of something pleasant, which surprises the mind, sends the animal spirits equally quickly into the nerves that open the orifices of the heart. The only effect of admiration in this context is that, because of the surprise involved, it increases the force of the motion that causes joy and, with the orifices of the heart opened suddenly, it causes the blood, which enters the heart through the vena cava and exits through the arterial vein, to inflate the lungs suddenly.

The same external signs that usually accompany the passions may sometimes also be produced by other causes. Thus a red face does not always result from shame; it can also result from the heat of the fire or from taking exercise. And the kind of laugh that is called sardonic is only a convulsion of the nerves in the face. Likewise, even if someone sighs only out of habit or as a result of some sickness, that does not prevent sighs from being external signs of sadness or desire in those cases where they result from such passions . . .

As for remedies for excessive passions: I agree that they are difficult to implement and even that they cannot be enough to prevent disorders which occur in the body; they merely prevent the soul from being disturbed so that it can retain its judgement free. To realize that, I do not think it is necessary to have a detailed knowledge of everything, nor to foresee in detail every event that may occur – that would be impossible! It is enough to have imagined in a general way more distressing things that someone has already experienced and to be prepared to cope with them. Nor do I think that one ever sins by excess in desiring things that are necessary for life; we only need to control desires for what is evil or superfluous. For those who strive only for what is good, it seems to me that the more noble they are, the better they are. And although I wished to indulge my own faults by including some kind of inertia among the excusable passions, I have a much greater appreciation of the diligence of those who are always keen to do what they believe is in some way their duty, even when they do not hope for much reward for doing so.

Descartes to Henry More, 5 February 1649

I am happy to reply to the queries you sent me.

1. The first one was: why, in defining body, I said that it is an extended substance rather than a substance that is perceptible, tangible or impenetrable. But it is clear that, if it is called a perceptible substance, it is defined by its relation to our senses; in that way only one of its properties is explained rather than its full nature, which certainly does not depend on our senses, since it could exist even if there were no human beings. Thus I do not see why you say that it is absolutely necessary for all matter to be perceptible. On the contrary, there is no matter that would not be obviously imperceptible if it were divided into parts that are much smaller than the particles of our nerves and if the individual parts were moved quickly enough.

I adopted that argument of mine which you call 'clever and almost sophistical' only to refute the opinion of those who, like you, think that every body is perceptible and in my opinion I have clearly and demonstratively refuted that. For a body may retain its nature as a body completely even if it is not soft or hard, cold or warm, or if it has no perceptible quality at all.

In order for me to fall into the mistake that you seem to want to attribute to me by using the analogy of the wax – which, although it may not be square nor round, must have some shape or other – I would have to conclude that, according to my principles, all perceptible qualities consist only in the fact that the small parts of a body move or are at rest in certain ways, and therefore a body could exist even if none of its particles were in motion or at rest. But that never even entered my mind. Thus a body cannot be defined correctly as a perceptible substance.

Let us now examine whether it would be more appropriate to say that it is an impenetrable or tangible substance in the sense you explained.

However, tangibility and impenetrability in a body are similar to the ability to laugh in the case of human beings, a property of the fourth type according to the common rules of logic and not a genuine, essential difference, whereas I contend that extension is such an essential difference. Therefore, just as human beings are not defined as animals capable of laughter but as rational animals, so likewise body is not defined by impenetrability but by extension. This is confirmed by the fact that tangibility and impenetrability involve a relation between parts and presuppose the concept of division and of a limit; but we are capable of conceiving of a continuous body of indeterminate size or which is indefinite, in which we think of nothing more than extension.

'But,' you claim, 'even God or an angel, and anything that subsists in itself is extended, and therefore your definition is wider than what is defined.' I am not in the habit of disputing about words; therefore if someone says that, from the fact that God is everywhere he is in some sense extended, I would accept that. But I deny that genuine extension, as it is commonly understood by everyone, is found in God, in angels, or in our mind, or finally in any substance that is not a body. For by 'an extended thing' everyone usually understands something imaginable (I leave aside, for the moment, the question whether it is a real being or a being of reason), and in this entity they can distinguish by the imagination various parts of a determinate size and shape, none of which can in any way be identical with another. One could imagine some of these parts being transferred to the place of others but one could not imagine two parts being in one and the same place. However, nothing like that can be said about God or, indeed, about our mind; for they are not imaginable but are only intelligible, nor are they distinguishable into parts, especially parts which have a determinate size and shape. Besides, we can understand easily that it is possible for the human mind, God, and many angels to be in one and the same place simultaneously. It follows clearly that no non-physical substances are, properly speaking, extended. I understand them rather as powers or forces of some kind which are such that, although they are applied to extended things, it does not follow that they themselves are extended, just as there is fire in a white-hot piece of iron but it does not follow that the fire itself is iron. Although some people confuse the notion of a substance with the notion of an extended thing, this results from a false prejudice because they think that nothing exists or is intelligible unless it is also imaginable, and, indeed, nothing is imaginable that is not in some way extended. Just as one can say that only human beings can be healthy but, nonetheless, medicine, a temperate climate and many other things may be said to be healthy by analogy, so likewise I apply the term 'extended' only to what is imaginable, that is, whatever has parts outside parts of a determinate size and shape, even if other things may also be said to be extended by analogy.

2. Let us now consider your second objection. If we investigate the extended entity that I described, we shall surely find that it is identical with space, which people commonly think about as being sometimes full and sometimes empty, or sometimes as real and at other times as imaginary. But in space – no matter how imaginary and empty it may be – everyone easily imagines different parts of a determinate size and shape, and in their imagination they can move some parts into the place of others but they cannot in any way conceive of two parts that simultaneously interpenetrate in one and the same place because it implies a contradiction for this to happen unless some part of space is removed. Since I think that such properties, which are so real, can exist only in real bodies, I dared to claim that there cannot be a space which is completely empty, and that every extended entity is a real body. Nor did I hesitate to disagree on this issue with great men, such as Epicurus, Democritus and Lucretius,[61] for I saw that they did not follow any sound reason but rather the false prejudice with which all of us have been imbued from our earliest years. That is, our senses do not always reveal external bodies to us as they are in themselves, but only insofar as they are related to us and are capable of being harmful or

beneficial, as I indicated earlier in Part II, article 3;[62] however, we all judged, when we were still children, that there is nothing in the world apart from what our senses reveal, and consequently that there are no bodies apart from those that we can perceive and that all the spaces in which we perceive nothing are empty. Since this prejudice was never rejected by Epicurus, Democritus or Lucretius, I ought not to follow their authority.

I am surprised that someone who is so perceptive about other things, and who realizes that he cannot deny that there is some substance in every space because all the properties of extension are genuinely found there, prefers to say that divine extension fills the space in which there are no bodies than to concede that there cannot be any space without body. For, as I said already, the alleged divine extension cannot in any way be the subject of the real properties that we perceive very distinctly in every space. Nor, indeed, is God imaginable or distinguishable into parts that have some size and shape.

But you admit without difficulty that there is no naturally occurring vacuum. You are concerned about the power of God which, you think, can remove everything from a container and at the same time can prevent the sides of the container from collapsing. In contrast, I know that my intellect is finite and that the power of God is infinite, and therefore I never determine anything about God's power. I only consider what may or may not be perceived by me and I am very careful that none of my judgments ever differs from my perceptions. For that reason I boldly claim that God is capable if doing everything that I perceive as possible. But I do not rashly deny, on the contrary, that he can do what I cannot conceive; I say simply that it involves a contradiction. Thus since I realize that I cannot conceive how, if all body is removed from a container, it would continue to have an extension that is not conceived by me otherwise than as I had previously conceived of the body which it contained, I say that it implies a contradiction that such an extension would remain in the container when all body has been removed, and therefore the sides of the container should collapse. This is completely consistent with my other views. For elsewhere I claim that every motion is in some sense circular;[63] it follows that it is unintelligible for God to remove some body from a container unless we understand that some other body, or the very sides of the container, takes its place as a result of a circular motion.

3. In the same way I claim that it implies a contradiction to say that there are atoms which are conceived simultaneously as extended and indivisible. Although God could have made them in such a way that it would be impossible for any creature to divide them, we surely cannot understand that he could have deprived himself of the power to divide them. It does not work to make a comparison with things which, once they have been done, cannot be undone. For we do not take it as a sign of impotence that someone cannot do something that we do not understand as possible; it is a sign of impotence only if someone cannot do something that we perceive distinctly as possible. But we definitely perceive that it is possible for an atom to be divided since, by supposition, it is extended. Therefore, if we judge that it cannot be divided by God we shall judge that God cannot do something which, nonetheless, we perceive as possible. But we do not likewise perceive that it is possible for what has been done to be undone; on the contrary, we perceive clearly that this is impossible. Therefore it is not a defect in God's power that he does not do so. But the same reasoning does not apply to the divisibility of matter. Even though I cannot enumerate all the parts into which matter is divisible and I would therefore say that their number is indefinite, I cannot, however, claim that their division by God is never realized because I know that God can do many more things than I can include in my thought. I granted in article 34 that such an indefinite division of the parts of matter does actually occur.[64]

4. In my opinion it is not an affected modesty on my part, but a necessary caution, to say that some things are indefinite rather than infinite.[65] I understand God alone as being positively infinite. I confess that I do not know in the case of other things – such as the extension of the world, the number of parts into which matter is divisible, and similar things – whether they are or are not absolutely infinite. All I know is that I am not aware of any limit to them and therefore, from my point of view, I call them indefinite.

Although our mind is not the measure of things or of truth, it certainly should be the measure of whatever we affirm or deny. For what is more absurd or less reasonable than to wish to pass judgement about things if we concede that our mind cannot perceive them?

I am surprised, however, that you seem to want to do this when you say, 'if extension is infinite only in relation to us, then it will be genuinely infinite, and so on . . .' But you also wish to imagine some divine extension that extends further than the extension of bodies, and thus to suppose that God has parts outside each other and that he is divisible, and you wish to attribute to God absolutely the whole essence of a physical thing.

Lest any difficulty remain, let me say: when I claim that the extension of matter is indefinite, I think this is enough to prevent anyone from imagining a place outside space into which the particles of my vortices could escape; wherever that place might be thought to be, there is already some matter there according to my view. For in claiming that it is indefinitely extended, I claim that it extends further than anything which is humanly conceivable.

But, nonetheless, I think there is the greatest difference between the dimensions of that bodily extension and the vastness – I shall not say extension since, properly speaking, there is none – of the divine substance or essence. And therefore I call the latter simply infinite and call the former indefinite.

Besides, I do not agree with what you suggest, in your exceptional generosity, namely, that the rest of my views could stand even if what I wrote about the extension of matter were refuted. For that is one of the primary and, in my view, the most certain foundations of my Physics and I acknowledge that none of the arguments in that Physics satisfy me unless they exhibit the necessity that you call logical or conceptual, once we make an exception for things that can be known only by experience, such as: that there is only one sun and only one moon around the earth, and similar things. Since you do not disagree with me about other things, I hope that you will readily agree with these also, if only you consider that it is a prejudice that many people think that an extended thing in which there is nothing that would affect our senses is not a genuine bodily substance but merely an empty space; and that there are no bodies apart from those that we can perceive and no substances apart from those that can be imagined and are therefore extended.

5. There is no prejudice to which we have become more accustomed than that which convinced us, from our earliest years, that brute animals think. There is no reason to make us believe this except that, when we observed that many animals' organs are not very different from ours in external shape and movement and we believed that there is a unique principle of those movements in our own case – namely, the soul, which both moves the body and thinks – we felt certain that a similar soul was required in the case of animals.

But when I later recognized that two different principles of our movements should be distinguished – one is completely mechanical and physical, relies solely on the force of animal spirits and the structure of the organs, and could be called a physical soul; the other is non-physical, namely the mind or soul that I defined as a thinking substance – I investigated carefully whether the movements of animals arise from these two principles or only from one of them. And when I saw clearly that they could all result from that principle alone, which is physical and mechanical, I took it as certain and demonstrated that it is impossible for us to prove that there is some kind of thinking soul in animals. I am not surprised at the cleverness and cunning of dogs and foxes, nor at anything else that is done by brute animals out of fear, or for food or sexual pleasure. For I claim that I can explain all those things very easily as resulting merely from the structure of their organs.

Although I think it has been demonstrated that it cannot be proved that there is any thought in brute animals, I do not think that it is therefore possible to prove that there is none, because the human mind does not reach into their innermost lives. But by investigating what is most probable about this question, I see no reason to support the claim that animals think, apart from the following: they have eyes, ears, a tongue and other sense organs like ours and, therefore, it is probable that they have sensations like ours. But since thought is included in our way of sensing, a similar thought should also be attributed to animals. Since this reason is very well known, it has engaged the minds of everyone from their earliest years. But there are other reasons, much stronger and more numerous but not equally well known to everyone, that convince us completely of the opposite conclusion. One of them is this: the claim that all worms, flies, caterpillars and other animals are endowed with an immortal soul is not as probable as the claim that they are like machines.

Firstly, because it is certain that within the bodies of animals, as in our own bodies, there are bones, nerves, muscles, blood, animal spirits and other organs so arranged that, on their own and without any thought, they could give rise to all the movements that we observe in animals. This is evident from convulsions when the machine of the body moves itself, despite the mind, often more violently and in ways that are more varied than it usually moves with the assistance of the will.

Secondly, it seems to be reasonable, since art copies nature and human beings are able to construct various machines that move without any thought, that nature could also produce its own automata, which are made, however, much more elegantly than by human art – namely, all the brute animals. This is especially so since we do not know of any reason why thought should be present whenever this structure of organs is found that we see in animals. Therefore, it is much more surprising that a mind should be found in every human body than that there is none in many of the brute animals.

But the principal reason that convinces us that animals lack thought is, in my view, that some animals are more perfect than others of the same species, as we find among human beings. This can be seen in horses and dogs, some of which learn what they are taught much better than others. And although they all signify to us their natural impulses, such as anger, fear, hunger and the like, by using their voice or other bodily movements, no brute animal has so far ever been observed that reached a level of perfection at which it used genuine speech, that is, by indicating something by its voice or signs that could be referred exclusively to thought and not to some natural impulse. Such speech is the only certain sign that thought is hidden in a body. All human beings use it – even those who are most stupid and mentally defective or who are deprived of a tongue and vocal organs – but no animal does.

Therefore, this can be taken as a genuine specific difference between human beings and brute animals.

For the sake of brevity I omit the other reasons for denying thought to animals. However, I would like to point out that I am speaking of thought, not about life or sensation. For I do not deny that any animal has life – which, I claim, consists only in the heat of the heart. Nor do I even deny sensation to animals, insofar as it derives from a bodily organ. Thus my view is not so much cruel to beasts but respectful to human beings (as long as they are not committed to the superstition of the Pythagoreans), whom it absolves from any suspicion of crime whenever they kill or eat animals.

Perhaps I have written about all these things at greater length than the sharpness of your intelligence requires. I wanted thereby to testify that, to date, the objections of very few people were as welcome as yours.

Descartes to More, 15 April 1649

Replies to the first counter-objections

It seems to me that, in relation to a thing that is perceivable, to be perceivable is nothing more than naming something by reference to something else. Nor is it adequate even to the thing itself, because if 'perceivable' is defined in relation to our senses it does not apply to the smallest particles of matter. If it is defined by reference to other imaginary senses that you may think could be fabricated by God, then angels and souls may also be said to be perceivable. For I do not find it any easier to understand sensory nerves, which are so subtle that they can be moved by the smallest particles of matter, than some faculty by which our mind could have an immediate sensation or perception of other minds. Although we understand easily the relation of parts of extension to each other, I still seem to perceive extension better even when I do not think clearly about the relation of the parts to each other. You have more reason to concede this than I have, because you conceive of extension in such a way that it applies to God, despite the fact that, at the same time, you deny that God has any parts.

'It has not yet been demonstrated that tangibility or impenetrability are properties of extended substance.'

If you conceive of extension in terms of the relation of parts to each other, you do not seem to deny that it is possible for each of its parts to touch others which are adjacent. And this tangibility is a genuine property, which is intrinsic to the thing in question and is not the same as that which is named after the sense of touch.

Moreover, it is unintelligible that one part of an extended thing should penetrate another similar part, unless one understands thereby that half of its extension is removed or annihilated. If it is annihilated, it does not penetrate something else; thus, in my view, it is demonstrated that impenetrability belongs to the essence of extension but not to anything else.

'I claim that there is another extension, which is equally genuine.'

Here, at last, we agree about some reality and there only remains a question about a name, whether this other extension is to be classified as an equally genuine extension. As far as I am concerned, I do not understand that there is any extension of a substance in God, in angels and in our mind, but only the extension of a power in the sense in which an angel could exercise its power at one time in a large part, at another in a small part, of a physical substance. For if there were no body, I would understand that there is also no space with which an angel or God would be co-extensive. But that someone would attribute the extension of a substance to what has only the extension of a power is, I think, the same prejudice as assuming that every substance, including God himself, is imaginable.

Replies to the second counter-objections

'Some parts of empty space would absorb others, etc.'

I repeat here that, if they were absorbed, then half of the space is removed and ceases to be. That which ceases to be does not penetrate anything else; therefore we should admit that every space is impenetrable.

'The space between worlds would have its own duration, etc.'

I think it involves a contradiction to conceive that there is some duration between the destruction of a prior world and the creation of a new one. For if we refer this duration to a succession of divine thoughts or to anything similar, that would be a mistake in understanding, not a genuine perception of anything.

I have already replied to the subsequent point by pointing out that the extension which is attributed to non-physical things is only the extension of a power, not that of a substance. This power, which is merely a mode in the thing to which it is applied, cannot be understood as extended if the extension with which it co-exists is removed.

Replies to the penultimate counter-objections

'God is positively infinite, that is, he exists everywhere, etc.'

I do not agree with this 'everywhere'. For here you seem to locate God's infinity in the fact that he exists everywhere; I do not agree with this view but think that God is everywhere by reason of his power. But he has no relation at all to any place by reason of his essence. Since power and essence are not distinguished in God, I think it is more satisfactory to reason about such things in the case of our mind or the angels, as realities that are more suited to our perception, rather than in the case of God.

All the remaining difficulties seem to me to arise from the same prejudice, that we are too accustomed to imagine every substance as extended, even those that we deny are physical, and to philosophize carelessly about beings of reason by attributing the properties of an entity or thing to what is a non-entity. But it should be remembered carefully that a non-being cannot have any real properties and that there is no way of understanding it in terms of part and whole, subject, attribute, etc. Therefore you are right to conclude 'that the mind plays with its own shadows' when it thinks about logical entities.

'A certain and finite number of states would be enough, etc.'

But it is inconsistent with my concept to attribute any limit to the world, nor do I have any criterion for what I should affirm or deny apart from my own perception. I claim, therefore, that the world is indeterminate and indefinite because I do not know of any limits to it. But I do not dare to describe it as infinite because I perceive God as greater than the world, not by reason of his extension – as I have often said, I do not understand that there is any extension is the strict sense in God – but by reason of his perfection.

Replies to the final counter-objections

I am not certain that the rest of my philosophy will ever see the light of day, because it presupposes many experiments and I do not know if I will ever have an opportunity to do them. However, I hope to publish this summer a small treatise on the passions[66] from which it will be clear how, in our own case, I think that all the movements of our limbs which accompany our passions result not from the soul but solely from the machinery of the body.

However, that 'dogs wag their tails, etc.' are only movements which accompany passions and I think they should be distinguished carefully from speech, which alone demonstrates that there is thought hidden in a body.

'Nor are there any infants, etc.'

The explanation of children is different from that of brute animals. I would not judge that children were endowed with a mind unless I saw that they had the same nature as adults; but brute animals never develop to a stage where any certain sign of thought can be detected in them.

Replies to your questions

To the first:

It is inconsistent with my understanding or, what amounts to the same thing, I think it involves a contradiction for the world to be finite or limited, because I cannot fail to conceive of a space beyond whatever limits of the world you presuppose. Such a space is, for me, a real body.

Nor do I care if others call it imaginary and the world is thus thought to be finite; for I recognize the prejudices from which that mistake arose.

To the second:

By imagining a sword piercing through the limits of the world you show that you do not conceive of the world as finite either; for you conceive of every space that the sword reaches as a genuine part of the world, even though you call what you thus conceive a vacuum.

To the third:

I cannot explain any better the reciprocal force in the mutual separation of two bodies from each other than if I put before your eyes a small boat which is stuck in the mud on the bank of a river, and there are two men – one of whom stands on the bank and pushes the boat with his hands in order to move it away from the land, and the other stands in the boat and, in the same way, pushes the bank of the river with his hands to move the boat likewise from the land. If the forces exerted by these two men are equal, the effort of the one on the land makes no less a contribution to the boat's motion than the effort of the other man who is moved with the boat. It is clear from this that the action by which the boat recedes from the land is no less on the land itself than on the boat. Nor is there any problem about someone who moves away from you while seated; since I am speaking here about translation, I understand only that which occurs in the separation of two bodies which immediately touch each other.

. . .

To the fifth:

I do not assume that there is any resistance or tenacity in the smallest parts of matter, apart from what occurs in larger parts which are perceivable – that is, that which depends on the motion and rest of the particles. But it should be noted that those striated particles are formed from very subtle matter, which is divided into innumerably many or an indefinite number of particles that are joined together to form them, so that I think there are more distinct minute parts in each striated particle than are commonly thought to be in much larger bodies.

To the sixth:

I tried to explain most of the issues you raised about my treatise on the passions. I add simply that nothing has so far occurred to me about the nature of material things for which I could not easily think of a mechanical explanation. But just as it is no disgrace for a philosopher to think that God can move a body without thinking that God is physical, so likewise it is no disgrace to make the same judgement about other non-physical substances. And although I think that there is no way of acting that applies univocally to God and to creatures, I confess, nevertheless, that I find no idea in my mind that represents the way in which God or an angel can move matter apart from that which shows me the way in which I am conscious of being able to move my body by my thought.

Nor can my mind extend or contract itself spatially by reason of its substance; it can so do only by reason of its power, by applying itself to larger or smaller bodies.

. . .

To the ninth:

From what I just said about the two men, one of whom is moved with the boat while the other remains immobile on the riverbank, I have shown sufficiently that I think there is nothing more positive in one man's motion than in the other one's rest.

Comments on a Certain Manifesto

1648

NOTE ON THE TEXT

This brief reply to critics and misguided supporters was written by Descartes during a period in which there was frequent discussion and criticism of his theories in the Netherlands. Henricus Regius or Henri De Roy (1598–1679) was a professor of medicine and botany at the University of Utrecht. Soon after his appointment in 1638 he began to be influenced by Cartesian theories, especially by Descartes' scientific essays of 1637: *The Discourse on Method, and the Dioptrics, Meteorology and Geometry*. He developed his philosophical ideas over a number of years and published them in various disputations, some of which gave rise to controversies involving his Aristotelian and theological colleagues at Utrecht, including the Rector, Gysbertus Voet (or Voetius). Although accused by his academic colleagues of introducing unorthodox Cartesian theories, Regius was also at odds with Descartes. On a number of occasions Descartes had made suggestions about how to avoid needless controversy and how to present the new philosophy without antagonizing the devotees of antiquity. When Regius published a treatise on the foundations of physics, *Fundamenta Physices* (1646), he seemed to be presenting Cartesian views that were significantly at variance with those of their original author. Descartes replied critically in his Preface to the French edition of the *The Principles of Philosophy* (1647) and this in turn provoked Regius to publish, anonymously, a summary of his views in the form of a manifesto or '*programma*'. Descartes composed his reply during December 1647, and it was published in January 1648.

In his *Comments on a Certain Manifesto*, Descartes also mentions other pamphlets which, in his view, did not deserve a formal reply. These were probably *A Theological Consideration of Descartes' Method*, written by the theologian Jacobus Revius or Jacques de Rives (1586–1658), and a disputation published by Adam Stuart (1591–1654), who was professor of philosophy at the same Statencollege in Holland.

Comments by René Descartes on a Certain Manifesto which was published in Belgium towards the end of 1647, under the title: An Explanation of the Human Mind or the Rational Soul, which explains what it is and what it may be.

AMSTERDAM, 1648

A few days ago I received two pamphlets, in one of which I am attacked openly and directly,[67] and in the other only covertly and indirectly. The first one does not bother me; I am even grateful to its author because, by his inept work, he merely collected futile quibbles and slanders that no one could believe and he has thereby testified that he could find nothing in my writings that he could justifiably criticize. He has thus confirmed the truth of my writings better than if he had praised them, and all this at the expense of his own reputation. The other pamphlet disturbs me more, even though it does not explicitly identify me anywhere and is published without the name of its author or publisher. However, it contains views which I think are pernicious and false, and it is published in the form of a manifesto which can be pinned to church doors and may be read by anyone who wishes. It is also reported to have been printed earlier in a different format, which included the name of someone, as author, who is believed by many people to teach views which are the same as mine. Therefore I am forced to expose its errors so that they will not be attributed to me by those who may see these publications but have not read my writings.

The following is the Manifesto in the format in which it was published most recently.

AN EXPLANATION OF THE HUMAN MIND OR THE RATIONAL SOUL, WHICH EXPLAINS WHAT IT IS AND WHAT IT MAY BE.

1. The human mind is that by which acts of thinking are first performed by human beings, and it consists solely in the faculty and internal principle of thinking.
2. As far as the nature of things is concerned, it seems possible for the soul to be either a substance or a mode of a physical substance. Or, if we follow some other philosophers who stipulate that extension and thought are attributes which are present in certain substances as their subjects, then since these attributes are not opposites but are just different from each other, there is nothing to prevent the mind from being an attribute of some kind which applies to the same subject as extension, even though neither attribute is included in the concept of the other.
3. Those are mistaken, therefore, who claim that we necessarily conceive of the human mind, clearly and distinctly, as really distinct from the body.
4. However, it has been revealed to us in many places in Holy Scripture that the mind is nothing but a substance, or an entity that is really distinct from the body and is inseparable from it in reality, and that it can subsist on its own apart from the body. Thus something that may be doubtful for some people when they rely on natural knowledge (if we are looking for reliable, rather than merely probable, knowledge and the truth about things)[68] is already indubitable as a result of divine revelation in the Sacred Scriptures.
5. Nor is it an objection that we are able to doubt the body while not doubting the mind. That only shows that, as long as we doubt the body, we cannot say that the mind is a mode of the body.
6. The human mind, although it is a substance which is really distinct from the body, is organically present in all its actions as long as the mind is in the body. Therefore, the thoughts of the mind vary in accordance with different dispositions of the body.

7. Since the mind is by nature different from the body or the disposition of the body, and since it cannot result from the latter, it is incorruptible.
8. The concept of the mind contains no parts and no extension; therefore it is futile to ask whether it is totally in the whole body or totally in individual parts.
9. Since the mind may be affected equally by imaginary things and by real things, it follows (if we are looking not for probable truth but for the accurate, precise truth of things)[69] that it is doubtful, according to nature, whether there are any bodies that we truly perceive. Divine revelation in the Scriptures removes this doubt too; it is undoubtedly true that God created, and that he continues to conserve, heaven and earth and everything they contain.
10. The bond by which the soul is joined to the body is a law of the immutability of nature, according to which everything remains in whatever condition it is until it is changed by something else.
11. Since the rational soul is produced as a new substance in the course of generation, it seems that the most correct view is that it is produced by God by means of an immediate creation in the course of generation.
12. The mind does not need innate ideas, notions or axioms. Its faculty of thinking alone is enough for it to perform its actions.
13. Therefore, all the common notions that are found in the mind originate either in the observation of things or in what we are taught.
14. Thus even the idea of God that is put in the mind derives from divine revelation, from what we are taught, or from the observation of things.
15. Our concept of God, or the idea of God which is present in our minds, is not a sufficiently strong reason for proving the existence of God because not all the things of which we have a concept exist. And this idea, insofar as it is conceived by us – imperfectly, it should be said – does not exceed our powers of thinking any more than the concept of anything else.
16. The thinking of the mind is twofold: understanding and willing.
17. Understanding is perception and judgement.

18. Perception is sensation, remembering and imagining.
19. All sensing is the perception of some physical movement; this does not require any intentional species,[70] and it takes place not in the external senses but exclusively in the brain.
20. The will is free and is indifferent to opposites in the order of nature, as is testified by our consciousness.
21. The will determines itself; it should not be described as blind, any more than vision should be described as deaf.

'No one acquires a reputation for great piety more easily than those who are superstitious or hypocritical.'[71]

AN EXAMINATION OF THE MANIFESTO FOLLOWS

Comments on the Title

I notice in the title that we are promised not bald assertions about the rational soul but its *explanation.* Thus we should take it for granted that this manifesto includes all the reasons or, at least, the principal reasons that the author had not only for proving but for explaining what he proposed and we should expect that he has no other reasons apart from these. I applaud the fact that he calls the rational soul the 'human mind'; he thereby avoids the equivocation of the term 'soul' and, in doing so, he follows my example.

Comments on the Individual Articles

In the first article, he seems to want to *define* the rational soul, but he does so imperfectly because he omits the genus,[72] that is, whether it is a substance, a mode, or something else. He gives only the specific difference, which he borrowed from me because, as far as I know, no one before me claimed that it consists solely in thought, or in a faculty and internal principle for thinking.

In the second article he begins to inquire into the genus of the soul, and says that 'as far as the nature of things is concerned, it seems possible for the human mind to be either a substance or a mode of a physical substance'.

This claim involves no less of a contradiction than if I said that the nature of things allows for a mountain either to have or not to have a valley. However, we must distinguish between things which by their very nature may change (for example: that, at the moment, I am writing or not writing, or that one person is prudent and another imprudent) and other things which never change. The latter include anything pertaining to the essence of something, and philosophers are agreed about this. There is no doubt that, in the case of contingent things, one could say that the nature of things leaves it possible for them to be in one condition or another; for example, I may be writing or not writing. But in the case of the essence of something, it is obviously wrong and contradictory to say that the nature of things leaves open the possibility for it to be other than it is. It belongs to the nature of a mountain that it cannot occur without a valley; equally, the nature of the human mind is whatever it is. Thus it is a substance if it is a substance, or it is certainly a mode of a physical thing if, indeed, it is such a mode. Our author tries here to convince us that it is a mode and in order to prove it he adds these words, 'or, if we follow some philosophers, etc.' where, by the phrase 'some philosophers' he clearly means me. For I was the first to identify thought as the principal attribute of a non-physical substance and extension as the principal attribute of a physical substance. But I did not say that it was possible for those attributes to be present in substances as if they were distinct subjects; one has to be careful here lest we understand the word 'attribute' as nothing other than a mode. For whatever we recognize as attributed to the nature of something – whether it is a mode, which can change, or the absolutely immutable essence of a thing – we call it an attribute of that thing.

Thus there are many attributes in God but no modes. Likewise it is one of the attributes of any substance that it subsists on its own. And the extension of any body may take on various different modes; if a body is spherical, that is one of its modes and, if it is cubic, that is another. But the extension itself which, when considered in itself, is the subject of these modes is not a mode of a physical substance but an attribute that constitutes its essence and nature. Finally, there are also various modes of thought, because to make an affirmation is a different mode of thought from denying something, and so on. But the thought itself, insofar as it is an internal principle from which these modes arise and in which they are located, is not conceived of as a mode but as an attribute which constitutes the nature of some substance. Whether the substance is physical or not remains to be seen.

He adds that 'these attributes are not opposites but are different from each other'. There is also a contradiction in these words. When we are discussing the attributes that constitute the essence of certain substances, it is impossible for them to be more opposite than by being different from each other. So when someone concedes that one is different from another, that is equivalent to saying that one is not the other, for 'to be' and 'not to be' are contraries. He says: 'Since these attributes are not opposites but are just different from each other, there is nothing to prevent the mind from being an attribute of some kind which applies to the same subject as extension, even though neither attribute is included in the concept of the other.' There is a clear contradiction in these words. For he draws a conclusion about some attributes that can be true only of modes in the strict sense of the term, but he never proves that the mind or the internal principle of thought is such a mode. On the contrary, it is not a mode, as I will show below from his very own words in article 5. As regards other attributes that constitute the natures of things, it is impossible to say that those which are distinct from each other, and are such that one is not included in the concept of the other, can be present in one and the same subject. That is the same as saying that one and the same subject has two different natures. That implies a contradiction, at least when the subject in question is simple (as is the case here) and not compound.

But there are three things to note here; if they had been well understood by this writer he would not have fallen into such obvious mistakes.

The first is that it belongs to the nature of a mode that, although we can understand any substance without a mode, we cannot vice versa understand a mode clearly unless we conceive at the same time of the substance of which it is a mode. I explained this in Part I of the *Principles*, article 61, and all philosophers agree on this. Our author, however, did not pay attention to this rule, as is obvious from his article 5 above, where he concedes that we can doubt the existence of the body while at the same time not doubting the existence of the mind. It follows from this that we can understand the mind without the body and, therefore, that the mind is not a mode of the body.

The second thing that I would like to emphasize is the difference between simple and compound entities. An entity is compound if we find it has two or more attributes, each of which can be understood distinctly without the other. From the fact that one attribute is thus understood without the other, it is known that one is not a mode of the other but is a thing or an attribute of a thing that can subsist without the other. A simple entity, however, is one in which such attributes are not found. It follows from this that a subject in which we understand only extension and various modes of extension is a simple entity; so, likewise, is a subject in which we recognize only thought and various modes of thought. However, an entity in which we think of extension and thought simultaneously is composite, that is, a human being, consisting of a soul and body, while our author seems to have assumed here that it is only a body of which the mind is a mode.

Thirdly, it should be noted here that in subjects that are composed of a number of substances, one of them is often primary. We think of this primary substance in such a way that whatever we add to it from other substances is only a mode. Thus a clothed person may be considered to be a composite of a person and clothes; and the clothes may be considered, in relation to the person, as just a mode even though the clothes are substances. In the same way our author was able to consider, in a human being who is composed of a soul and body, that the body is the primary thing and, consequently, to be animated or to have thought is only a mode. But it is a mistake to conclude from this that the soul itself, or that by which the body thinks, is not a substance which is distinct from the body.

However, he tries to prove what he said by means of this syllogism:

'If we can conceive of something, then it is possible for it to exist. But we are able to conceive of the mind as either a substance or a mode of a physical substance – for nothing here implies any contradiction. Therefore, etc.' It should be noted that this rule, 'If we can conceive of something, then it is possible for it to exist,' is my own rule and that it is true as long as we have a clear and distinct perception in which the possibility of the thing is contained, because God can do anything that we conceive clearly as possible. But this rule should not be exploited, with temerity, because it can easily happen that someone thinks they understand something properly which, however, they do not understand because they are blinded by some prejudice. That is what happens to this author when he denies that it implies a contradiction for one and the same thing to have either of two completely different natures, namely, to be either a substance or a mode. If he had said simply that he had no reasons for believing that the human mind is a non-physical substance rather than a mode of a physical substance, his ignorance could be excused. Even if he said that human ingenuity is unable to discover any reasons by which either position could be proved, his arrogance would be culpable but his claim would not be self-contradictory. However, when he says that the nature of things allows the same thing to be a substance or a mode, he speaks in a completely contradictory way and shows the absurdity of his own mind.

In article 3 he offers his judgement on me. For I am the one who wrote that the human mind can be perceived clearly and distinctly as a substance that is distinct from physical substance. However, our author pronounces that I am mistaken, despite the fact that he provides no reasons other than those that involve the contradictions I explained in the previous article. But I shall not delay on this. Nor shall I examine the words 'necessarily' [art. 3] or 'really' [art. 4], which are somewhat ambiguous, because they are not of great significance.

I do not wish to examine what is said in article 4 about the Sacred Scriptures, lest I seem to arrogate to myself a right to inquire into other people's religion. I shall simply say that we should distinguish three types of question here. Some things are believed on faith alone, such as the mysteries of the Incarnation, the Trinity, and the like.

There are other things, however, which, although they pertain to faith, may be investigated by natural reason; the existence of God and the distinction of the human soul from the body are usually included in this group by orthodox theologians. Finally, there are others, which have nothing to do with faith but pertain exclusively to human reasoning, such as squaring a circle, making gold by using alchemical skills, and so on. It is an abuse of the words of Sacred Scripture to believe that one can derive the third kind from a faulty explanation of Scripture; likewise, it is a derogation from the authority of Scripture to try to demonstrate the first kind by arguments derived exclusively from philosophy. But all theologians claim that these mysteries should be shown to be compatible with the natural light of reason and they devote their studies primarily to this task. Questions of the second kind, however, are not only considered as not inconsistent with the natural light of reason but philosophers are urged to demonstrate them as best they can by using rational arguments. But I have never seen anyone who claimed that the nature of things allows for the possibility of something being otherwise than is taught by Sacred Scripture unless they wish to indicate, indirectly, that they do not believe in Scripture. But since we were born human before we were made Christian, it is not credible that, in order to cling to the faith which makes them a Christian, someone would seriously adopt views that they believe are inconsistent with the right reason that makes them human.

Perhaps this is not what our author says, for his words are as follows: 'Thus something which may be doubtful for some people when they rely on natural knowledge is already indubitable as a result of divine revelation in Sacred Scripture.' I find two contradictions in this. The first is in claiming that the essence of one and the same thing does not remain always the same: he supposes that, by nature, it is doubtful and therefore changeable (for, if one supposes that it changes, by that very fact it will become a different thing, which would require a different name). The other contradiction is in the phrase 'some people'; since nature is the same for everyone, something that may be doubtful only for some people is not doubtful by nature.

Article 5 should be referred to the second article rather than the fourth. For here the author is concerned not with divine revelation but with the nature of the mind and whether it is a substance or merely a mode. In order to prove that it is possible to defend the view that the mind is merely a mode, he tries to answer an objection which is taken from my writings. I wrote that we cannot doubt that our mind exists because from the very fact that we doubt it follows that it exists. But we are able to doubt at the same time whether any bodies exist. From this I concluded and demonstrated that the mind is clearly perceived by us as a thing that exists or as a substance, even if we do not conceive clearly of any bodies and even if we deny that any bodies exist. Therefore the concept of the mind does not include in itself any concept of body. He thinks that he can demolish this argument by saying that 'it only shows that as long as we doubt the body we cannot say that the mind is a mode of the body'. Here he shows that he is completely ignorant of what philosophers call a mode. For the nature of a mode is such that it cannot be understood in any way without including, in its concept, the concept of the thing of which it is a mode, as I explained above. Our author, however, admits that the mind can sometimes be understood without a body, namely when the body is being doubted. It follows from this that, at least during that time, it cannot be said to be its mode. But whatever is true of the essence or nature of something at one time is always true of it. Despite this, he claims that 'as far as the nature of things is concerned, it seems possible for the soul to be a mode of a physical substance'. These two claims are manifestly inconsistent.

I do not understand what he is trying to do in article 6. I remember hearing it said in the schools that 'the soul is the act of an organic body'. But I have never before heard of the soul itself being called 'organic'. Therefore I ask our author's pardon if I set out my conjectures – not as if they were true but merely as conjectures – for I am not writing anything here that I think is certain. It seems to me that there are two claims here which are incompatible. One is that the human mind is a substance which is really distinct from the body; our author says this explicitly, even though he uses arguments as much as possible to show the opposite and claims that it is possible to prove it only on the authority of Sacred Scripture. The other claim is that the very same human mind is organic or instrumental in all its actions.

That means that it does nothing on its own and acts only insofar as the body uses it in the same way as it uses the structure of its limbs and other bodily modes. He thereby claims – not in so many words, but in effect – that 'the mind is merely a mode of the body', as though he had lined up all his arguments to prove this one thesis. These two claims are so clearly inconsistent that I do not think our author wants readers to believe both of them simultaneously but that he mixed them together intentionally in order to satisfy in some way, by the authority of Scripture, less sophisticated readers and his own theologians. But, meanwhile, more perceptive readers recognize that he is speaking ironically when he says that 'the mind is distinct from the body', and that he is completely convinced that the mind is merely a mode.

In articles 7 and 8, however, he seems to be speaking only ironically and he uses the same Socratic style in the latter part of article 9. But in the earlier part of it his claim is supported by an argument and it seems, therefore, as if we should believe that he is speaking seriously there. He teaches 'that it is doubtful, according to nature, whether there are any bodies which we truly perceive'. The reason he offers is 'that the mind may be affected equally by imaginary things and by real things'. In order for this reason to work, one would have to suppose that we cannot use our understanding in the strict sense of that term and that all we can use is the faculty which is usually called 'common sense'.[73] This is the faculty in which the intentional species of things, both real and imaginary, are received so that they can then affect the mind; it is a faculty that philosophers commonly attribute even to brute animals. But even if people are affected not only by images from real things but also by images that occur in the brain as a result of other causes (as happens in sleep), evidently they are not made like horses or mules; they have an understanding and can distinguish very clearly one type of image from another by the light of reason. In my writings I explained how this can be done correctly and reliably; I have done this so carefully that I am confident that no one who reads it and is able to understand could remain sceptical.

In the tenth and eleventh articles, one might think that he is still writing ironically. However, if the soul is believed to be a substance, it is ridiculous and silly to say that 'the bond by which the soul is joined to the body is a law of the immutability of nature, according to which everything remains in whatever condition it is'. For whether things are joined together or separated, they remain equally in the same state as long as nothing changes that condition. That is not in dispute; the question is, rather, how it happens that the mind is joined with the body and is not separated from it. However, on the supposition that the mind is a mode of the body, it is correct to say that there is no need to look for any other bond by which they are joined together apart from the fact that the soul remains in whatever condition it is, because the only condition that modes can have is to inhere in the things of which they are modes.

In article 12 he seems to disagree with me only verbally. When he says that 'The mind does not need innate ideas or notions or axioms' while conceding to it a faculty of thinking (apparently, natural or innate), he clearly affirms the same reality as I do although he denies it verbally. I never wrote or claimed that the mind needs innate ideas which are anything other than its faculty of thinking; but when I noticed that I had certain thoughts that did not come from external objects or from the determination of my own will but resulted exclusively from my faculty of thinking, I called them 'innate' in order to distinguish the ideas or notions which are the forms of those thoughts from others that were acquired or constructed. In the same sense, we say that generosity is innate in certain families whereas, in others, various diseases such as gout or stones are innate. That does not mean that the children of those families suffer from such conditions in their mother's womb but that they are born with a certain disposition or capacity for contracting them.

He draws a surprising conclusion in article 13 from the previous article. He says: 'Therefore (from the fact that the mind does not need any innate ideas but that a faculty of thinking alone is enough for it), all the common notions which are found in the mind originate either in the observation of things or in what we are taught.' This suggests that the faculty of thinking could not provide anything itself apart from what it receives from observing things or from what it has been taught, that is, from the senses. That is so false that, on the contrary, anyone who has an accurate understanding of the scope of our senses and of what exactly can reach our faculty of thinking from the senses must admit that no ideas are presented to us from the senses in the way in which we form them in our thought. Thus there is nothing in our ideas which was not innate in the mind or in the faculty of thinking, apart from the circumstances that pertain to experience – viz. that we judge that such and such ideas, which we have at present, are related to certain external things. This is not because those external objects transmitted these very ideas to our mind through the sense organs but because they transmitted something that provided the mind with an occasion to form those ideas, by means of an innate faculty, at one time rather than another. Thus nothing is transmitted from external objects through the sense organs to our mind apart from certain physical movements, as our author himself claims in article 19, based on my *Principles*. But neither the movements themselves nor the shapes that result from them are conceived by us in the same manner as they occur in the sense organs, as I explained previously in the *Dioptrics*.[74] It follows that the ideas themselves of those motions are innate in us. There is an even stronger reason why the ideas of pain, colour, sounds and so on must be innate if our mind is to have those ideas on the occasion of certain physical movements, because the ideas have no similarity with the physical movements. Could anything more absurd be imagined than that all the common notions that are present in our mind would result from such physical movements and would be incapable of existing without them? I would ask our author to explain to me which physical movements could form some common notion in our mind, for example the following one: 'things which are equal to a third thing are equal to each other', or any similar notion. All such physical movements are particular, whereas the common notions are universal; they do not resemble such movements and are not related to them in any way.

He goes on to say, in article 14, that the idea of God that we have does not originate in our faculty of thinking, in which it is innate, but that it results 'from divine revelation, from what we are taught, or from the observation of things'. We shall recognize the error of this claim more easily if we consider that one thing can be said to result from another either because the other thing is its proximate and primary cause without which it could not exist, or because it is only its remote and accidental cause, viz. that which provides an occasion to the primary cause to produce its effect at one time rather than another. Thus all artisans are the primary and proximate causes of whatever they make, whereas those who command them to make them or promise to pay them for their work are the remote and accidental causes because, without instructions, they would not have done what they did. Now, there is no doubt that being taught or observing things is often the remote cause that invites us to think about the idea that we are able to have of God and to bring it before our thought. But no one could say that it is the effective proximate cause of that idea unless they think that we never understand anything about God apart from the name 'God' or the kind of physical shape which is used by painters to represent God to us. For observation, if it is visual, can present nothing to the mind by its own proper power apart from pictures and, indeed, pictures which are constituted simply by various physical shapes, as our author himself teaches. If an observation is auditory, it is constituted by nothing but words and voices; if, however, an observation is made by using some other sense, there is nothing in it that can be referred to God. But clearly, it is obvious to anyone that, in a strict sense, vision by itself provides nothing but pictures and hearing by itself provides nothing but voices and sounds. Thus everything else, apart from voices and pictures that we think about as signified by them, is represented to us by means of ideas that derive only from our faculty of thinking and which, therefore, are innate in us along with that faculty. That is, they are always potentially in us. For to be in some faculty is not to be actually present but to be there only potentially, because the term 'faculty' means nothing other than a potentiality. But no one can claim that we can know nothing about God apart from his name or physical effigy, except those who openly admit to being atheists and who lack all understanding.

After our author has expounded this view of his about God, he rejects in article 15 all the arguments with which I demonstrated God's existence. Here the man's arrogance is very surprising, for he thinks he can overturn easily and in so few words everything that I composed in a lengthy and careful meditation and which required a whole book to explain. But all the arguments that I marshalled in this context eventually come down to two. The first is that I showed that we have a notion or idea of God which is such that, if we pay sufficient attention to it and consider the issue in the way that I explained, we know from that consideration alone that it is impossible for God not to exist because the concept of God includes an existence that is not simply possible or contingent, as is the case with the ideas of all other things, but is absolutely necessary and actual. I am not alone in thinking of this argument as a certain and evident demonstration; many others who have examined it carefully, and who are more intelligent and learned, have come to the same conclusion. The author of the manifesto rejects this argument as follows: 'Our concept of God or the idea of God which is present in our minds is not a sufficiently strong reason for proving the existence of God, because not all the things of which we have a concept exist.' This shows that he has indeed read my writings but that he is either incapable or unwilling to understand them in any way. For the strength of my argument does not depend on ideas in general, but on a peculiar property that is most evident in the idea that we have of God and cannot be found in the concepts of anything else; it depends on the necessity of the existence that is required for the supreme perfection without which we cannot understand God.

The second argument by which I demonstrated that God exists was drawn from the fact (one that I proved clearly) that we would not have had a faculty for understanding all the perfections that we know about in God if it were not true that God exists and that we were created by him. Our author thinks he can refute this argument completely by saying, 'this idea, insofar as it is conceived by us – and we do so imperfectly – does not exceed our powers of thinking any more than the concept of anything else'. In saying this, if he means that the concept we have of God without the aid of supernatural grace is just as natural as all the concepts we have of other things, then I agree with him; but then there is nothing here with which to argue against me. However, if he thinks that this concept does not include intentionally many more perfections than are found in all other concepts taken together, he is clearly mistaken. For I have drawn my argument simply from this abundance of perfections by which our idea of God surpasses all other concepts.

Our author has nothing worth mentioning in the remaining six articles, except that when he wishes to distinguish the properties of the soul, he talks about them in a completely confused and inappropriate way. I certainly said that all the properties relate to two principal properties, one of which is the perception of understanding and the other is the determination of the will – which our author calls, respectively, understanding and willing. Then he divides what he calls understanding into perception and judgement, and here he differs from me. For when I saw that, besides the perception which is a prerequisite for judging, one needs an affirmation or negation to provide the form of a judgement and that we are often capable of withholding our assent even when we perceive something, I did not assign the act of judging, which consists only in assent (that is, in affirmation or negation) to the perception of the understanding but to the determination of the will. He then enumerates only sensing, remembering and imagining among the types of perception. One could draw the conclusion that he does not accept any pure understanding, that is, an understanding that is not concerned with physical images; and therefore he thinks that we have no knowledge of God or the human soul, or of other non-physical things. I cannot imagine any other explanation of this except that the thoughts he has about these realities must be so confused that he never notices any pure thought in himself which is independent of all physical images.

At the conclusion, then, he adds the following words which were taken from one of my writings: 'No one acquires more easily a reputation for great piety than those who are superstitious or hypocritical.' I do not know what he wishes to express by these words, except perhaps that there is some hypocrisy involved in his using irony in so many places. But I hardly imagine that he can achieve a great reputation for piety in that way!

For the rest, I have to admit that I am full of shame for having praised this author in the past as a man of very keen intelligence and for having written that 'I do not think that he teaches any views which I would not acknowledge as my own.'[75] But when I wrote that, I had not yet seen any samples of his writing that were not faithful reproductions of my ideas, apart from once, in a single expression, which caused him so many problems that I dared hope that he would not do anything like it ever again.[76] I also noticed that on other issues he strongly endorsed views that I thought were completely true, and I attributed this to his intelligence and insight. Now, however, I am forced by many experiences to think that he is motivated not by a love of truth but of novelty. And since he thinks that everything he learned from others is old and out of date and that nothing is novel enough for him unless it emerges from his own brain, his own discoveries are so useless that I find not a single thing in any of his writings (apart from what he borrowed from others) which, in my view, is free from mistakes. For these reasons I should warn anyone who is convinced that he defends my views that he expounds them all poorly and falsely, not only in metaphysics in which he clearly opposes me but also in physics, which he discusses in some of his writings. Thus I find it much more disturbing that this professor treats my writings in the way he does and that he assumes the task of interpreting or misinterpreting them, than if others were to attack them sharply.

For I never found any sharp critics who did not attribute to me views that were completely at variance with my own and which were so absurd and inept that I had no fear that any intelligent person could believe that they were mine. Thus, even as I write, I have come across two new pamphlets which were written by such critics. In the first one it says: 'There are some fanatics for novelty who abolish all reliable trust in the senses and claim that philosophers can deny God and doubt his existence and who, at the same time, claim that there are actual notions, species and ideas which are inserted by God into the human mind.' In the second pamphlet one finds the following: 'These fanatics for novelty proclaim boldly that God should be described as the efficient cause of himself, not in a negative but in a positive sense.' But what is really going on in both pamphlets is simply that many arguments are strung together to prove, firstly, that we have no actual knowledge of God in our mother's womb and, therefore, that there is no actual species or idea of God that is innate in our mind; secondly, that one should not deny God and that those who deny God are atheists and should be punished by law; and thirdly, that God is not the efficient cause of himself.

I could pretend that none of these things were written against me because my name does not appear in the pamphlets and I consider all the views that are attacked in them to be completely false and absurd. However, these views are not unlike others that have often been attributed to me maliciously in the past by similar critics, and there is no one else to whom they could be attributed. Finally, there are many people who have no doubt that I am the target of these pamphlets. Therefore I shall take this opportunity to advise their author as follows.

Firstly, by 'innate ideas' I have never understood anything else apart from what he himself explicitly claims as true, on page six of his second pamphlet, namely: 'that we have in us a natural power by which we are capable of knowing God'. I have never either thought or written that the ideas in question are actual, or that they are species which are in some unknown way distinct from the faculty of thinking. Besides, I am opposed more than anyone else to the completely useless fabrications of scholastic entities, so that I cannot refrain from laughing when I see the large number of arguments which this gentleman – who possibly is not at all malicious – has laboriously put together to prove that infants in their mother's womb have no actual knowledge of God, as if he were thereby launching a magnificent attack on me!

Secondly, I have never taught that 'God should be denied or that he can deceive us, or that we should doubt everything, or abolish all trust in the senses or that being asleep and being awake should not be distinguished,' and the like, which have sometimes been alleged against me by ignorant detractors. But I have explicitly rejected all those claims and have rejected them with very strong arguments – stronger, I dare say, than any that were used to refute them before me. To do this more easily and effectively, I proposed at the beginning of my *Meditations* to treat them all as doubtful; I was not the first to discover them, because they had been repeated for a long time by sceptics. Is there anything more iniquitous than to attribute to a writer the views to which he refers merely for the sake of refuting them? What is more inept than to suppose, at least during the time when these views were suggested and not yet refuted, that I was teaching them and that anyone who refers to the arguments of atheists is a temporary atheist? What is more childish than to say, if someone were to die before discovering or writing down the demonstration they were looking for, that they died an atheist and that in the mean time they were teaching a pernicious doctrine, and that 'evil should not be done so that good may come of it', and so on? Someone may object that I did not introduce those false views as if they belonged to others, but as if they were my own. So what, as long as I refuted them all in the book in which I introduced them? One could gather from the very title of the book that I was completely opposed to believing them, since the title promises proofs of God's existence. Is there anyone so obtuse as to think that whoever wrote that book did not know, while writing the earlier pages, what he would undertake to prove in the later pages? I proposed objections as if they were my own because that is required by the literary style of meditations which, I thought, was most suitable for explaining my arguments. If this explanation is not enough for our critics, I would like to know what they say about Sacred Scripture – with which no human writings are comparable – when they see there many things that they cannot understand properly unless they are assumed to have been said by the impious or, at least, by someone other than the Holy Spirit or the prophets. For example, these sentences from Ecclesiastes, Chapter 2: 'Is it not better to eat and drink, and to shew his soul good things of his labours? And this is from the hand of God. Who shall so feast and abound with delights as I?'[77] And in the following chapter: 'I said in my heart concerning the sons of men, that God would prove them, and shew them to be like beasts. Therefore the death of man and of beasts is one, and the condition of them both is equal. As man dieth, so they also die: all things breathe alike, and man hath nothing more than beast: etc.'[78] Do they believe that the Holy Spirit teaches us here that we should indulge our stomachs and fill them with delights, and that our souls are no more immortal than the souls of beasts? I do not think that they are that mad. But they should not slander me either because, when I was writing, I did not use precautions that were not observed by any other writers, not even by the Holy Spirit.

Thirdly, and finally, I warn the author of those pamphlets that I never wrote that 'God should be described as the efficient cause of himself, not only in a negative but also in a positive sense,' as he very rashly claims on page eight of his second pamphlet. Let him examine, read and look through my writings. He will never find anything like that in them, but the complete opposite. Everyone who has read my writings, who knows me at all or, at least, who does not think that I am completely stupid, knows very well that I am as far as possible from such dangerous views. That is why I wonder what could be the aim of such slanders. If they wish to convince people that I wrote things that are completely the opposite of what is found in my writings, they should have taken the trouble first to suppress everything that I published and even to delete them from the memories of people who had read them. As long as they have not done this, they harm themselves more than me. I also wonder why they attack me with such bitterness and zeal – someone who has never troubled or harmed them, even though I could have harmed them if I had been provoked – whereas they take no action against many others who devoted whole books to refuting their teachings and who deride them as simpletons and blindfolded gladiators. However, I do not wish to add anything further here that might stop them from their habit of attacking me in their pamphlets. I am glad to see that they think I am so important but, in the mean time, I hope they get sensible.

Written in Egmond, Holland, towards the end of December 1647.

Notes

1. 'Natural' is contrasted here with 'supernatural'. Throughout these texts Descartes relies on a familiar distinction between what we learn by supernatural means, i.e. what is revealed to us by God in the Bible, and what we are capable of discovering simply by using the cognitive faculties that are common to all human beings and are therefore called 'natural reason' or 'the natural light' of reason.
2. Wisdom 13:8–9.
3. Epistle to the Romans 1:19.
4. A reference to the *Discourse on Method*, published in French in 1637.
5. The Faculty of Theology at the Sorbonne had established an almost unique authority and independence in deciding the orthodoxy or otherwise of different points of view in the theological controversies of the period, especially in France, and in persuading the civil authorities either to protect someone like Descartes or denounce him as a heretic.
6. *Discourse on Method*, Part VI, AT VI, 75.
7. In Latin, the word used is '*objective*'. See above (pp. 6–7) for a note on translating this scholastic term.
8. i.e. metaphysics, or the most fundamental questions in philosophy. These were not 'first' in the sense that one has to resolve them before doing any other work in philosophy but they were so fundamental, conceptually and methodologically, that a philosopher's answers to all other questions presupposed answers to these questions.
9. This sentence was added on the advice of Antoine Arnauld and was put in parentheses to indicate that it was a later addition.
10. According to scholastic theories of causality, a cause could give rise to an effect if it literally (or formally) possessed the effect it causes (e.g. something that is hot can make something else hot), or if the cause is so superior that, although it does not literally possess the same effect that it causes, it has a power to do so (and it is then said to contain the effect eminently). This latter part of the theory was necessary to explain, for example, how God could cause material effects without being material himself.

11. See the discussion of primary and secondary qualities in the Introduction (pp. xxxii–xxxiii).

12. Descartes borrows a distinction from scholastic philosophy between having an idea of God which, although it is inadequate to God's reality, is enough to make it possible to think and talk meaningfully about God, and 'comprehending' some reality by understanding it fully. Given God's infinity, we cannot comprehend God. See *The Principles of Philosophy*, Part I, art. 25 (p. 121).

13. According to this terminology, a marble statue is said to be in a block of marble 'in potency' if it is possible to convert the marble into a statue. Likewise, I could be said to have God's perfections in potency if it were possible for me to acquire them, even though I do not have them at present.

14. In the *Principles*, I, 60, Descartes explains that there is what he calls a real distinction in a strict sense of the term only between two substances. There is only a distinction of reason (*ibid.*, I, 62) involved if we think about one and the same reality in two different ways. In that case, there is a distinction between our two ways of thinking about it but there is only one reality to which both descriptions apply. In this context, Descartes claims that the action by which God creates everything is identical with the action by which he conserves everything in existence.

15. Here Descartes excludes as illegitimate the search for teleological explanations of natural phenomena (i.e. explanations in terms of purposes). According to this thesis, we may speculate about the efficient causes that give rise to natural phenomena but we cannot hope to discover intrinsic purposes in them that express the intentions of their Creator. See also *The Principles of Philosophy*, Part I, art. 28 (p. 122).

16. Added in the French edition of 1647.

17. Here Descartes presents a version of the ontological argument for God's existence, which was made famous by St Anselm in his *Proslogion* (1078).

18. A reference to the pineal gland, which was identified by Descartes as the likely locus of interaction between the mind and the body because, unlike other parts of the brain, which were duplicated in the right and left hemispheres, it seemed as if there was only one gland like this.

19. From a Catholic theologian from Holland, Johan de Kater. In this edition I have added (a), (b) etc., to the text of the selected objections, and likewise to Descartes' replies, in order to correlate the replies and objections.

20. An *ens rationis* is an entity that does not exist independently of our thought but, on the contrary, has only a mental existence as a construction of our mind. For example, a genus or species is a mental classification, which, as such, exists only in virtue of our thinking about things in a certain way.

21. From Fr Marin Mersenne, one of Descartes' most frequent correspondents, who lived in Paris.

22. i.e. to Kater, see note 19.

23. Fifth Meditation, pp. 55–6.

24. First principles are known because they are self-evident in some sense. 'Scientific knowledge' was reserved here as a term for whatever we know as a result of knowing first principles, usually by deducing other propositions from them.

25. A proposition that is true by definition or that is true simply in virtue of its logical structure.

26. From Thomas Hobbes (1588–1679).

27. In the Third Objections and Replies, Descartes adopted a different format by presenting the objections one at a time and then following them immediately with his own reply to each rather than, as in the preceding cases, giving all the objections first and then answering them all in order. I have followed the format of the original edition here.

28. Second Meditation, p. 25.

29. Ibid., p. 26.

30. From Antoine Arnauld (1612–94), a very prominent theologian associated with Port-Royal and Jansenism.

31. Added by the translator.

32. Sixth Meditation, p. 61.

33. Ibid., p. 62.

34. From Pierre Gassendi (1592–1655), who was later the author of further counter-objections to Descartes' replies.

35. Fourth Meditation, p. 46.

36. Refers to earlier objections by Gassendi, which are not included in this edition.

37. Bucephalus was the name of Alexander the Great's horse.

38. Sixth Meditation, p. 67.

39. Second Meditation, p. 25.

40. Lucretius, *De Rerum Natura*, 1, 305.

41. These objections were compiled by Marin Mersenne.

42. The term 'real accidents' was used by scholastic philosophers and theologians to designate properties of a substance that are not themselves substances (e.g. the colour or shape of something) and, for that reason, they were called accidents. But it was also claimed that they could exist apart from the substance of which they are properties and the qualification 'real' was added for that reason. Descartes objected that this terminology involved a category mistake; it identified features that were not substances but that acted as if they were.

See the Introduction (p. xxiii) for the relevance of this distinction for theological disputes about transubstantiation.

43. I.e. reason which has completed a reasoning process and is bound by its own conclusions.

44. Discourse VI of the *Dioptrics* (1637), AT VI, 130 ff.

45. Genesis I: 10: 'And God saw that it was good.' A similar phrase is repeated frequently in the first chapter of Genesis, after each stage of God's creation.

46. Intentional species were rather mysterious theoretical entities in medieval theories of perception, which were supposed to travel from the object of perception to the appropriate sensory organ and impress on it the 'form' of the object of perception. The senses thereby became 'informed' by the object of perception and this perceptual activity was capable, in turn, of informing the mind.

47. In Discourse VI of the *Dioptrics*, AT VI, 130 ff.

48. Descartes formulated the sine law of refraction in Discourse II of the *Dioptrics* (AT VI, 93 ff.). This involved using our intellect to construct a theory about an apparent perceptual error and not simply comparing the sensations derived from different senses and putting our trust in one of them rather than another.

49. This does not refer back to the subtitle but to the claim in the previous paragraph that we know the idea of God more clearly than ideas of physical things.

50. The Latin text does not include the phrase 'general notions' but seems to imply that duration, order and number are kinds of thing. Descartes, however, classifies duration, etc., as modes or qualities of substances. In a letter to Princess Elizabeth, which was written at about the same time as this section of the *Principles* (21 May 1643) and is translated below, Descartes writes as follows: 'There are certain primitive notions in us which are like originals, on the model of which we construct all our other knowledge. There are very few such notions. For apart from the most general notions of being, number, duration, etc., which apply to everything that we can conceive . . .'

51. This is found in Part IV, articles 189–91 of the original text.

52. Descartes was familiar with a distinction that was traditionally taught in universities and was derived from the writings of Thomas Aquinas and F. Suarez (among others). According to this, a term was applied univocally if it was applied to different things with exactly the same meaning. However, if the meaning changed from one case to another, but not so much that it was completely different, the term was said to apply equivocally or analogically. The term 'substance' does not apply to created substances and to God in

exactly the same sense, but there is enough overlap in the two usages to apply the same term in both cases.

53. AT VII, 120.

54. *Principles*, Part II, 43–44, where Descartes distinguishes between motion in the strict sense of the term, which is the translation of a body from the vicinity of one group of bodies to the vicinity of others, and the force or power that causes that translation.

55. 'Animal spirits' was the name given to a very subtle fluid material, which, according to Cartesian physiology, flowed through narrow tubes connecting the brain with various parts of the body and functioned as nerve connections. In order to move a limb, for example, the brain would have to send animal spirits to the appropriate muscles. The term 'to determine' was used in Cartesian physics as a technical term which meant 'to affect the direction of a body's motion'. Elizabeth is asking how a purely non-physical mind could affect the motion of a physical fluid so that the agent could perform a specific, voluntary human action. This objection had been raised earlier, in the Fifth Objections, (d) above.

56. Elizabeth had asked Descartes, in her letter of 24 May 1645 (AT III, 208), whether he thought drinking the waters from Spa might be therapeutically helpful, since her doctors had suggested this remedy and had offered to arrange for transport of some Spa water to the Hague.

57. Descartes had spent considerable time in doing anatomical dissections and, based on his observations, had drafted a short treatise on animals, which he had also shown at about the same time to Regius.

58. A Greek philosopher who advocated suicide.

59. Members of a Dutch reformed church that rejected the Calvinist theology of predestination.

60. Descartes had left a draft copy of his *Treatise on the Passions* with Princess Elizabeth and invited queries about it.

61. Epicurus (*c.* 341–270 BC), Democritus (*c.* 460–370 BC), and the author of *De rerum natura*, Lucretius (*c.* 99–55 BC), were all early proponents of an atomic theory of matter, which presupposed empty space. Descartes' theory of matter implied that all particles of matter are divisible and therefore there are no atoms; secondly, anything that is extended is material and therefore space is not empty.

62. See the *Principles*, AT VIII-1, 41.

63. Cf. the *Principles*, Part II, art. 33 (AT VIII-1, 58).

64. *Principles*, AT VIII-1, 59.

65. The distinction between the infinite and the indefinite was discussed on pp. 121–2 in *The Principles of Philosophy*, Part I, arts. 26, 27.

66. Descartes' *Passions of the Soul* was published in Amsterdam and Paris in November 1649.

67. Apart from the manifesto by Regius, the other pamphlet referred to here is probably the *Consideratio Theologica* (1648) by Jacobus Revius. Its official publication date was 1648, but the text was evidently available during the previous December.

68. The phrase in parentheses was added as a note to the first edition.

69. Likewise added as a note to the first edition.

70. See note 46 above to Descartes' Replies to the Sixth Objections.

71. Quoted from Descartes' letter of dedication of the *Principles* to Princess Elizabeth (p. 109).

72. A definition was expected by scholastic philosophers to indicate the most general class of things to which something belonged (i.e. what was called the genus), and the characteristic quality that distinguished the reality being defined from other members of the same class (i.e. what was called the specific difference). For example, human beings were often defined as belonging to the genus 'animal', and the specific difference was 'rational'. For Descartes, the first part of the definition was expected to specify whether or not the reality in question was a substance and, if it was, whether it was a material or a spiritual substance.

73. See note 46 above, on intentional species. There were thought to be intentional species proper to each sensory organ and, according to the medieval theory, they affected our senses separately and were then transmitted to a central processing unit in the brain. This was called 'common sense' because it was able to perceive or register the sensory information gathered by all the senses and, therefore, functioned almost as a single common sense.

74. AT VI, 109.

75. Letter to Voetius (1643), AT VIII-2, 163.

76. Descartes refers to the phrase 'human beings are only accidental entities', which he challenged in his letter to Regius, December 1643 (AT III, 460).

77. Ecclesiastes 2: 25–26.

78. Ibid., 3: 18–19.

Index